Kaleidoscope

Bibliography Series

Kaleidoscope

A Multicultural Booklist for Grades K–8

Third Edition

Junko Yokota, Editor,

and the Committee to Revise the Multicultural Booklist
of the National Council of Teachers of English

National Council of Teachers of English
1111 W. Kenyon Road, Urbana, Illinois 61801-1096

Prepress Services: Precision Graphics
Production Editor: Bonny Graham
Interior Design: Doug Burnett
Cover Design: Precision Graphics
Series Cover Design: R. Maul
The cover illustration by Holly Meade is from the cover of *Hush!* by Minfong
Ho, illustrated by Holly Meade. New York: Orchard Books, 1996. Used with
permission.

NCTE Stock Number: 25409-3050

ISSN: 1051-4740

ISBN: 0-8141-2540-9

Contents

About the NCTE Bibliography Series

The National Council of Teachers of English is proud to be part of a tradition that we want to share with you. In our bibliography series are four different booklists, each focused on a particular audience, and each updated regularly. These booklists are *Adventuring with Books* (pre-K through grade 6), *Kaleidoscope* (multicultural literature, grades K through 8), *Your Reading* (middle school/junior high), and *Books for You* (senior high). Together, these volumes list thousands of recent children's and young adult trade books. Although the works included cover a wide range of topics, they all have one thing in common: they are good books that students and teachers alike enjoy.

How are these volumes put together? The process begins when an educator who knows literature and its importance in the lives of students and teachers is chosen by the NCTE Executive Committee to serve as booklist editor. That editor then works with teachers and librarians who review, select, and annotate hundreds of new trade books sent to them by publishers. It is a complicated process that can last three or four years. But because of their dedication and strong belief in the need to let others know about the good literature that is available, these professionals volunteer their time and serve as an inspiration to all of us. The members of the committee that compiled this volume are listed in the front of the book, and we are truly grateful for their hard work.

As educators know, no single book is right for every reader or every purpose, so inclusion in this booklist is not necessarily an endorsement from NCTE. But it does indicate that the professionals on the booklist committee feel that the works listed here are worthy of teachers' and students' attention, whether for their informative or aesthetic qualities. Similarly, exclusion from an NCTE booklist is not necessarily a judgment on the quality of a given book or publisher. Many factors—space, time, availability of certain books, publisher participation—may influence the final shape of the list.

We hope that you'll find this booklist a useful resource for discovering new titles and authors, and we hope that it will encourage you to consult the other booklists in the series. Our mission is to help improve the teaching and learning of English and the language arts, and we hope you'll agree that the quality of our booklists contributes substantially toward that goal.

Zarina M. Hock
Senior Editor
National Council of Teachers of English

Acknowledgments

Creating a booklist such as *Kaleidoscope* is a major undertaking, and many people contributed to the creation of this third edition. This project was made possible only because of the voluntary efforts of all participants, and their contributions are gratefully acknowledged:

- The members of the Committee to Revise the Multicultural Booklist, listed opposite the title page, who provided all of the reviews contained in this book. They spent countless hours reading, rereading, discussing, researching, and preparing thoughtful reviews. Each review is followed by the initials of the reviewer.

- The publishers who sent review copies of their multicultural books. Without their generosity, this project would not have been possible.

- Friends and colleagues in Chicago who served as an early advisory group, particularly as we tried to answer some of the big questions regarding the direction of the project: Barbara Elleman, Peter Fisher, Judy O'Malley, Hazel Rochman, Bill Teale, and Carl Tomlinson. I am especially grateful to Bill Teale for his feedback and editing in helping me develop the introduction.

- The clerical work and organizational support of numerous people at National-Louis University, particularly Darlene Porteus, Joan Stahl, and Lucy Goldberg, and my colleagues in the Reading and Language Department, as well as our work-study students.

- The editors of the first two editions of *Kaleidoscope,* for establishing a clear template that I could use as a guideline. I am deeply indebted to Rudine Sims Bishop, Rosalinda Barrera, Verlinda Thompson, and Mark Dressman. In particular, the appendixes of this third edition are updates of the work that they and their committees compiled for the first two editions.

- NCTE editor Pete Feely, who always offered extraordinary support, and the NCTE Editorial Board, for their careful reading of the manuscript, helpful feedback, and support in bringing this project to completion.

Introduction

Kaleidoscope: A Multicultural Booklist for Grades K–8 is an annotated bibliography of books for children and young adults about African Americans, Asian Americans, Latino Americans, and Native Americans. It also includes books related to them—books set in their countries of origin or those of their ancestors, books about their coming to America, and books that deal with religious and cultural practices that can be traced to the countries of their ancestral roots. The precedent for this focus was set by the first two editions of *Kaleidoscope* (Barrera, Thompson, and Dressman 1997; Bishop 1994).

Some of the books in this bibliography are exclusively about the people of these defined populations. Others are not solely about them, but include central characters from these populations. In all cases, however, the books annotated in *Kaleidoscope* offer stories and information that give insight into the people from the cultures identified as central to this book.

Why does *Kaleidoscope* define multicultural literature as literature of ethnic diversity—by and about people of color? The issue of how to make *Kaleidoscope* as inclusive as possible has been debated continuously from the earliest days of the first edition. In some ways the field of children's literature, like that of language arts education in general, has certainly opened itself to defining multicultural literature more broadly and inclusively. Yet, at another level, it is clear that multicultural literature is still mainly regarded as literature by and about people of color. Despite ongoing discussion of this topic, the decision for the third edition was to maintain the original focus of *Kaleidoscope*. This decision was fundamentally a theoretical one, based largely on the thoughts about the meaning of multicultural literature outlined in the "Issues and Continuing Concerns" section of this introduction (see pp. xii–xviii).

There was also a technical reason for maintaining *Kaleidoscope*'s focus on books by and about people of color: this is how publishers generally define the multicultural category. The process for compiling *Kaleidoscope* involves publishers sending multicultural books to the committee, who then apply selection criteria to those books and review the ones that meet the criteria. So few books were sent by the publishers on types of diversity other than cultural that it was impossible for the committee to adopt a definition that went beyond people of color. Resources were simply not available to *Kaleidoscope* for systematically locating and reviewing books that address sexual orientation, age, gender, class, and other differences. Although this was one of many considerations in determining what to include in this third edition, ultimately the focus remained on multiethnic books.

Some of the books annotated in this edition of *Kaleidoscope* fit Sims's (1992) definition of "culturally generic or neutral" literature. That is to say, their illustrations indicate that the characters are ethnically diverse, but the stories could just as easily have been about "mainstream" or "Anglo" characters. In such cases, the cultural backgrounds of the characters are more incidental than purposeful.

Other books annotated in this volume depict characters whose ethnicities are central to their identities and therefore to the story or information presented in the book. Such "culturally specific" (Bishop 1992) books are rich with details that bring the characters' cultural experiences alive.

Both culturally neutral and culturally specific books contribute to the body of literature available to readers. Incorporating differing degrees of cultural emphasis into classroom or library selections allows neither underemphasis nor overemphasis of culture to become the dominant means of viewing multiculturalism. Including culturally diverse characters in a book should not always be a way of saying, "look how different we/they are." Varying degrees of cultural emphasis within a collection of books allows a more natural look at diversity in U.S. society—offering images that, sometimes purposefully while sometimes only incidentally, accurately reflect our diversity.

Issues and Continuing Concerns

Over the course of the three editions of *Kaleidoscope*, literacy educators and librarians have seen a heightened interest in multicultural books, debate about the appropriate role of multicultural books in the curriculum, and in many cases, greater acceptance of the place of multicultural books in classrooms. But even after years of such advancement in the status of multicultural literature, it still comes across as a relatively new concept to many audiences, both lay and professional. Thus, there is a continuing need to promote basic awareness.

Multicultural Literature Defined

The term *multicultural literature* has been defined in innumerable ways. During the late 1980s and early 1990s, the term was commonly interpreted as meaning literature by and about people of color. However, adopting the belief that multicultural literature is about "people who have been misrepresented and underrepresented and who are outside the sociopolitical mainstream" (Bishop 1992) has broadened the definition to include far more than ethnic diversity. In fact, in *Using Multiethnic Literature in the K–8 Classroom,* Harris (1997) considers relevant books that feature people of color, the elderly, gays and lesbians, religious minorities, language minorities, people with disabilities, gender issues and concerns about class. Some in the field have gone so far as to maintain that all literature is multicultural, and that we simply must read it from that perspective (Fishman 1995; Shannon 1994).

Cai (1998) categorizes the various definitions of multicultural literature into three groups:

1. those that assume that *multiple + culture = multiculturalism,*
2. those that focus on "people of color," and
3. those that assert that *all* literature is multicultural.

He analyzes the effects of each of these perspectives as follows:

- The first perspective, which results in a "tourist" approach that includes as much exposure to as many cultures as possible by giving equal treatment to unequal groups, is overly idealistic.

- The reasons for focusing on "people of color" are rooted in the "discrimination, oppression, and exploitation" of some groups of people who have been marginalized by others. However, the inclusion only of ethnic groups entails the unjustifiable exclusion of other groups who have also experienced such treatment (e.g., religious minority groups, gay and lesbians, etc.).

- Seeing all literature as multicultural leads to a degree of inclusiveness that dilutes the focus so much that it becomes meaningless.

Each of these approaches has merit. Despite the breadth of the first approach, seeking even a cursory inclusion of as many cultures as possible allows at least an introduction at a basic level to a wide range of cultures. Despite its exclusiveness, the specific focus of the second approach on people of color gives voice to one subset of the population: those who have historically been silenced. And with the final approach, the possibility that all literature is multicultural rests on the reasonable belief that it is one's interpretation of literature—how a book is read—that is the ultimate definition. This belief follows from the fact that we are all members of multiple cultures—a result of the intersections of gender, class, ethnicity, religion, and so forth—and that the totality of one's identity is a combination of simultaneous membership in many cultural groups.

My own attempt to define multicultural literature has shifted over time. Initially, I argued that all books offering specific insights into a cultural group—"literature that represents any distinct cultural group through accurate portrayal and rich detail"—should be considered multicultural literature (Yokota 1993, 157). At that time, relatively few books met these criteria. Moreover, groups other than those defined in terms of ethnicity were significantly less visible in children's literature. However, as I have studied and written about diversity from various angles—e.g., ethnic diversity, socioeconomic and social diversity, children of gay and lesbian parents, children with special needs (Temple, Martinez, Yokota, and Naylor 1998; Henkin and Yokota 1999; Yokota and Owens 1999)—I find the potential for children's literature to address the many perspectives on diversity both praiseworthy and overwhelming. I have now come to believe that a focus of issues related to "people of color," a multiethnic literature, needs to be distinguished from the larger, more inclusive perspective of multicultural literature. It is not that people of color deserve more or less attention than people of other cultural groups. Rather, a focus on ethnicity-related issues in literature allows us to consider the sociopolitical, economic, and cultural issues shared by ethnic groups that lie outside the mainstream. I am not proposing an exclusionary attitude toward other kinds of cultural diversity. Rather, broadening our perspective on diversity overall is important. But it is also important to recognize that different kinds of diversity are not necessarily parallel in their issues and that although some issues affecting a range of diverse groups are the same or at least similar, others are quite different. From this perspective, then, *Kaleidoscope* continues to be a book of multiethnic literature, rather than of multicultural literature broadly defined.

Empowerment or Divisiveness?

In *On the Brink: Negotiating Literature and Life with Adolescents*, Susan Hynds (1997) examines the role of literature in the lives of five teenagers. The teens' teacher, Meg, is firmly committed to the inclusion of multicultural literature in the reading materials of her students. She believes in the ability of such literature to empower her students to overcome racial barriers and to celebrate their heritage. Indeed, in their responses, her students express their connection to such literature. However, over time, Meg also realized that merely making multicultural literature available is not enough. Availability is necessary, but taking more active and direct steps to understand and counteract bias is also required. Meg uses multicultural literature as the impetus for the kinds of learning that need to take place in order to empower her students.

Although many agree about the ability of multicultural literature to empower the whole, there is also concern about the divisiveness that results from treating multicultural literature as a separate genre. For example, when libraries place stickers on spines of books designating them as "multicultural," or when bookstores create a "multicultural section," some readers take that to mean, "not for me." When books are set aside with a special designation or as a special collection, whether in a library, bookstore, or classroom, it may make such books more visible to those who are seeking them already, but it can also limit their visibility to others.

In another example of a problem related to the separate treatment of multicultural literature, some have expressed concern about featuring African American literature only during Black History Month, as this leads many to slot the literature into a narrow time period and ignore it the rest of the year. Many other ethnic and cultural groups have fallen prey to this "calendar" approach, designating a day, week, or month to study and celebrate them. Such an approach has led to an overemphasis on "holidays and heroes," with inadequate attention paid to who the people are or what it means to be a person from that culture. Still another problem is that only a few cultures receive highlighted treatment in this way; many cultures that do not have a designated place on the calendar receive little, if any, attention.

Moreover, some resent the very notion that multicultural literature should receive special consideration, believing that certain groups are merely asking for extra attention or preferential treatment. This has led to expressions of protest by those who regard themselves to be without culture when cultures of European origin are excluded; they are left feeling colorless and invisible (Schmidt 1999).

At one extreme of this debate about the alleged divisiveness of multicultural literature is the claim by Stotsky (1999) that some literature used in school curricula stresses the flaws of the mainstream majority in order to raise the status of minorities. The inclusion of what is termed "victim lit" or "white-guilt lit," which focuses on how minority groups have been victimized by White Americans, fosters resentment and division at the expense of learning. Stotsky faults the ascendance of the social goals of multiculturalism, which are said to interfere with primary academic and aesthetic goals.

Still others have protested more generally that emphasis on diversity in the classroom creates attitudes of divisiveness. They, like Schlessinger (1992), call for putting aside differences and for placing more emphasis on the united identity all people of the United States share.

Inclusivity or Dilution?

In recent years, we have heard some call for multicultural literature to be more inclusive (Harris 1994). Such a call is partially in response to the fact that focusing only on a smaller subset of the population (e.g., people of color) has made many feel excluded. In fact, those who used to be in the "majority" and in the mainstream now may feel excluded in discussions of multiculturalism. For example, Polish Americans may ask, "What about us? We have a distinct culture, and we have often been oppressed as the ones out of favor with the public. Does our culture not count because we are not 'of color'?" Some lament that they do not have a recognizable culture because they are from a variety of White cultural backgrounds.

The need for multicultural literature became apparent because for so long there had been a lack of attention given to literature that reflects diversity. But now, the call for expanding the definition of multicultural literature threatens to dilute its focus.

Then there is the debate of what is meant by *multi*cultural—is a focus on only one cultural group *multi*cultural? Is there a need now to seek more literature that shows cultures interacting? Or does this debate arise due to the fact that many claim membership in multiple cultural groups simultaneously? Some accept a wide definition of what constitutes a "cultural group" and argue that we are all members of multiple cultures, with our identities shifting fluidly between cultures over time. With the classification of cultural groups encompassing race, nationality, ethnicity, religion, and gender, and with class, age, geography, education, occupation, family status, and sexual orientation constituting secondary areas of cultural classification, it is easy to see how one would have membership in multiple cultural groups (Fishman 1995).

Ethnic American Stories, Country of Origin Stories

When attention first began to be paid to multicultural literature on a large scale, there was so little available that any book that seemed to connect to ethnic diversity was grabbed and identified as multicultural. This ended up blurring the distinction between ethnic Americans and those who still lived in the country of origin. Immigrants typically bring their cultural heritage to their new country, hold onto some traditions, adopt some new ones, and even blend the cultural practices of the home country with those of the new country in interesting and novel ways.

In reality, many ethnic Americans have never even been to the country of their origin, and often those who do go find that they feel more an outsider there than in the United States, especially if they are several generations removed. In classrooms and in libraries across the United States, should there be more emphasis on ethnic Americans rather than on literature set in countries outside the United States? To apply the metaphors used by Rudine Sims Bishop, *mirrors* (to show reflections of self) and *windows* (to view lives beyond our own), could it be that ethnic American experiences are "mirrors" while experiences outside the United States may often feel more like "windows"? This is not to imply that experiences in other countries are less important, but rather to emphasize how they may not feel like reflections of experiences known to ethnic Americans as "their own." Thus, it is important to acknowledge these related yet different kinds of experiences and to provide readers with contexts for both.

Mulicultural Literature, International Literature

With the current call for children to become more astute as global citizens, there has also been an increasing awareness of international literature. International literature is defined as books originally published outside the United States that are translated into English (as needed) and published for U.S. readers. The publication of Tomlinson's (1999) *Children's Books from Other Countries* made available for the first time a compilation of annotations of books that were originally published outside the United States. The United States Board on Books for Young People (USBBY) and its parent organization, the International Board on Books for Young People (IBBY), have championed the cause of international children's literature. But even some of those who are extremely committed to the cause ask, "What is international literature?" Some books published in the United States feel more "international" from a reader perspective than those published abroad. In fact, the second edition of *Children's Books from Other Countries* plans to include a section on books published in the United States that have international settings.

Do some books fit into both the international and multicultural categories? Will some be overlooked that could be valuable if included? For the purpose of this edition of *Kaleidoscope*, international literature has been included only when the books also fit the criteria for multicultural literature set forth in this introduction.

The Selection Process and the Organization of Annotations

During the latter half of the 1990s, literature by or about people of color accounted for approximately 6 percent of the total books published for children and young adults (Kruse, Horning, and Schleisman 1997). The contributions of small, independent presses to this total are not to be overlooked. Their focused commitment to creating high-quality, authentic literature has resulted in many new and overlooked authors and illustrators gaining recognition. But few of these independent publishers sent books to the *Kaleidoscope* committee to be reviewed. Attempts were made to contact small press publishers who exhibited their books at various conferences (e.g., at Book Expo, the annual convention of booksellers) and to request review copies. We can only speculate as to why many did not follow up. The most likely explanation is lack of resources—both in terms of personnel available to do the clerical work in sending out books, as well as the financial resources needed to provide examination copies. Sadly, when books are not reviewed, it is unlikely that they will find their way into classrooms and libraries.

Categorization by strict definition is not what is important in reading and using multicultural books. But in creating a booklist such as *Kaleidoscope*, it became a major point of consideration. It meant that some books were included and some were not. In part, the annotations that appear depended on what publishers sent us. Because *Kaleidoscope* relies on the generosity of publishers who send their books for review, publishers' decisions about what books would be appropriate for this volume placed limits on what sorts of books were available to our reviewers. In fact, our initial attempts to broaden the definition for what should be included led us to review many books that ultimately had to be left out. This process produced such an uneven set of books, straying considerably beyond our working definition of ethnic diversity, that we realized this approach was unfair to the larger market of books that could have been reviewed and made available to readers.

Approximately six hundred books are annotated in this third edition of *Kaleidoscope*. The first criterion for selection was the following:

- Is the book a piece of quality literature?

That is to say, the text had to be written well, and the illustrations had to be of high quality. In addition, the following specific criteria, adapted from Temple, Martinez, Yokota, and Naylor (1998), were applied to each selection considered:

- Do the author and illustrator present insider (culturally authentic) perspectives?
- Is the culture portrayed multidimensionally?
- Are cultural details naturally integrated?
- Are details accurate and interpretations current?
- Is language used authentically?

Books found to be of poor literary quality, or those that included cultural interpretations deemed so erroneous as to be inappropriate, were not annotated and do not appear in this book. A few books generally met the criteria for inclusion, but had some noteworthy drawbacks; their annotations typically contain a precautionary note about such shortcomings.

The annotations included in this edition are organized into chapters similar to those of the two preceding editions. "Picture Story Books" are primarily for the younger child, but some picture books for older students and for "all ages" are included in this chapter as well. Works of realistic fiction that are not picture books are in the chapter of "Realistic Fiction Novels." History and historical fiction are combined in a single chapter. (One interesting note about books classified as "history" and "historical fiction" is that the traditional definitions for what is classified as history and historical fiction are changing, and authors as well as teachers and children are identifying books set in the fairly recent past—1950s and 1960s—as historical.) Nonfiction books can be found in chapters on "Ceremonies and Celebrations," "Biographies and Autobiographies," and "Informational Books." Poetry, rhymes, and songs make up a single chapter. The chapter "Folktales, Myths, and Legends" includes traditional folktales as well as newly written original tales that draw upon folk traditions.

Because categorization of a book is often difficult, the subject index should prove helpful in guiding readers to books on specific topics. Additionally, the index makes it possible to access book annotations by cultural group. An author index, an illustrator index, and a title index are also included.

Each book was annotated in the following manner:

Author. **Title.** Illustrator. Publisher, copyright year. ISBN (International Standard Book Number, for the hardback trade edition unless otherwise indicated). Number of pages. Age range. Genre.

Annotation of the book. (Initials of reviewer).

Awards.

The appendix "Award-Winning Books" lists major awards, most of which pertain in some way to multicultural literature (though not all books for these awards are multicultural). For the years included in the third edition of *Kaleidoscope,* all of the winners of the following awards (listed in alphabetical order by award) are included in the appendix:

Jane Addams Award

Américas Award

Mildred L. Batchelder Award

Pura Belpré Award

Randolph Caldecott Medal

Coretta Scott King Award

NCTE Award for Excellence in Poetry for Children

NCTE Orbis Pictus Award for Outstanding Nonfiction for Children

John Newbery Medal

Notable Books for a Global Society

Scott O'Dell Award for Historical Fiction

In addition, at the end of the "Award-Winning Books" appendix several other booklists are described, but the lists of honored books were too lengthy to include in their entirety. If a title annotated in this edition of *Kaleidoscope* received one of the following awards, the award is listed in its bibliographic entry, immediately following the annotation. The booklists, in alphabetical order, are:

American Library Association Best Books for Young Adults

American Library Association Notable Children's Books

American Library Association Quick Picks for Young Adults

International Reading Association Children's Choices, Teachers' Choices, Young Adults' Choices

Notable Children's Trade Books in the Field of Social Studies

A second appendix provides a list of publishers and their addresses.

Future Directions

Perhaps a time will come when the parameters of *Kaleidoscope* are more inclusive of groups beyond multiethnic diversity within the United States. But this will take considerable discussion about the purpose of *Kaleidoscope* and will require careful communication with publishers who make the books available. Most of all, we should thoughtfully consider the implications of such a change in what is included in future editions of *Kaleidoscope*.

The annotations in this book reflect the books themselves. But what happens when these books make it into our libraries and classrooms? How do librarians and teachers make use of these books? How do students respond to their reading of the books? For it is not the book alone that makes a difference in our students' lives, but also the discussion that accompanies their readings and the learning experiences linked to the reading of the books. All of that, of course, depends on the adult's beliefs and perceptions about the role of multicultural literature in the classroom and in students' lives. How we, as adults, believe the reading of multicultural literature should take place is extremely influential in the learning and attitudes of our students. In fact, Fang, Fu, and Lamme (1999) suggest that some ways of incorporating multicultural literature into the classroom can do more harm than good; they found classrooms in which readings and discussions served to build and reinforce stereotypes. Their research considered what happens when a teacher inappropriately scaffolds the reading of multicultural books, and what happens with appropriate scaffolding. Most important, they suggest that multicultural literature should not be reduced to a disembodied text, a tool that serves as the vehicle fulfilling various curriculum objectives. Rather, they stress the importance of keeping in mind the goals of social, cultural, and literary theories when guiding student discussion.

In my own observations, I have found it important for teachers and librarians to keep in mind that the less intimate knowledge a student has of the culture presented, the more scaffolding the student will need. In fact, the less experience a teacher or librarian has with the culture, the more support he or she will need. Ultimately, as professionals we must commit ourselves to continuing our own personal and professional growth in learning about cultures and the sociopolitical issues that influence the people of those cultures. In other words, teachers and librarians must themselves be readers of multicultural literature and join in discussion with each other.

Some suggested guidelines for teachers and librarians are the following:

- Look for books that offer authentic and accurate portrayals of the culture.
- Ask someone from the given culture to give you feedback.
- In preparing to share the book with students, focus on how the culture is presented.
- Allow students opportunities to respond personally to the literature.
- When discussing responses, monitor the discussion and guide, redirect, and focus the discussion in ways that enhance cultural understandings.
- Weed classroom and library collections to rid them of multicultural books that contain inappropriate and/or outdated information or images.

Finally, in looking toward the future of multicultural literature, we all need to reconsider our own positions on the issues, continue to engage in discussions with others, and analyze the responses we get from our students. Most of all, we must keep reading multicultural books and talking with each other about the implications of such literature for our lives.

References

Barrera, R. B., Thompson, V. D., and Dressman, M., eds. 1997. *Kaleidoscope: A Multicultural Booklist for Grades K–8*, 2nd ed. Urbana, IL: NCTE.

Bishop, R. Sims, ed. 1994. *Kaleidoscope: A Multicultural Booklist for Grades K–8*. Urbana, IL: NCTE.

Bishop, R. Sims. 1992. "Multicultural Literature for Children: Making Informed Choices." In *Teaching Multicultural Literature in Grades K–8,* edited by V. Harris, 37–54. Norwood, MA: Christopher-Gordon.

Cai, M. 1995. "Can We Fly Across Cultural Gaps on the Wings of Imagination? Ethnicity, Experience, and Cultural Authenticity." *The New Advocate* 8: 1–16.

Cai, M. 1998. "Multiple Definitions of Multicultural Literacy: Is the Debate Really Just 'Ivory Tower' Bickering?" *The New Advocate* 11: 311–324.

Dudley-Marling, C. 1997. "'I'm Not from Pakistan': Multicultural Literature and the Problem of Representation." *The New Advocate* 10: 123–134.

Fang, Z., Fu, D., and Lamme, L. L. 1999. "Rethinking the Role of Multicultural Literature in Literacy Instruction: Problems, Paradox, and Possibilities." *The New Advocate* 12: 259–276.

Fishman, A. R. 1995. "Finding Ways In: Redefining Multicultural Literature." *English Journal* 84: 73–79.

Harris, V. J. 1994. "Multiculturalism and Children's Literature: An Evaluation of Ideology Publishing, Curricula, and Research." In *Multidimensional Aspects of Literacy Research, Theory, and Practice: Forty-third Yearbook of The National Reading Conference,* edited by C. K. Kinzer and D. J. Leu. 15–27. Chicago, IL: The National Reading Conference.

Harris, V. J., ed. 1997. *Using Multiethnic Literature in the K–8 Classroom.* Norwood, MA: Christopher-Gordon.

Henkin, R., and Yokota, J. 1999. "Inclusive Reading: Literature Portraying Families with Gay and Lesbian Parents." *Democracy & Education* 13 (3): 60–61.

Hynds, S. 1997. *On the Brink: Negotiating Literature and Life with Adolescents.* New York: Teachers College Press, and Newark, DE: International Reading Association.

Kruse, G., Horning, K., and Schliesman, M., with T. Elias. 1997. *Multicultural Literature for Children and Young Adults: A Selected Listing of Books by and about People of Color,* vol. 2. Madison, WI: Cooperative Children's Book Center.

Schlessinger, Jr., A. M. 1992. *The Disuniting of America: Reflections on a Multicultural Society.* New York: Norton.

Shannon, P. 1994. "I Am the Canon: Finding Ourselves in Multiculturalism." *Journal of Children's Literature* 20 (1): 1–5.

Schmidt, P. R. 1999. "Know Thyself and Understand Others." *Language Arts* 76: 332–340.

Stotsky, S. 1999. *Losing Our Language: How Multicultural Classroom Instruction Is Undermining Our Children's Ability to Read, Write, and Reason.* New York: The Free Press / Simon & Schuster.

Temple, C., Martinez, M., Yokota, J., and Naylor, A. 1998. _Children's Books in Children's Hands: An Introduction to Their Literature._ Boston: Allyn & Bacon.

Tomlinson, C. M., ed. 1998. _Children's Books from Other Countries._ Lanham, MD: Scarecrow Press.

Yokota, J. 1993. "Issues in Selecting Multicultural Children's Literature." _Language Arts_ 70: 156–167.

Yokota, J. and Owen, V. 1999. _Finding Identity in Children's Literature: Voices and Cultural Images._ Paper presented at the 1999 TASH Conference, Chicago, IL.

1 Picture Story Books

1.1 Antle, Nancy. **Staying Cool.** Illustrated by E. B. Lewis. Dial, 1997. ISBN 0803718772. 29 pp. 4–8. Fiction.

Curtis, an African American child, spends most of his time at his grandfather's gym, where he works toward his goal of participating in the Golden Gloves boxing competition and making his grandfather proud of him. Other young men are also encouraged to use the gym; they are not charged a fee if they maintain good grades on their report cards. This is a story not only of the training and commitment necessary to compete in a boxing tournament, but of the bond between a grandfather and his grandson. After Curtis loses his "cool" while practicing one day, he must prove to his grandfather that he can maintain his composure in order to be allowed to participate in the competition. The illustrations are beautifully rendered and portray feelings as well as the actions described. (SSG)

1.2 Bell, William. **River My Friend.** Illustrated by Ken Campbell. Orca, 1997. ISBN 1551430843. 32 pp. 4–8. Fiction.

The son of a poor fisherman, Gang-gang enjoys playing in the river and watching his father at work. When his family catches enough fish to earn a silver coin, however, Gang-gang takes a new interest in what the river has to offer. Returning alone to the river one night, Gang-gang mistakes moonlight dancing on the water for silver coins and hurts himself while attempting to net them. Recovering from his injury and wishing to learn more from his father, Gang-gang requests his own fishing net in order to earn more silver coins for his family. (CP)

1.3 Blackstone, Stella. **Grandma Went to Market.** Illustrated by Bernard Lodge. Houghton Mifflin, 1996. ISBN 0395740452. 24 pp. 4–7. Fiction.

Grandma goes to market to buy a flying carpet that sweeps her across the world collecting souvenirs in various countries. At each stop along her journey she increases her purchase by one, making this a delightful counting book. Blackstone inserts definitions of unclear symbols and language, which serve as learning tools to understand the text. Lodge's colorful illustrations spread across facing pages, leaving a narrow outer margin for the text. The story culminates when the last page folds out several times to reveal all of Grandma's purchases. (CMH)

1.4 Bradby, Marie. **The Longest Wait.** Illustrated by Peter Catalanotto. Orchard, 1998. ISBN: 0531068714. 32 pp. 4–8. Fiction.

Dramatic and effective watercolor illustrations of a blizzard open this story of an African American family. The father, a mail carrier, is going out to deliver the mail on horseback, and although his mother is worried, Thomas is confident that his father can do anything. Warm and safe at home, Thomas imagines all of the things he and his father will do together upon his return. These visions are well integrated into the background of the illustrations. When his father arrives late, cold and ill, everyone is relieved to see him. (LS)

1.5 Bunting, Eve. **Going Home.** Illustrated by David Diaz. Joanna Cotler / HarperCollins, 1996. ISBN 0060262966 (trade). ISBN 0060262974 (library binding). Unpaged. 9–12. Fiction.

Bold, colorful illustrations and text set in a font created by the illustrator tell the moving story of a Mexican American migrant family's trip to Mexico for Christmas. As Mama and Papa take Carlos and his sisters "home" for the holidays, the children begin to realize that their parents have left their beloved home to labor in the fields of California so that the family can have better opportunities for work and education. The closeness and warmth of a Mexican American family, as well as the linguistic, cultural, and generational differences that migrant families face, are evident in this lovingly told story. (KB)

1.6 Bunting, Eve. **Moonstick: The Seasons of the Sioux.** Illustrated by John Sandford. HarperCollins, 1997. ISBN 006024805X (library binding). ISBN 0060248041 (trade). 5–8. Unpaged. Fiction.

With his father's moonstick, a young Sioux boy links the notches of the passing months with the signs of nature and his tribe's activity. From the Moon of the Birth of Calves when his father cuts the moon-counting stick to keep in the tipi, to the Moon of the Yellow Leaves when the brightness and yellowness of the moon are almost as strong as the sun's, to the Sore-Eyes Moon when the starkness of winter threatens the survival of the Sioux, readers will find the lyrical text and carefully detailed paintings a subtle

celebration of Sioux culture. The poignancy of time and generations is captured as the Sioux boy—now a grandfather himself—
takes his grandson to cut another moon-counting stick. (KW)

Notable Social Studies Trade Books for Young People

1.7   Bunting, Eve. **Your Move.** Illustrated by James E. Ransome.
Harcourt Brace, 1998. ISBN 0152001816. Unpaged. 6–10. Fiction.

A realistic story about a ten-year-old boy who cares for his six-
year-old brother while his mother works at night. One night they
go to meet friends who insist they are not members of a gang.
When the friends dare the two boys to vandalize property and a
rival gang shows up with a gun seeking revenge, the older boy
must make an important decision. Should he join the gang or
refuse his friends? This book can generate an important discussion in the classroom. The colorful painted illustrations also add a
deep visual realism to the text. (MP)

1.8   Burleigh, Robert. **Hoops.** Illustrated by Stephen T. Johnson.
Harcourt Brace, 1997. ISBN 0152014500. 32 pp. 5 and up. Fiction.

Using powerful verse and detailed drawings, the author and
illustrator take the reader into the intense power and motion of
the game of basketball. *Hoops* is about the game: how it feels to
live, breathe, and play basketball. Through each verse, we can feel
the experience of the game as if we were a part of it. The poetic
verse is made stronger by the powerful drawings in color pastel;
their hues of light and dark bring readers more emotionally into
the text. (RF)

ALA Notable Books for Children

1.9   Carling, Amelia Lau. **Mama and Papa Have a Store.** Dial, 1998.
ISBN 0803720440 (trade). ISBN 0803720459 (library binding).
32 pp. 4–8. Fiction. Autobiographical story.

Drawing from childhood memories of growing up in Guatemala
City, the author has written and illustrated a typical day in the life
of her Chinese immigrant family. After escaping from China during early World War II, the author's parents set up a fabric store in
Guatemala City where Mayan- and Spanish-speaking clientele
shop throughout the day. What is particularly delightful about
this book is the way Chinese and Guatemalan customs, language,

and culture are blended within the family's life. The author's vibrant watercolor illustrations abound with details of this rich blend of cultures. (KYR)

Pura Belpré Award Honor Book for Illustration

1.10 Carter, Dorothy. **Bye, Mis' Lela.** Illustrated by Harvey Stevenson. Foster / Farrar, Straus and Giroux, 1998. ISBN 0374310130. 32 pp. 4–8. Fiction.

Until her death, Mis' Lela provided warm and loving care to a small African American girl while her mother was at work. From the perspective of a young child, the subjects of the death of a loved one and its accompanying loneliness are tastefully approached in this touching story. Stevenson's luminous paintings in lush shades of yellow, orange, gold, blue, green, and purple create moods of joy, sadness, and remembrance. (JHC)

1.11 Cherry, Lynne, and Mark J. Plotkin. **The Shaman's Apprentice: A Tale of the Amazon Rain Forest.** Illustrated by Lynne Cherry. Gulliver / Harcourt, 1998. ISBN 0152012818. Unpaged. 5–9. Fiction.

In the great Amazon rain forest, in the Tirio Indian village of Kwamala, Kamanya lies sick and motionless, burning with fever. With the help of the village shaman, Kamanya becomes well and healthy again. But the shaman's place of honor is threatened when another tribesman carries malaria into the Tirio village, and Nahtahlah, the shaman, is unable to cure it. It is through another outsider that the tribespeople come to learn the importance of their own knowledge and natural medicines. (KW)

Notable Social Studies Trade Books for Young People

1.12 Choi, Sook Nyul. **Yunmi and Halmoni's Trip.** Illustrated by Karen Dugan. Houghton Mifflin, 1997. ISBN 0395811805. Unpaged. 5–8. Fiction.

In a beautifully written story, Sook Nyul Choi brings us a world where cultural and generational boundaries are crossed as Yunmi and her grandmother, Halmoni, go to Korea to commemorate Grandfather's birthday. But as Halmoni busies herself with the festivities, Yunmi longs for the days when she had Halmoni's attention all to herself. The heartwarming ending will leave all readers with smiles on their faces. Karen Dugan's watercolor illustrations add a scrapbook memory quality to Choi's story. (KW)

1.13 Clements, Andrew. **Temple Cat.** Illustrated by Kate Kiesler. Clarion, 1996. ISBN 0395698421. 32 pp. 6–11. Fiction.

This is the tale of a tawny cat who is considered a god at the cat temple where he lives in pharaonic Egypt. The cat is bored with his life of luxury and yearns for a more authentic existence. He eventually wanders away and, after three days of hunger and thirst, meets a farmer and his family and decides to say good-bye to the royal life. The touching final page is reminiscent of "The Velveteen Rabbit" or other children's classics loved by adults, giving this book a secondary market as "inspirational" adult reading. The honey-gold coloring of the illustrations is effective. (KL)

1.14 Corpi, Lucha. **Where Fireflies Dance / Ahi, donde bailan las luciérnagas.** Illustrated by Mira Reisberg. Children's Book Press, 1997. ISBN 0892391456. Unpaged. 6–10. Fiction.

While flickering fireflies dance in the night air, Lucha Corpi remembers what it was like growing up in Jáltipan, Mexico. She reminisces about exploring the haunted house of Juan Sebastián with her brother, discovering her first jukebox at the local cantina, snuggling with her father as he sang ballads to her, and listening to the stories of her grandmother. Readers of all ages will be inspired to reflect on their own lives and wonder if they are doing what they were born to do. Mira Reisberg's vibrant illustrations and the accompanying bilingual text bring the memories to life. (KW)

1.15 Cox, Judy. **Now We Can Have a Wedding!** Illustrated by Dyanne DiSalvo-Ryan. Holiday House, 1998. ISBN 082341342X. 30 pp. 4–8. Fiction.

Sally is getting married today. Her sister takes the reader on a culinary journey to each of her neighbors' apartments, where traditional wedding foods are being prepared for Sally's celebration. Each episode of Cox's text integrates a new motif before and after each visit. DiSalvo-Ryan's gentle illustrations introduce the customs and traditions of various cultures in this story of friendship and love. Although some readers may find the central premise—an open wedding invitation to all tenants in Sally's building—somewhat unrealistic, it serves as a useful device to introduce the reader to the cuisines and customs of a variety of cultures. (CMH)

1.16 Czernecki, Stefan. **Zorah's Magic Carpet.** Illustrated by Stefan Czernecki. Hyperion, 1996. ISBN 1895340063. 32 pp. 6–10. Fiction.

This story of adventure and travel begins when Zorah, a Berber farm woman living in Fez, Morocco, unwittingly saves the life of a magic goat. From its hair she weaves a magic carpet and is able to fly to places around the world, including Kiev, Bombay, and Beijing, each time bringing back an exotic souvenir. Zorah ultimately becomes a famed carpet maker, and her expertise brings wealth and happiness to her husband and herself. The illustrations are framed in colorfully edged squares, giving the appearance of Persian tiles. Whether read aloud or silently, the tales of Zorah's journeys are sure to please anyone who admires adventurous and enterprising women. (KL)

1.17 Curtis, Gavin. **The Bat Boy and His Violin.** Illustrated by E. B. Lewis. Simon & Schuster, 1998. ISBN 0689800991. 32 pp. 4–8. Fiction.

Reginald's Papa is the manager of the Dukes, the worst team in the Negro National League. For Reginald, baseball is not nearly as important as his violin. He fills the house with beautiful music, but his papa worries that he is spending too much time inside. So when Papa needs a bat boy, Reginald is recruited. Not doing well as a bat boy, Reginald plays his violin in the dugout instead. The team responds to the beautiful music by improving their game, and eventually plays against the best team in the Negro League. This is an honestly told story that also presents information on an important part of African American history. (CC)

Coretta Scott King Illustrator Award Honor Book

1.18 Davol, Marguerite W. **The Paper Dragon.** Illustrated by Robert Sabuda. Atheneum / Simon & Schuster, 1997. ISBN 0689319924. 29 pp. 5–10. Fiction.

Davol combines history and fiction to create this charming, adventurous story about Mi Feu, a famous Chinese scroll painter of the Sung dynasty. When a dragon, Sui Jen, awakens after one hundred years of sleep and threatens to destroy the countryside, the townspeople panic and run to humble Mi Feu for his assistance. Accepting the challenge, Mi Feu politely asks the dragon to go back to sleep. The dragon agrees on the condition that Mi Feu perform three tasks. Mi Feu's resourcefulness and strength of character allow him to subdue the dragon. Illustrator Sabuda entices the reader with his colorful paper cutout interpretation of Chinese art. The folded page extensions reflect Mi Feu's scroll-making. Both story and illustrations convey the message that love conquers all. (CMH)

ALA Notable Books for Children, Notable Social Studies Trade Books for Young People, Notable Books for a Global Society

1.19 DeFelice, Cynthia. **Willy's Silly Grandma**. Illustrated by Shelley Jackson. Orchard, 1997. ISBN 0531300129 (trade). ISBN 0531330125 (library binding). 32 pp. 5–8. Fiction.

Willy's grandmother believes in magic and superstition. When she warns Willy against cutting his toenails on Sunday or singing before breakfast, he stubbornly disobeys her just as soon as her back is turned. After a week of disproving her superstitions, Willy ventures near the swamp at night. He gets his "fearsome fright," however, as the Bogeyman rises out of the darkness screeching and wailing. His "silly" grandma is the one to reassure him that there is no Bogeyman "for true." Exaggerated crayon and ink drawings enhance the humor and suspense of this ultimately reassuring story. (SM)

1.20 Dengler, Marianna. **The Worry Stone.** Illustrated by Sibyl Graber Gerig. Rising Moon, 1996. 40 pp. 4–8. Fiction.

When Amanda was just a girl she found a worry stone, prompting her grandfather to tell the story passed down among the people in the Chumash Indian tribe. The small, smooth stones symbolize the tears shed by a widow, and people found that holding the stones and rubbing them eased their worries. Years later Amanda shares this story, and her stone, with a young boy who seems very lonely and sad just like her. This story integrates three separate narratives, as we learn about the origin of the worry stones, the relationship between Amanda and her grandfather, and, finally, the friendship Amanda begins on a park bench with the young boy. (MR)

1.21 English, Karen. **Just Right Stew.** Illustrated by Anna Rich. Boyds Mills, 1998. ISBN 1563974878. 32 pp. 4–8. Fiction.

Is dill, lemon pepper, cumin, garlic powder, or red pepper the secret ingredient in Big Mama's oxtail stew? Victoria's mother, her neighbors, and aunts speculate and argue about the additive that will make the stew taste just right for Big Mama's birthday dinner. Each family member thinks that he or she knows what the missing ingredient is. Only Victoria knows, however, as Big Mama, Victoria's grandmother, has shared the secret only with her. Anna Rich's vibrant oil paintings represent well the emotions and actions of the characters in this warm story of an African American family. (JHC and SF)

1.22   Fleming, Candace. **Gabriella's Song.** Illustrated by Giselle Potter. Anne Schwartz / Atheneum, 1997. ISBN 0689809735. 40 pp. 4–8. Fiction.

Hearing the sounds of the city on her way home one day, Gabriella hums a catchy tune that gets everyone humming and whistling and singing, from the baker, to the widow, to the gondolier, and finally to the frustrated composer who turns it into his greatest symphony. Giselle Potter uses simple illustrations to capture the rhythmic tone of this story and of the city of Venice. (MR)

ALA Notable Books for Children

1.23   Gage, Amy Glaser. **Pascual's Magic Pictures.** Illustrated by Karen Dugan. Carolrhoda, 1996. Unpaged. 8–11. Fiction.

What do you get when you combine a camera, a boy, and mischievous howler monkeys? In the Guatemalan marketplace, Pascual works hard to save enough money to buy a disposable camera. Soon he is able to photograph the howler monkeys that live in the rain forest near his home. With help from the monkeys, Pascual gets some wonderful pictures of the monkeys and even of himself! This enchanting and humorous story, complemented with colorful, vivid illustrations, will put a smile on anyone's face. (KW)

1.24   Garay, Luis. **Pedrito's Day.** Illustrated by Luis Garay. Orchard, 1997. ISBN 0531095223. 32 pp. 4–8. Fiction.

Pedrito lives with his mother and grandmother while his father, Pedro, has gone north to work. Each morning, Mama and Pedrito go to work in the market. Mama sells tortillas and tamales, while Pedrito shines the shoes of the men who work in the big offices. Pedrito saves some of his earnings each day in hopes of buying his own bicycle, to help his mother carry the loads to market and also to ride it like a stallion. But when misfortune strikes Pedrito must give up his savings in an act of courage and maturity. The colorful full-page illustrations place the reader with Pedrito throughout the entire story. (CC)

1.25 Garland, Sherry. **My Father's Boat.** Illustrated by Ted Rand. Scholastic, 1998. ISBN 0590478672. Unpaged. 5–8. Fiction.

This story about a Vietnamese immigrant shrimp fisherman and his son emphasizes very little about Vietnamese culture, but focuses instead on the universal aspects of the fishing experience. Even so, references to the South China Sea and fields of rice, and pictures of sampans and straw fishermen hats give the story a generalized "Asian" feel. Although more specifics about Vietnamese culture might have offered deeper insight into the characters of this story, it offers readers instead a perspective on the connection all immigrants in the United States have with their homelands. (KW)

1.26 Geeslin, Campbell. **In Rosa's Mexico.** Illustrated by Andrea Arroyo. Knopf, 1996. ISBN 067986721X (trade). ISBN 0679967214 (library binding). Unpaged. 4–7. Fiction.

In three separate tales, the magical crowing of El Gallo brings forth *violetas* with which Rosa rescues her family, a burro, and a bride with a kind heart. Are the *violetas* magical or is it Rosa's own magic? Readers become more convinced that it is Rosa's own wondrous magic with each story. Illustrated with vibrant colors, this is an enchanting tale that is perfect for a read-aloud for all ages. A brief Spanish–English glossary adds to the overall accessibility of these delightful tales. (KW)

1.27 Geeslin, Campbell. **On Ramon's Farm.** Illustrated by Petra Mathers. Atheneum, 1998. ISBN 0689811349. 40 pp. 5–8. Fiction.

Ramon is a little boy who lives on a farm in Mexico. His chores include taking care of the animals, including a pig, a rooster, a goat, and twin lambs. A silly little story is presented about each of the five animals. Because many Spanish words appear in the text, a brief glossary precedes each story. (SF)

1.28 George, Jean Craighead. **Arctic Son.** Illustrated by Wendell Minor. Hyperion, 1997. ISBN 0786803150 (trade). ISBN 0786822554 (library binding). Unpaged. 6–9. Fiction.

At the center of this story is Luke, a boy who is born in a small town on the Arctic Ocean near the North Pole. Following Arctic custom, a family friend gives him a second name, the Eskimo name "Kupaaq." As Kupaaq grows, he experiences such Arctic phenomena as the northern lights, dog sled travel, ice fishing, a whale hunt and celebration, and extended seasons in which the sun never sets or never rises. The illustrations vividly juxtapose a vast, treeless landscape with stunningly beautiful wildlife and the hearty people who make their homes in this remote area of the world. The author and illustrator spent time researching their subjects by traveling to Alaska and visiting an Inupiat Eskimo village leader. (SJ)

1.29   Gershator, David, and Phillis Gershator. **Palampam Day.** Illustrated by Enrique O. Sánchez. Cavendish, 1997. ISBN 0761450025. Unpaged. 5–8. Fiction.

On Palampam Day in the West Indies, when the full moon becomes truly blue, anything can talk—from coconuts and parrots to fish and carrots. But Turo needs to find something to keep his own stomach from talking! Papa Tata Wanga gives Turo some magical words of wisdom, and they work! Colorful tropical illustrations are combined with the playful Papiamento vocabulary to create a delightful story for all ages. (KW)

1.30   Gottlieb, Dale. **Where Jamaica Go?** Illustrated by Dale Gottlieb. Orchard, 1996. ISBN 0531095258. 32 pp. 5–7. Fiction.

Jamaica is a little girl who has a busy day filled with things to do and places to go. Where Jamaica go? To the beach, downtown, and finally home with Daddy. This story is set in the Caribbean, and is written in a call-and-response format (great for two voices) with an "island beat." This book simply begs to be read aloud. (SF)

1.31   Gray, Libba Moore. **Little Lil and the Swing-Singing Sax.** Illustrated by Lisa Cohen. Simon & Schuster, 1996. ISBN 0689806817. Unpaged. 6–9. Fiction.

Published posthumously, this lyrical book tells of urban hard times in an African American family, and a young girl's delight in her uncle's saxophone playing. She trades in her special ring so her uncle can get his sax back from the pawnshop, but the kind pawnshop owner understands her sacrifice and returns both ring and sax. Bright, black-lined, childlike drawings are effective here. This is a great read-aloud book. (KL)

1.32 Hanson, Regina. **The Face at the Window.** Illustrated by Linda Saport. Clarion, 1997. ISBN 0395786258. 32 pp. 6–8. Fiction.

Dora is frightened to walk past Miss Nella's house because the old woman seems to see things that aren't there and has "such strange and scary ways." Her parents learn how scared Dora is, and take her to meet Miss Nella. They help her understand that their neighbor is mentally ill but will not harm her. Set in Jamaica, the narrative reflects the natural rhythms of island dialect. This is a compassionate look at how the mentally ill are set apart from the community and how understanding can help assuage the fear and discrimination associated with the mentally disabled. (GG)

Américas Award

1.33 Heide, Florence Parry, and Roxanne Heide Pierce. **Tio Armando.** Illustrated by Ann Grifalconi. Lothrop, Lee & Shepard, 1998. ISBN 0688121071 (trade). ISBN 068812108X (library binding). Unpaged. 6–9. Fiction.

The title page illustration reveals anticipation, uncertainty, and possibility as Tio Armando comes to live with Lucitita's family. The tiny Mexican American girl and her uncle spend his final year together exchanging ideas and sharing family bonds and simple gifts of kindness. Lucitita learns Tio Armando's loving ways and, after he is gone, realizes that he has passed along his gifts of happiness and love. The story is told in a month-by-month format, and each watercolor and pencil illustration conveys the intimacy shared by this closely knit family. (KB)

1.34 Hoffman, Mary. **An Angel Just Like Me.** Illustrated by Cornelius Van Wright and Ying-Hwa Hu. Dial, 1997. ISBN 0803722656. 32 pp. 4–8. Fiction.

Tyler has many questions: Why do they all have gold hair? Why do they all look like girls? Why are they always pink? Aren't there any Black angels? Tyler makes it his special project to find a new angel for his family's tree—one that resembles them. But it is not until Christmas day that Tyler discovers that angels, just like people, can come in all colors. This is an inspiring text with festive and realistic watercolor illustrations. (GG)

Notable Social Studies Trade Books for Young People

1.35 Huth, Holly Young. **Darkfright.** Illustrated by Jenny Stow. Atheneum, 1996. ISBN 0689801882. 32 pp. 4–8. Fiction.

Darkfright is afraid of the night that creeps over her Caribbean island when the sun sinks into the sea. She stays up all night pretending it is day in an effort to keep the bad things that come with the darkness out of her house, As a result, Darkfright sleeps all day and misses the light that she loves so well. Her neighbors try to help her, but their efforts are in vain. One night, a broken star bursts through her door. Darkfright's determination to heal the star helps her see the night in a different light. The sprinkling of Caribbean traditions, the rhythm of the dialect, and occasional rhymes bring the text to life. The colorful illustrations suggest the warm glow of the islands. (BK)

1.36 Hru, Dakari. **The Magic Moonberry Jump Ropes.** Illustrated by E. B. Lewis. Dial, 1996. ISBN 0803717555. 28 pp. 5–8. Fiction.

April and Erica just love to jump double dutch. Unfortunately, they can't find a third person for their game. Uncle Zambezi drops by with a present for the girls: new jump ropes. The ropes are from Tanzania. He tells them the jump ropes are magical. When April and Erica jump with the ropes and make a wish, the wish will come true. The book includes an author's note on jump ropes and the jump rope jingles included in the story. (SF)

1.37 Igus, Toyomi. **Two Mrs. Gibsons.** Illustrated by Daryl Wells. Children's Book Press, 1996. ISBN 0892391359. Unpaged. 5–8. Fiction.

This beautifully told tribute to two women celebrates the joy of growing up in a racially mixed family. Memories of Toyomi's vibrant, bear-hugging African American grandmother, and her soft-spoken, peaceful Japanese mother—the two Mrs. Gibsons—are woven together into a sweet story that is perfect to be read aloud by parent and child. (KW)

1.38 Jackson, Isaac. **Somebody's New Pajamas.** Illustrated by David Soman. Dial, 1996. ISBN 0803715498 32 pp. 4–8. Fiction.

This is a delightful story of the friendship that develops between two young African American boys from different social groups. Robert invites his friend Jerome for a sleepover, and they become friends as they share and learn about each other's lifestyle and family traditions. At the same time their differences become apparent, as Robert does not own pajamas, and therefore sleeps in his underwear. The experiences shared by the boys, and their recognition that people from different social and economic backgrounds can be friends nonetheless, make for delightful reading. The beautiful, bright watercolor illustrations enrich the story even more. (RF)

1.39 Jiménez, Francisco. **La mariposa.** Illustrated by Simón Silva. Houghton Mifflin, 1998. ISBN 0395816637. ISBN 0395917387 (Spanish edition). 40 pp. 4–8. Autobiographical story.

La mariposa is a true story based on the author's childhood experiences in school. Francisco, a Mexican American boy, shares his struggles learning to fit into an English-only classroom during his first year of school. His friend, Arthur, speaks a little Spanish and they play together at recess; however, the teacher gets angry if she hears them speaking Spanish. He spends his time daydreaming and watching the caterpillar in a jar by his desk. By the time the caterpillar begins its transformation into a butterfly, Francisco has changed as well. He has learned some English, become quite an artist, and made a friend. Simón Silva's warm, sun-drenched illustrations beautifully depict Francisco's largely biographical story of alienation and triumph. The author includes some Spanish words in the text to depict Francisco thinking in his native language. A glossary of Spanish words at the back of the book makes the story more accessible to nonbilingual readers. (ER & MS)

1.40 Johnson, Angela. **The Rolling Store.** Illustrated by Peter Catalanotto. Orchard, 1997. ISBN 0531300153. Unpaged. 8–11. Fiction.

A young African American girl remembers her grandfather in this delightful tale of memories mixed with childhood fantasies. As the young girl and her friends work together to bake cookies, string beads, and illustrate pictures, she recalls her grandfather's rolling store. Watercolors bring to life the moving store and the African American communities it served. As they remember the past, they prepare to bring the tradition to life again. (SS)

1.41 Johnson, Dolores. **Grandma's Hands.** Illustrated by Dolores Johnson. Cavendish, 1998. ISBN: 0761450254. 32 pp. 6–9. Fiction.

Billy must live with his grandmother in the country, while his mother returns to the city to "get herself together." He is unsure about living with his grandmother, whom he hasn't seen in a long time and who seems "rough and scratchy." His unwillingness to accept his grandmother's overtures dissolves over time because of his loneliness. Grandmother offers him love by making him part of the daily routine of her life. He comes to accept her and the farm, and when his mother reappears to take him home many months later, he isn't sure he wants to go. (GG)

1.42 Johnston, Tony. **The Magic Maguey.** Illustrated by Elisa Kleven. Harcourt Brace, 1996. ISBN 0152509887. 29 pp. 4–8. Fiction.

Miguel lives on a pueblo in Mexico. Down the road from his house there is a huge maguey plant. Everyone in the pueblo loves this maguey; people often gather around the large cactus, which gives them shelter from the sun and rain. Miguel's family often uses fallen leaves from the plant to make thread or tile their roof. It is truly a magical plant. When a wealthy landowner threatens to uproot the maguey, Miguel has an idea that saves the plant, just in time for Christmas. The illustrations are whimsical and rich with the colors of Mexico. (ER)

1.43 Khan, Rukhsana. **The Roses in My Carpets.** Holiday House, 1998. ISBN 0823413993. 32 pp. 9 and up. Fiction.

A young Afghanistani boy relates the story of his life in a refugee camp, where he lives in a mud hut with his mother and sister. His father was killed while plowing his field, and the family now must subsist on bread and water or tea. Each day after prayers and school, while honing his skills in carpet weaving, he dreams of a world that is free from war, death, nightmares, and hunger. One day his sister is hit by a truck, and the narrator confronts death once again. While the depiction of life in war-torn Afghanistan may seem realistic, the number and intensity of tragedies that befall the young boy within such a brief time frame may strain believability for some readers. (SG)

Notable Books for a Global Society

1.44 Kleven, Elisa. **Hooray, a Piñata!** Illustrated by Elisa Kleven. Dutton / Penguin, 1996. ISBN 0525456058. Unpaged. 4–8. Fiction.

When Clara chooses a small, brightly colored dog piñata for her birthday party, her imagination transforms it into a real pet named "Lucky" who walks, sniffs, digs in the sandbox, and eats dog biscuits. As the days go by, Clara's friend Samson becomes worried that the piñata will be too worn out to fill with candy and break open at the party. Clara, however, worries about having to break Lucky at all. The thoughtful Samson decides to get Clara a different piñata to break so that her special friend can stay in one piece. The fancifully detailed illustrations, of watercolor and collage, perfectly complement this warm, lighthearted story about friendship. (SJ)

1.45 Knutson, Kimberley. **Beach Babble.** Illustrated by Kimberley Knutson. Cavendish, 1998. ISBN 0761450262. 32 pp. 4–7. Fiction.

Three children go to the beach for a day of fun. They swim, wade, crabwalk, and build sandcastles. The reader is drawn into the action with sensory language that helps one to see, hear, and smell a day at the seaside. (SF)

1.46 Kroll, Virginia. **Can You Dance, Dalila?** Illustrated by Nancy Carpenter. Simon & Schuster, 1996. ISBN 0689805519. 28 pp. 5–7. Fiction.

Dalila is inspired to dance after watching ballroom dancing on television in February. However, her first attempts to learn prove unsuccessful. During the winter and spring, Dalila is introduced to several new forms of dance. She tries them all, but she just cannot seem to get them right. In July, Dalila goes to a festival where she finds just the right form of dance for her. (SF)

1.47 Kroll, Virginia. **Faraway Drums.** Illustrated by Floyd Cooper. Little Brown, 1998. ISBN 0316504491. 32 pp. 4–8. Fiction.

Jamila Jefferson, her younger sister Zakiya, and their mother have just moved into a new city apartment. Left in charge while her mother works, Jamila uses the stories her great-grandma told her about Africa to transform the frightening nighttime sounds into scenes that soothe both girls' fears. Voices on the street become hyenas fighting over food; car horns become elephants at a water hole. Illustrated in warm, hazy tones, this story demonstrates how creativity and love can overcome the tough realities of inner-city life. (KYR)

1.48 Kudler, David. **The Seven Gods of Luck.** Illustrated by Linda Finch. Houghton Mifflin, 1997. ISBN 0395788307. 32 pp. 4–8. Fiction.

This beautifully illustrated story begins with a brief discussion of the seven Japanese gods of luck. Following the introduction is the story of Sachiko and Kenji, two Japanese children who learn from their mother that they are too poor to celebrate a New Year's feast this year. The two head to town and exchange various homemade items they have brought for hats from a merchant they meet. After the children place the hats on the statues of the seven gods of luck, the gods awake and reward the children and their family with a surprise New Year's feast. (CP)

1.49 Kurtz, Jane, and Christopher Kurtz. **Only a Pigeon.** Illustrated by E. B. Lewis. Simon & Schuster, 1997. ISBN 0689800770. 40 pp. 4–8. Fiction.

Ondu-ahlem is a young boy from Ethiopia who raises and cares for his pigeons. Each morning he makes sure they have survived the dangers of the night. Ondu-ahlem attends school for only a half day, due to overcrowding, then returns home to check on his pigeons again. The rest of the afternoon he spends shining shoes in town. The young boys in town meet to show and race their cherished birds. One day Chinkay, his prized pigeon, is pitted against another pigeon in a contest. The excitement of the race reveals Ondu-ahlem's pride and love for his pets. The text and detailed watercolor illustrations capture life in the city of Addis Ababa. (CC)

1.50 Lee, Huy Voun. **In the Park.** Illustrated by Huy Voun Lee. Henry Holt, 1998. ISBN 0805041281. 26 pp. 4–8. Fiction.

Xiao Ming's walk through the park on an early spring day turns into a lesson on Chinese writing. His mother shares with him the Chinese characters for words like *fruit, nest,* and *river.* The lessons of nature and mankind come together for Xiao Ming in this caring story about the relation between a mother and child. The simplicity of the story and the connections the mother shows her child are what make this book so inviting. (SKA)

1.51 Lewin, Betsy. **What's the Matter, Habibi?** Illustrated by Betsy Lewin. Clarion, 1997. ISBN 039585816X. 32 pp. 4–8. Fiction.

Ahmed's beloved camel, Habibi (which means "darling" in Arabic), gives children camel rides every day. One day the camel will not cooperate, so Ahmed offers his own slippers for Habibi's sore feet. Habibi runs off in them, then trades them for a fez, which makes him vain. Finally he returns to carry the children in his new finery, and all is forgiven. Along with the fanciful plot, the sketchy cartoon drawings on large white spaces make this a humorous and whimsical book to read aloud. Lewin has traveled in many Middle Eastern countries with author/illustrator Ted Lewin. (KL)

1.52 Lewin, Ted. **The Storytellers.** Illustrated by Ted Lewin. Lothrop, Lee & Shepard, 1998. ISBN 0688151787. 40 pp. 5–10. Fiction.

Set in Fez, Morocco, in the modern age, the story shows young Abdul with his grandfather, the town storyteller, going through a typical day's work. The watercolor paintings show dappled light streaming through the slats of the covered market as people work below, creating an almost tactile effect. The story line is as pleasing as the setting and the illustrations, and raises themes of the value of elders, legacy, and family tradition. The story is also a reminder that language is, at its root, oral, and that books are often renderings of stories that have been told aloud for millennia. (KL)

Notable Social Studies Trade Books for Young People, Notable Books for a Global Society

1.53 Lillegard, Dee. **The Poombah of Badoombah.** Illustrated by Kevin Hawkes. Putnam, 1998. ISBN 0399227784. 32 pp. 4–8. Fiction.

Children will love to follow along with this rhyme, set in India, as the Poombah of Badoombah uses his magical powers to *poombah* everything. His amusing antics finally catch up with him when he *poombahs* a nabob (government official), tipping his elephant and scattering everything aboard. The angry townspeople quickly chase the Poombah out of town. The Poombah finds peace in the countryside, where he grows magic beans. The delightful and colorful illustrations will make this a favorite for many children. (MR)

1.54   Lomas Garza, Carmen, as told to Harriet Rohmer. **In My Family /
En mi familia.** Illustrated by Carmen Lomas Garza. Edited by
David Schecter. Translated by Francisco X. Alarcón. Children's
Book Press, 1996. ISBN 0892391383. Unpaged. 8–11. Autobio-
graphical story.

Through her own vibrant pictures and words, Carmen Lomas
Garza tells a beautiful story of life in her hometown of Kingsville,
Texas. She brings to life what it is like to grow up in a Mexican
American community: from hitting piñatas at a backyard barbe-
cue, to making empañadas in the kitchen, to witnessing a healer
help the younger sister communicate with her mother. The Spanish translation opens up Garza's family's story to a wider audience. (KW)

Pura Belpré Honor Book for Illustration, Américas Award

1.55   London, Jonathan. **Ali, Child of the Desert**. Illustrated by Ted
Lewin. Lothrop, Lee & Shepard, 1997. ISBN 0688125603. 32 pp.
5–9. Fiction.

Young Ali is crossing a part of the Sahara desert for the first time,
on the way to a camel market in Rissani, Morocco, but loses his
father and the camel train in a terrible sandstorm. An old Berber
shepherd befriends him, and Ali spends the night in his tent. The
next day, Ali is left alone again, with his camel, a dwindling food
supply, and a musket lent by the Berber. By shooting the rifle at
regular intervals, he signals to his father, who finally finds him.
The impressive watercolors spread across facing pages depict the
sandstorm's gritty fury, the old shepherd's illuminated face at the
campfire, and the dazzling starry sky. Culturally authentic, with a
universal theme of a child using his wits to survive, this book is
spellbinding. A brief glossary of Arabic terms is found in the back
of the book. (KL)

Notable Social Studies Trade Books for Young People

1.56   London, Jonathan. **Fireflies, Fireflies, Light My Way**. Illustrated
by Linda Messier. Viking, 1996. ISBN 0670854425. 32 pp. 6–10.
Poetry.

A bright, rhyming poem about following fireflies into the world of
nature is richly illustrated with creamy, colorful paintings that
bleed off each page. In each verse the text breaks for a page turn

just at its point of suspense, making the book a good choice for reading aloud. The poem is an adaptation of a Mesaquakie (a Native American Great Lakes tribe) lullaby. (KL)

1.57 London, Jonathan. **The Village Basket Weaver**. Illustrated by George Crespo. Dutton, 1996. ISBN 0525453148. 32 pp. 5–8. Fiction.

Tavio spends time every morning before school with his grandfather, Policarpo, the village basket weaver. He is the only one in the village who knows how to weave baskets, but he is becoming old and weak. One day when Tavio arrives, his grandfather is not there. Tavio learns that Policarpo has become too old to weave. Policarpo had not finished weaving a basket for cassova bread. If he does not finish it, the village will have no bread to eat. Can Tavio find a way to save the village? (SF)

1.58 Lorbiecki, Marybeth. **Just One Flick of a Finger**. Illustrated by David Diaz. Dial, 1996. ISBN 0803719485 (trade). ISBN 0803719493 (library binding). 32 pp. 9 and up. Fiction.

This first-person cautionary tale is told in rhythmic free verse that begs to be read aloud. Jack, a White teenager, and his African American friend Sherms are hounded by a bully called Reebo. In a school culture where "The rule / at my school / is you're a fool / if you can't get / your hand on a gun," the two friends attempt to protect themselves by avoiding trouble. When that proves impossible, Jack steals his sleeping father's handgun. When Jack threatens Reebo with the gun Sherms intervenes, and both are wounded. While the contrived conclusion and didactic tone of the text may limit the story's effectiveness, it could prompt meaningful discussions. Diaz's larger-than-life illustrations, set against digitally enhanced photographic backgrounds, enhance the drama of the story. (SM)

1.59 MacDonald, Margaret Read, reteller. **Pickin' Peas.** Illustrated by Pat Cummings. HarperCollins, 1998. ISBN 006027235X. Unpaged. 5–8. Fiction.

This southern U.S. folktale is about a young girl, her garden, and a pesky rabbit who loves to eat her peas. As the story proceeds, the girl and then the rabbit sing a poetic rhyme to each other whenever they continue their game. Children will love the energetic rhythm of the book and the bold colorful illustrations of the African American girl and her new "friend"! (MP)

1.60   McDonald, Megan. **My House Has Stars.** Illustrated by Peter Catalanotto. Orchard, 1996. ISBN 0531095290. 32 pp. 4–8. Fiction.

McDonald celebrates diversity around the world by sharing glimpses of children from the Philippines, Nepal, Ghana, Japan, the American Southwest, Mongolia, Brazil, and Alaska, and the houses in which they live. Each country is described from the point of view of a child living there. While characters and settings are different, a common view shared by every child around the world includes the stars in the sky and the earth that serves as a home for all. The text and illustrations depict life in countries around the world. (MS)

1.61   Melmed, Laura Krauss. **Little Oh.** Illustrated by Jim LaMarche. Lothrop, Lee & Shepard / Morrow, 1997. ISBN 0688142087 (trade). ISBN 0688142095 (library binding). Unpaged. 5–8. Fiction.

This enchanting story tells of an origami doll who comes to life for the woman who created her, her "mother." As she is separated from her mother in the busy marketplace, Little Oh's adventures lead her to a sad crane, with whom she exchanges stories of loss and sorrow. Flying on the crane's back in search of her mother, Little Oh mistakenly reaches the house of a motherless boy and his father. When Little Oh finally reunites with her mother, the paper girl magically becomes human, and she and her mother form a new family with the lonely man and his son. Children will be entranced by the Japanese story complemented by soft mixed-media illustrations that portray authentic images of Japan. (MP & KW)

ALA Notable Books for Children, Notable Social Studies Trade Books for Young People

1.62   Mollel, Tololwa M. **Kele's Secret.** Illustrated by Catherine Stock. Lodestar, 1997. ISBN 0525675000. 32 pp. 5–7. Fiction.

Kele's grandmother has a hen with a peculiar habit: she lays eggs in strange places. Kele's job is to find the eggs and give them to his grandmother. The eggs can then be sold at the market. One day, even Kele cannot find where the hen has laid the eggs. His search takes him on a journey that requires courage. (SF)

1.63 Namioka, Lensey. **The Laziest Boy in the World.** Illustrated by YongSheng Xuan. Holiday House, 1998. ISBN 0823413306. 32 pp. 4–8. Fiction.

Xiaolong is the laziest boy in the village, maybe the laziest in the province, maybe the laziest in all of China! So starts this funny, tongue-in-cheek tale that cuts across cultures to examine spoiled, lazy children. Ms. Namioka's descriptions of Xiaolong's laziness and how he conquers it make for a fun read-aloud that encourages children to fully participate in life's simple pleasures. Mr. Xuan's illustrations include details in dress and household that give an authentic sense of Chinese culture. (KYR)

1.64 Ogburn, Jacqueline K. **The Jukebox Man.** Illustrated by James E. Ransome. Dial, 1998. ISBN: 0803714297. 32 pp. 4–8. Fiction.

Donna's grandfather is a jukebox man; he owns and fixes jukeboxes in diners, fish camps, and truck stops all over the state. Donna goes with Poppaw one Saturday to change records and service machines. As the music begins and the jukeboxes invitingly flash different colors of light onto the floor, Donna discovers a whole new world. The fact that Ogburn's grandfather really was a jukebox man adds authenticity and sensitivity to this tale. (GG)

1.65 Padt, Maartje. **Shanti.** Illustrated by Milo Freeman. DK Ink, 1998. ISBN 0789425203. 28 pp. 5–8. Fiction.

This stunningly illustrated picture book follows Shanti, a zebra, who gets lost and wanders the South African plain seeking her fellow zebras. The story uses a curious repeating line, as she is told by many forest animals, "You won't be alone much longer." The listener/reader is delighted and surprised to find that Shanti soon gives birth. The book is a natural for reading aloud, and the brightly hued batik paintings make joyous backdrops to the plot. (KL)

1.66 Pinkney, Brian. **The Adventures of Sparrowboy.** Illustrated by Brian Pinkney. Simon & Schuster, 1997. ISBN 0689810717. Unpaged. 5–8. Fiction.

Every child (and adult) will enjoy this story of Henry who, after a near collision with a sparrow, finds himself able to fly just like his favorite comic book hero, Falconman. Readers will be able to imagine themselves as a superhero, here to save the day, defend the helpless, battle evil, and still deliver the newspapers on his paper route! Readers will delight in Pinkney's scratchboard illustrations, which connect seamlessly with his lively, imaginative story. (KW)

Boston Globe–Horn Book Award Winner—Picture Book

1.67 Pirotta, Saviour. **Turtle Bay**. Illustrated by Nilesh Mistry. Farrar, Straus and Giroux, 1997. ISBN 0374378886. 25 pp. 4–8. Fiction.

In this touching story that crosses generational lines, Taro, a young boy, befriends Jiro-San, an old and wise man who is full of secrets and immense patience. He takes Taro into his confidence and shares one of the secrets of nature: how turtles migrate to shallow waters and come ashore to lay their eggs. Taro shares this knowledge with his sister, Yuko, and the two are intrigued and captivated by the hatching of the sea turtles and their struggle to make their way back to the ocean where they belong. The two learn a lesson about the impact of humans on the habitats of different creatures, and how humanity must learn to respect and protect the environment in which they live. (SKA)

Notable Social Studies Trade Books for Young People

1.68 Pomerantz, Charlotte. **You're Not My Best Friend Anymore.** Illustrated by David Soman. Dial, 1998. ISBN 0803715595 (trade). ISBN 0803715609 (library binding). 30 pp. 4–8. Fiction.

Molly and Ben live in a two-family house, and spend their days frolicking around the neighborhood, creating new inventions, and going to school together. The even make plans to celebrate their two different birthdays together on the same day in June. But a disagreement tears them apart, and they refuse to talk to each other. It is not until their joint birthday party that they realize that the presents they give each other are exactly what each wanted. Without words, their angry division disappears. Pomerantz reminds readers that even good friends can disagree, but they remain friends. Soman's watercolors expressively depict children in happy times and angry times. Images of Molly, with her blonde hair, blue eyes, and white skin, playing with Ben, who has black hair and brown skin, depict diversity in friendships. (CMH)

1.69 Reiser, Lynn. **Tortillas and Lullabies / Tortillas y cancioncitas.** Illustrated by Corazones Valientes. Translated by Rebecca Hart.

Greenwillow, 1998. ISBN 0688146287 (trade). ISBN 0688146295 (library binding). 40 pp. 4–8. Fiction.

In both English and Spanish, this book tells a story of family love within Costa Rican culture. The illustrations' festive, folk art style, rendered by Corazones Valientes, an organization of Costa Rican women artists, complements the tale. The four chapters describe from a historical perspective pastimes such as preparing tortillas, gathering flowers, doing washing, and hearing lullabies. Children will enjoy seeing and reading this bilingual book. (MP)

1.70   Reiser, Lynn. **Cherry Pies and Lullabies.** Illustrated by Lynn Reiser. Greenwillow / Morrow, 1998. ISBN 0688133916 (trade). ISBN 0688133924 (library binding). 40 pp. 4–8. Fiction.

This is a book about mothers and daughters and changing family traditions. Whether depicting baking a cherry pie, making a crown of flowers, creating a quilt, or singing a lullaby, the bright and attractive illustrations give the reader a sense of the warmth of one family's home. Children may be inspired to reflect on their own family traditions and history, and create stories or songs about their homes and families. (MP)

1.71   Riecken, Nancy. **Today Is the Day.** Illustrated by Catherine Stock. Houghton Mifflin, 1996. ISBN 0395739179. 28 pp. 5–8. Fiction.

Yesenia's father has left his home in a Mexican village to find work, and has been gone for six months. Finally, the family receives a letter telling them that he is coming home. Yesenia spends the day filled with anticipation of her father's arrival. She goes to town to wait for the bus. However, her older sister has doubts that he will return. (SF)

1.72   Rochelle, Belinda. **Jewels.** Illustrated by Cornelius Van Wright and Ying-Hwa Hu. Lodestar, 1998. ISBN 0525675027. Unpaged. 5–8. Fiction.

Every year Lea Mae spends her summer vacation in rural North Carolina visiting her great-grandparents, Ma Dear and Pop Henry. Lea Mae enjoys the neighbors who come by and loves to frequent familiar places around the small town with her great-grandparents. Her visits are filled with fun activities such as catching lightning bugs and playing in the rain. Most memorable of all, however, are the stories Lea Mae's grandmother tells of several generations of their family, using the family picture album. These are historical accounts of bravery and survival as well as tales of happiness and good times. Lea Mae promises herself that one day these "jewels" will be made more permanent through her writings. Van Wright and Hu's stunning and expressive paintings beautifully represent the love and devotion of this African American family. (SF and JHC)

Notable Social Studies Trade Books for Young People

1.73   Rosa-Casanova, Sylvia. **Mama Provi and the Pot of Rice.** Illustrated by Robert Roth. Atheneum / Simon & Schuster, 1997. ISBN 0689319320. 32 pp. 5–8. Fiction.

Mama Provi and her granddaughter, Lucy, live on different floors of the same apartment building. When Lucy gets the chicken pox and is unable to visit Mama Provi as usual, Mama Provi prepares a pot of *arroz con pollo* and begins the walk upstairs to Lucy. On the way, she stops at each floor and exchanges some of her chicken with rice for a variety of foods from neighbors on each floor. Watercolor illustrations vividly depict apartment life in this cumulative story. (CC)

1.74   Ryan, Cheryl. **Sally Arnold.** Illustrated by Bill Farnsworth. Cobblehill, 1996. ISBN 0525651764. 28 pp. 6–8. Fiction.

Jenny is spending the summer with her grandparents. She becomes curious about one of the residents of the town, Sally Arnold. Jenny suspects that Sally Arnold might be a witch. She looks like a witch and she does strange things, such as collect junk. It is not until Jenny actually gets to know Sally that she understands her peculiar behavior. (SF)

1.75   Sandoval, Dolores. **Be Patient, Abdul.** Illustrated by Dolores Sandoval. Margaret McElderry / Simon & Schuster, 1996. ISBN 0689506074. 32 pp. 6–10. Fiction.

A little boy tries to sell oranges to pay his school tuition. The story is set in Sierra Leone and has many bright paintings showing daily life and celebrations. Although the story is not completely clear, the exuberance comes through. This is a good book to read aloud, and children will enjoy trying to guess how it ends. (KL)

1.76 Say, Allen. **Allison.** Illustrated by Allen Say. Houghton Mifflin, 1997. ISBN 039585895X. 32 pp. 5–12. Fiction.

When Allison tries on her new kimono and looks in the mirror, she suddenly realizes she looks more like her doll, Mei Mei, with straight black hair and brown eyes, than like her parents, who have blonde hair and blue eyes. As she struggles to make sense of why her real mother gave her away, a stray cat helps Allison reach a new understanding of what it means to belong. Allen Say's beautiful watercolors and poetic text combine to make a heart-wrenching and unforgettable story. (KW)

1.77 Say, Allen. **Emma's Rug.** Illustrated by Allen Say. Houghton Mifflin, 1996. ISBN 0395742943. 32 pp. 4–8. Fiction.

Most children have favorite blankets or stuffed toys that they carry around. Emma has a small, shaggy bathroom rug, which she carries everywhere and stares at for hours. Her father calls it her television. When Emma begins to paint, the adults around her are amazed at her talent. But Emma is only "copying" the images she sees in her rug. When Emma's mother washes the rug, Emma is horrified, convinced she has lost her source of artistic inspiration. Emma soon learns, however, that her inspiration comes from imaginative interpretation of the world around her. Say's water-color illustrations immediately convey Emma's solitude and iso-lation. In most of the illustrations, she is by herself, but even when she is with others, she is not a part of her surroundings. This story provides an excellent opportunity to explore the concepts of cre-ativity and artistic inspiration with children. (BK)

1.78 Schick, Eleanor. **My Navajo Sister.** Illustrated by Eleanor Schick. Simon & Schuster, 1996. ISBN 0689805292. 32 pp. 4–8. Fiction.

A young girl and her family come to live on the Navajo reserva-tion. She is befriended by Genni, a young Navajo girl, and together the two girls explore the reservation, walking the back roads and climbing the canyon walls. Genni introduces her new friend to the Navajo culture. At a family picnic, Genni's mother calls the friend Sparrow, saying "She eats like a bird!" When Sparrow and her family move away from the reservation, she finds it difficult to leave her Navajo sister. The soft colors of the full-page illustrations present a realistic depiction of contempo-rary Navajo culture. (CC)

1.79 Scott, Ann Herbert. **Brave as a Mountain Lion.** Illustrated by Glo Coalson. Clarion, 1996. ISBN 0395667607. 31 pp. 4–8. Fiction.

What comes through in this story of contemporary Shoshone life is how a family lovingly works together to help solve a problem. Spider is proud of his perfect spelling test, but is afraid of participating in a spelling bee and standing before a large group. He seeks advice from his father, grandmother, and brother, and learns how they overcome their fear. In turn, Spider discovers his own individual way to be brave. Colorful watercolor illustrations capture the feelings of Spider and the affection of his family members. (KYR)

1.80 Shaik, Fatima. **The Jazz of Our Street.** Illustrated by E. B. Lewis. Dial, 1998. ISBN 0803718853 (trade). ISBN 0803718861 (library binding). 32 pp. 4–8. Fiction.

Residents of a New Orleans neighborhood emerge from their porches to follow an impromptu jazz parade, dancing to the shimmering music in a "second line." Told in first person by a young African American girl who, with her brother, joins in the celebration of music and community, this book illustrates how individual stories—whether musical or oral—come together to create and reinforce a common history. An author's note provides historical background on the city's tradition of marching bands and the resurgence of such organizations in recent years. Full-page watercolor illustrations capture the joy of both the music and the dance. (SM)

1.81 Shaw-MacKinnon, Margaret. **Tiktala.** Illustrated by Laszlo Gal. Holiday House, 1996. ISBN 0823412210. 28 pp. 6–8. Fiction.

Tiktala believes that she will someday become a famous and admired soapstone carver. Following the advice of an elderly villager, Tiktala goes in search of a spirit helper, who turns Tiktala into a harp seal. As a harp seal, Tiktala begins a journey with Tulimak, another harp seal, that teaches her about the dangers of the sea and the importance of friendship, trust, and the beliefs of her culture. The light-colored illustrations create an almost dreamlike setting in which to follow Tiktala on her journey. (MR)

1.82 Sisnett, Ana. **Grannie Jus' Come!** Illustrated by Karen Lusebrink. Children's Book Press, 1997. ISBN 0892391502. Unpaged. 5–8. Fiction.

Wit de bubblin rhythm of de Caribbean tongue, Ana Sisnett tells an enchanting story of a young girl who eagerly awaits the arrival of her grandmother. Set in Paraíso, Panama, the dialogue between the girl and her grandmother is told in the rhythmic dialect of Caribbean English, just right for a lively read-aloud. Readers of all ages will enjoy this loving story complemented by the joyous illustrations of Karen Lusebrink. (KW)

1.83   Sisulu, Elinor Batezat. **The Day Gogo Went to Vote: South Africa, 1994.** Illustrated by Sharon R. Wilson. Little Brown, 1996. ISBN 0316702676. 6–10. 32 pp. Fiction.

A young girl's great-grandmother, Gogo, wants to vote in the 1994 election in South Africa. Prior to this election, Black South Africans had not been allowed to vote. Since Gogo is the oldest person in town, Thembi, her granddaughter, worries about how Gogo will be able to walk, stand in line, and finally vote. Gogo does accomplish her dream of voting and Thembi learns an important lesson in democracy. The soft pastel illustrations by Sharon Wilson give the book a warm feel. (MP)

ALA Notable Books for Children, Notable Books for a Global Society

1.84   Smalls, Irene. **Because You're Lucky.** Illustrated by Michael Hays. Little Brown, 1997. ISBN 0316798673. Unpaged. 6–9. Fiction.

Kevin comes to live with his cousins Dawn and Jonathan, who have mixed feelings about accepting him as a member of the family. Dawn shuts her door and disappears, leaving Jonathan to struggle with sharing his clothes, his bedroom, and his school friends. After some ups and downs, Kevin and Jonathan learn to appreciate and even enjoy each other's company. The illustrations, though true to the text, have a stiff quality that tends to distance the reader from the characters and their difficulties. Although the mother clearly has good intentions, her explanation of why Kevin is there—"Because you're lucky"—seems obscure, and the tone throughout feels somewhat didactic. (SJ)

1.85   Soto, Gary. **Snapshots from the Wedding.** Illustrated by Stephanie Garcia. Putnam, 1997. ISBN 039922808. 32 pp. 4–8. Fiction.

Soto introduces us to Maya, a young flower girl, who takes us on a journey through her family's Mexican American wedding celebration. Through Maya's eyes, we see the various family members and characters who share in this special family occasion. She shares with us the traditional events of the wedding such as the ceremony, the kiss, the cake cutting, and the wedding toasts, as well as the less important side events. Readers will delight in Maya's naive account of this traditional celebration as seen by a child. Soto's simple verse and Garcia's very detailed three-dimensional artwork enhance this wonderful story. (RF)

Pura Belpré Award Winner for Illustration

1.86 Stanley, Sanna. **Monkey Sunday: A Story from a Congolese Village.** Illustrated by Sanna Stanley. Frances Foster / Farrar, Straus and Giroux, 1998. ISBN 0374350183. 32 pp. 4–8. Fiction.

Like most six-year-old children, Luzolo, a Congolese girl, is inquisitive and easily distracted. When asked by her father, a preacher, to sit still during the Matondo celebration of thanksgiving, Luzolo agrees. The celebration takes place under a palm thatch shelter with no walls, allowing animals to wander in and investigate. Tension builds for Luzolo when the animals are attracted to her like a magnet. She tries her best to ignore the animals and listen to her father preach, but the temptation is too great. Meanwhile, the other animals are helping themselves to the celebration food offerings, and a monkey swings in to cause havoc. Luzolo's mother beckons for help but Luzolo is torn between sitting still for Dad or helping Mother save the food. Luzolo decides to help escort the animals out of the shelter. Her father has learned a lesson about his daughter: she is most happy when she is allowed to be herself. The illustrations are simple but warm and friendly, in oranges, reds, beiges, and browns. (CMH)

1.87 Steptoe, John. **Creativity.** Illustrated by E. B. Lewis. Clarion, 1997. ISBN 0395687063. 32 pp. 6–9. Fiction.

There is a new student in Charles's class. The new student, Hector, is Puerto Rican. Charles agrees to walk him home from school and the boys become friends. Charles helps Hector adjust to a new way of life in the United States. This cross-cultural friendship helps Charles learn about and appreciate the similarities and differences between his and Hector's cultures. (SF)

1.88 Stevens, Jan Romero. **Carlos and the Skunk / Carlos y el zorrillo.** Illustrated by Jeane Arnold. Rising Moon, 1997. ISBN 0873585917. 32 pp. 4–8. Fiction.

Wanting to impress his friend Gloria, Carlos attempts to catch a skunk by its tail. The skunk sprays Carlos, who tries to wash off the scent by bathing in a river and then in a tub of tomato salsa. Even so, when Carlos goes to church with his family the next day the skunk odor remains on his shoes, and the church is permeated with the foul odor. The next day, his father takes Carlos to buy new shoes, and when he has the opportunity to catch a skunk again, Carlos quickly declines. Each page of the text is bilingual, with English on top and Spanish on the bottom. The story ends with a recipe for salsa. (CP)

1.89 Stevenson, Robert Louis. **The Bottle Imp.** Illustrated by Jacqueline Mair. Clarion, 1995. ISBN 0395721016. 60 pp. 9–12. Fiction.

Keawe buys a magic bottle, and in it is an imp who will grant his every wish. But the owner must sell the bottle at a loss prior to his death, or be doomed to a life in hell. As the story unfolds, Keawe finds the house of his dreams and the love of his life, Kokua. When Kokua discovers Keawe's destiny, she tricks him into selling the bottle to her in order to save his soul. Their love for each other knows no bounds. This is a wonderful story about greed and the price we pay for our desires. Jacqueline Mair's watercolor illustrations of the South Seas setting are so vibrant and intense that one looks forward to continuing the story just to get to the next picture. (MR)

1.90 Stuve-Bodeen, Stephanie. **Elizabeti's Doll.** Illustrated by Christy Hale. Lee & Low, 1998. ISBN 1880000709. Unpaged. 4–7. Fiction.

When Elizabeti gets a new baby brother, she also decides that she needs a doll to care for the same way that Mama cares for Obedi. Elizabeti finds the perfect rock to serve as a doll to love, whom she names Eva. When Mama bathes Obedi, Elizabeti bathes Eva (who only splashes a little). When Mama burps Obedi, Elizabeti burps Eva (who is too polite to burp). A near tragedy is avoided when Eva is lost and discovered by someone who does not realize the significance of the doll. Readers will enjoy this warm tale of love and tenderness, beautifully illustrated by Christy Hale's creative collage paintings, which is set in contemporary Tanzania. (KW)

ALA Notable Books for Children

1.91   Tamar, Erika. **The Garden of Happiness.** Illustrated by Barbara Lambase. Harcourt Brace, 1996. ISBN 0152305823. 32 pp. 4–8. Fiction.

The New York City neighbors of East Houston Street are transforming a garbage-filled empty lot into a "Garden of Happiness." As neighbors from a variety of cultures prepare for planting, young Marisol wants to plant something too. Unfortunately, there is no room left. Unwilling to be left out, Marisol borrows a seed from the pigeons being fed by Mrs. Garcia and plants it in a small crack in the sidewalk next to the garden. Soon Marisol's plant is the largest of them all, and then blooms into a brilliant sunflower that brightens the entire neighborhood. When fall approaches Marisol is saddened by the loss of her beautiful flower. Her sadness turns to joy when her flower is re-created in an outdoor mural painted by neighborhood teenagers. Vivid oil paintings with colorful borders illustrate the liveliness of the culturally diverse neighborhood. (CC)

Notable Books for a Global Society

1.92   Testa, Maria. **Nine Candles.** Illustrated by Amanda Schaffer. Carolrhoda, 1996. ISBN 0876149409. 30 pp. 4–8. Fiction.

Sunday is Raymond's favorite day of the week because he gets to visit his mother, who is in jail for larceny. Today is also a special day for Raymond because it is his seventh birthday. His father presents Raymond with gifts in the morning, but when Raymond visits his mother, he believes that she has forgotten all about his birthday. Soon enough, however, Raymond's mother presents her son with a birthday cake. She reminds him that when his cake has nine candles on it, she will be celebrating with him and his father at home. (CP)

1.93   Van Camp, Richard. **A Man Called Raven.** Illustrated by George Littlechild. Children's Book Press, 1997. ISBN 0892391448. Unpaged. 6–10. Fiction.

In a compelling contemporary story an elder teaches two young Indian brothers about having respect for life and for nature. Through the elder's story, the boys learn about an old man who hurt ravens and was transformed into a raven as punishment. But it is through being a raven that he learns kindness and compassion. George Littlechild's dramatic illustrations add to the magic of the story. (KW)

1.94 Van Camp, Richard. **What's the Most Beautiful Thing You Know about Horses?** Illustrated by George Littlechild. Children's Book Press, 1998. ISBN 0892391545. Unpaged. 5–8. Fiction.

Richard is from the Dogrib Nation of the Northwest Territories in Canada, where they have great respect for dogs but have never used horses because of the extreme cold. On the coldest day of the year, Richard consults family and friends and asks each person, "What's the most beautiful thing you know about horses?" He learns that they can run sideways, have secrets, always know their way home, and have super-cool hair! Children will delight in this playful tale, complemented by George Littlechild's bold and lively paintings. (KW)

1.95 Wells, Rosemary. **Yoko.** Illustrated by Rosemary Wells. Hyperion, 1998. ISBN 0786803959 (trade). ISBN 0786823453 (library binding). Unpaged. 4–8. Fiction.

Wells conveys a message of tolerance for diversity in this story about Yoko, a female cat of Japanese heritage. Yoko is very upset when the animals in her classroom exhibit disgust about sushi, her favorite food. After thinking for many hours, Mrs. Jenkins, Yoko's teacher, informs the parents of an upcoming International Food Day. Will this event successfully solve the problem? The references to ethnic differences are depicted through the illustrations: Yoko's mother wears a kimono, Valerie's mother wears a sombrero, and miniature flags representing each country are inserted into the dishes of food. (JC)

1.96 Willard, Nancy. **The Tortilla Cat.** Illustrated by Jeanette Winter. Harcourt Brace, 1998. ISBN 0152895876. 48 pp. 6–12. Fiction.

The members of the Romero family all come down with a fever, beginning with Mrs. Romero. Even though her husband is a good doctor, he cannot save her. Then the children become ill one by one. However, each of them awakens in the morning completely recovered. They each report that they were visited in the night by a singing cat who delivered a tortilla on a tray for them to eat. Dr. Romero is skeptical, and is convinced that the cat vision is the result of delirium from the fever. (SF and ED)

1.97 Wing, Natasha. **Jalapeño Bagels.** Illustrated by Robert Casilla. Atheneum, 1996. ISBN 0689805306. 24 pp. 5–8. Fiction.

Pablo must decide which of the delicacies from his parents' bakery to bring to school for International Day. Since his mother is Mexican American and his father Jewish, his final decision may not be much of a surprise; yet, the warmth of the family and the details of the individual cultures make for a realistic and reassuring story. Watercolor illustrations that bleed off the pages reinforce the intimacy of the family scenes. Spanish and Yiddish words are italicized in the text and a glossary with a pronunciation guide is appended, as are recipes for chango bars and the jalapeño bagels themselves. (SM)

1.98 Wolff, Ferida. **A Year for Kiko.** Illustrated by Joung Un Kim. Houghton Mifflin, 1997. ISBN 0395773962 . 32 pp. 4–8. Fiction.

Kiko, a playful child, shows how each month can bring about simple, playful experiences. From catching snowflakes in January, through planting flowers in May, to anticipating snow again in December, Kiko shows how to enjoy each month and each year by experiencing nature's wonders. (SKA)

1.99 Woodson, Jacqueline. **We Had a Picnic This Sunday Past.** Illustrated by Diane Greenseid. Hyperion, 1997. ISBN 0786802421 (trade). ISBN 0786821922 (library binding). Unpaged. 6–10. Fiction.

Teeka and Grandma are among the first to arrive at the park on Sunday to set up for a picnic. As family members and friends appear and the table fills with food, the reader gets the "inside story" on the new arrivals and their contributions. Through Teeka's blunt comments about Terrance, that "mean old cousin of mine," and Auntie Kim, "my all-time favorite," who teaches second grade, as well as Grandma's worries about the dryness of Cousin Martha's apple pie, the narrative moves quickly forward with contagious good humor. The casual, conversational tone is complemented by bright illustrations that seem to jump out from each two-page spread. They perfectly capture the lively and diverse personalities in this African American family gathering. (SJ)

1.100 Wyeth, Sharon Dennis. **Something Beautiful.** Illustrated by Chris K. Soentpiet. Bantam Doubleday Dell, 1998. Unpaged. 8–11. Fiction.

A little girl looks at her dismal surroundings: a dark alley, litter on the sidewalk, the word "die" painted on the wall, a homeless woman. Feeling dissatisfied with life, she goes in search of something beautiful to warm her heart. On her uplifting journey through the neighborhood, she finds a giggling baby, children dancing and laughing, boys playing a friendly game of basketball, and shiny apples at a nearby market. Her heart is filled with warmth as she discovers that she is indeed beautiful on the inside. This story, told with realistic watercolors, empowers us all to feel proud of what we have. (SS)

Notable Social Studies Trade Books for Young People, Notable Books for a Global Society

1.101 Yolen, Jane. **Miz Berlin Walks.** Illustrated by Floyd Cooper. Philomel, 1997. ISBN 0399229388. 32 pp. 5–8. Fiction.

Miz Berlin walks around the block talking to herself and sometimes singing fragments of a song, and everyone in Mary Louise's Virginia neighborhood assumes that she is just crazy. One evening, with nothing else to do, Mary Louise decides to catch up with Miz Berlin. Mary Louise discovers not a crazy old lady, but a wonderful storyteller who can create a whale of a tale as easily as she can relate a story from her own past. Floyd Cooper's rich illustrations convey the magical effect that Miz Berlin and her stories have on Mary Louise. Jane Yolen's intergenerational, interracial story is a warm and lovely reminder about the importance of storytelling and sharing the stories of our lives. (BK)

2 Realistic Fiction Novels

2.1 Abelove, Joan. **Go and Come Back.** DK Ink, 1998. ISBN 0789424762. 177 pp. 12 and up. Fiction.

Alicia, a young Isabo woman, is not interested in the "two old white ladies," the anthropologists, who have come to her village of Poincushmana in Peru. To Alicia they seem very stingy with their possessions, and know nothing about the villagers' way of life. They do not even understand the villagers' explanation of their belief about the purpose of sex. Alicia cannot understand how they could be so "dumb." Through their encounters, Alicia helps to teach the anthropologists the ways of her tribe. In turn, the anthropologists teach Alicia that there is more to the world than just her village. This book takes an honest look at the American way of life from a different cultural perspective. (ER)

ALA Notable Books for Children, Best Books for Young Adults

2.2 Belton, Sandra. **Ernestine and Amanda: Members of the C.L.U.B.** Simon & Schuster, 1997. ISBN 0689816111. 161 pp. 8–12. Fiction.

This is the third book in the "Ernestine and Amanda" series of stories about African American girls growing up in the 1950s. Now in the sixth grade, Ernestine and Amanda come to a new school and are placed in separate classrooms. As they struggle with their on-and-off friendship, they also must deal with divorce in their families, boy-girl relations, and membership in an exclusive club. An important element of the plot develops around an oratory contest, in which students must deliver speeches on notable African Americans. An appendix is included to provide additional historical information. (SF)

2.3 Belton, Sandra. **Ernestine and Amanda: Summer Camp, Ready or Not!** Simon & Schuster, 1997. ISBN 0689808461. 168 pp. 8–12. Fiction.

This is the second book in the "Ernestine and Amanda" series of stories about African American girls growing up in the 1950s. In this book Amanda and Ernestine go away to summer camp. Amanda goes to an integrated camp, while Ernestine goes to an African American camp. Back home, both of their families are going through some major changes. Both girls learn some valuable lessons at camp that will help them adjust to these changes when they return home. (SF)

2.4 Brooks, Martha. **Bone Dance.** Orchard, 1997. ISBN 0531300218. 179 pp. 14 and up. Fiction.

Alexandra's long-lost father dies and leaves her a cabin in Manitoba. She decides to go there to explore her Canadian Indian heritage. She learns about the father she never knew, the sacred land that he willed to her, the former landowner's son, Lonny, and the spirits that haunt them all. This is a beautifully written coming-of-age book about love and loss. (ER)

Best Books for Young Adults

2.5 Bruchac, Joseph. **Eagle Song**. Dial, 1997. ISBN 0803719191. 79 pp. 9 and up. Fiction.

This story chronicles the experiences and feelings of Danny Bigtree, a young Mohawk boy, as he leaves the reservation to live in Brooklyn, New York. Danny has trouble at his new school and is teased by his classmates because he is Native American. When his father shares cultural and historical information with Danny's class, he becomes more accepted and is able to interact more confidently with classmates. In this way, the story addresses important issues of stereotyping and misunderstanding of Native Americans, although the many distracting subplots of the book obscure this message somewhat. A glossary of Native American terms helps the reader better understand the realities of contemporary Native American life depicted in this book. (SSG)

Notable Social Studies Trade Books for Young People

2.6 Bruchac, Joseph. **The Heart of a Chief.** Dial, 1998. ISBN 0803722761. 153 pp. 10 and up. Fiction.

Chris Nicola would rather spend time on his special island in the heart of the Penacook Indian land than begin sixth grade off the reservation. While trying to retain his pride and his people's traditions, he assumes a leadership role both at school and at home. Some issues he must face include the use of Native American names for sports teams, casino gambling, and his father's struggle with alcoholism. Chris's Penacook name, which means *bridge,* becomes a symbol for his efforts to function in both Indian and White cultures. (SG)

2.7   Cameron, Ann. **More Stories Huey Tells.** Illustrated by Lis Toft. Farrar, Straus and Giroux, 1997. ISBN 0374350655. 118 pp. 6–9. Fiction.

The adventures of Huey and his older brother, Julian, continue in this chapter book for young readers. The two brothers, well-grounded in a secure family and a solid network of neighborhood friends, experience a series of adventures that are vaguely linked by the underlying theme of the father's efforts to stop smoking. Huey's naive innocence is underscored by his efforts to "feed" his dying sunflowers, and the nearly fatal attempts to accommodate the daredevil desires of his playmates as they dig a tunnel in sandy park soil in search of gold. Fans of the several books about these brothers will enjoy this offering; however, the convenient convergence of themes might seem too pat to some readers. Black-and-white drawings offer the only clues that Huey's family is African American. (SM)

2.8   Chambers, Veronica. **Marisol and Magdalena: The Sound of Our Sisterhood.** Jump at the Sun / Hyperion, 1998. ISBN 0786804378. 141 pp. 9–12. Fiction.

Marisol and Magdalena are thirteen-year-old best friends of Panamanian heritage. Although they were born in America and live in New York City, the girls are surrounded by family and friends who bring the culture of Panama into their daily lives. They enjoy eating Tía Luisa's special *frituras,* dancing to Latin music at family gatherings, and speaking the hybrid language called *Spanglish.* Through Marisol's first-person narration, the reader learns that it can be difficult balancing two cultures, especially while navigating adolescence. Marisol faces her greatest challenge when her mother, a single parent who is working and going to college, sends her to live for a year with her grandmother in Panama. Although the story centers on issues involving dual cultures, the characters' struggles are recognizable and accessible to readers of all backgrounds. The liberal intermingling of Spanish and English is gracefully done so that meaning and tone are clear. It is a compelling account of a teenager's coming of age. (SJ)

2.9 Dewey, Jennifer. **Navajo Summer.** Boyds Mills, 1998. ISBN 1563972484. 143 pp. 10 and up. Fiction.

In first-person narrative, twelve-year-old Jamie shares the devastation she feels upon learning that her parents are divorcing. She spends the summer living with the Wilson family in Navajo country, where she believes she can find peace and solitude. Jamie shares with readers her summer adventures such as horse racing and taking part in Navajo religious ceremonies. The story depicts her search for the inner peace and stability needed to cope with her parents' separation. (MS)

2.10 Farmer, Nancy. **A Girl Named Disaster.** Orchard, 1996. ISBN 0531095398. 309 pp. 12 and up. Fiction.

Life in the small African tribal village is hard for Nhamo. She is eleven and her family is gone. Knowing that it has been arranged for her to marry a cruel man with three other wives, she decides to run away. As we follow Nhamo through her adventurous flight in Mozambique and Zimbabwe, we come to know her as a survivor on a heroic journey to freedom and independence. (ER)

Newbery Honor Book, ALA Notable Books for Children, IBBY Honor Book, Best Books for Young Adults

2.11 Fenner, Carol. **Yolonda's Genius.** Simon & Schuster, 1995. ISBN 0689800010. 210 pp. 10–14. Fiction.

To provide a safer environment for her two children, Josie Blue, an African American widow, relocates her family from Chicago to a small town in Michigan. Eleven-year-old Yolonda is the overweight, yet confident, talented, and enterprising protagonist who is extremely protective of Andrew, her six-year-old brother. Andrew Blue is a struggling first-grade student with extraordinary musical ability. Yolonda believes that Andrew is a genius, one who "rearranges old material in a way never heard before." Rather than expressing himself verbally, Andrew plays his harmonica to exhibit his feelings and reactions. Yolonda's aim is to convince others, especially her mother, that Andrew is gifted. Fenner portrays urban and suburban living in a balanced manner, and makes abundant use of cultural markers without stereotyping. (JC)

Newbery Honor Book

2.12   Fleischman, Paul. **Seedfolks.** Illustrated by Judy Pedersen. HarperCollins, 1997. ISBN 0060274719 (trade). ISBN 0060274727 (library binding). ISBN 0064472078 (paperback). 80 pp. 9–14. Fiction.

Multiethnic residents of an inner-city Cleveland neighborhood slowly transform a trash-strewn vacant lot into a community garden, after a young Vietnamese girl plants a few bean seeds behind an abandoned refrigerator to honor her late father, who died before her birth. Each chapter is narrated by a different character as, one by one, each resident discovers that the garden enriches his or her life. These short but effective character sketches come together in a whole that is larger than the sum of its parts, as a deteriorating, largely immigrant neighborhood slowly becomes a true community. Pair this with Dyanne DiSalvo-Ryan's picture book, *City Green,* for another perspective on how a neighborhood garden can forge a link between young and old, neighbor and neighbor, across race, class, and ethnicity. (SM)

Best Books for Young Adults, Quick Pick for Young Adults, Notable Social Studies Trade Books for Young People, Notable Trade Books in the Language Arts

2.13   Giles, Gail. **Breath of the Dragon.** Illustrated by June Otani. Clarion, 1997. ISBN 0395764769. 104 pp. 9–12. Fiction.

Malila is only a small child when she must leave her home to live with her grandmother. After Malila's father is shot and killed by police during a robbery, her mother leaves her with Grandmother while she seeks a better life in America. Malila learns traditional Thai customs from her grandmother along with the truth about her father's life. Grandmother's unconditional love enables Malila to survive and overcome the stigma of being considered *suay* (unlucky) by others in their community. Malila grows in wisdom and courage with the lessons learned from Grandmother. When Grandmother becomes ill, Malila cares for her as Grandmother once cared for Malila. After Grandmother's death, Malila makes the decision to leave Thailand and join her mother in America. A glossary of Thai words is appended. (CC)

2.14   Glass, Tom. **Even a Little Is Something: Stories of Nong.** Illustrated by Elena Gerard. Linnet, 1997. ISBN 0208024573. 119 pp. 9–12. Fiction.

In a rural village of Thailand, Nong lives with her sister Oi and their widowed mother. Nong's story is told through brief episodes that combine to form an intricate portrayal of Nong and the people of her village. Eccentric characters are presented with humor, kindness, and realism. While the characters and settings may be unfamiliar to American readers, Nong's cares and concerns are common to eleven-year-old children from many cultures. (CC)

2.15 Green, Timothy. **Twilight Boy.** Rising Moon / Northland, 1998. ISBN 0873586700. 227 pp. 12 and up. Fiction.

Green writes a suspenseful mystery in this fictional story about a creature of Navajo mythology. Not knowing if the mysterious wolf is human or spirit keeps the reader entranced. The suspenseful climax occurs when the wolf is trapped and made to reveal his true nature. This book puts stereotypes and cultural misunderstandings into perspective, as the Native Americans view the *bilagaana,* or White people who live among them, as oddities who know little about Navajo ways. The ample use of the Navajo language, with translations provided, gives the story a sense of authenticity. (CMH)

2.16 Griffin, Peni. **Margo's House.** Margaret McElderry / Simon & Schuster, 1996. ISBN 0689809441. 122 pp. 8–10. Fiction.

Margo and her father share a very special relationship. Being a skilled craftsman, he builds a dollhouse with a brother and sister doll for Margo. Unexpectedly Margo's father has a heart attack and cannot finish the mother and father dolls for the house. Margo is worried about her father's severe condition but finds comfort in playing with the dollhouse he made for her. One evening that which is imaginary comes to life when Margo finds herself transformed into a living version of "Sis," the female four-inch wooden doll. Acting as Sis, she has a sense that she must go to her father's workshop where he built the dollhouse. Her father's spirit guides her on a long journey from her room to the workshop. (MS)

2.17 Grimes, Nikki. **Jazmin's Notebook.** Dial, 1998. ISBN 0803722240. 112 pp. 12 and up. Fiction.

Jazmin Shelby is an African American teenage girl who aspires to be a celebrated author. Through her daily journal entries, many adorned with eloquent poetry, the reader enters Jazmin's world to learn about her life in an urban neighborhood and the challenges her family faces. Jazmin is mature beyond her years as she shares her views on religion, interpersonal relationships, and a variety of other societal issues. (JC)

Coretta Scott King Author Honor Book

2.18 Hyppolite, Joanne. **Ola Shakes It Up.** Delacorte, 1998. ISBN 0385322356. 128 pp. 8–12. Fiction.

Ola Benson's family is moving from her beloved neighborhood of Roxbury, in Boston, to suburban Walcott Corners. They will be the first African American family in Walcott Corners, a community with strict rules and expectations. Ola devises several plans to prevent her family from moving. When those plans are unsuccessful, she schemes to convince her family to move back to Roxbury. When all fails, she begins to work on plans to survive in Walcott Corners. Her final plan not only makes life better for her, but also for the rest of the community. (SF)

2.19 Johnson, Angela. **Gone from Home.** DK Ink, 1998. ISBN 0789424991. 104 pp. 12 and up. Fiction.

Angela Johnson's twelve short stories poignantly describe the hardships and wonders of adolescence. In "Starr," a young girl looks to her eccentric, pierced, and bald babysitter for the maternal relationship she has never known. In the end, she discovers that Starr is bald because of her battle with cancer, which eventually separates the two. In "Souls," Greg and Mick go on a crusade to free all the pet store animals and give them away for free. Though they know stealing is wrong, they decide that nothing with a soul should be bought or sold. (ER)

2.20 Johnson, Angela. **Heaven.** Illustrated by Paul Zakris. Simon & Schuster, 1998. ISBN 0689822294. 138 pp. 12 and up. Fiction.

Marley, of Heaven, Ohio, is fourteen and believes she knows who she is and where she belongs in her world. She knows the routines of her neighbors in Heaven; bonds with Feather, the toddler she watches; befriends Shoogy, a girl pretending not to be bothered by her imperfections; and carries on a relationship through letters with Jack, a man she believes is her uncle. A combination of events force Marley to confront the untold truth: Marley's birth mother is dead, and the man she knew as Uncle Jack is in fact her father. Part Four of the novel touches on Marley's pain from being deceived, her struggle to forgive, and her rediscovery of herself. (JY)

Coretta Scott King Author Award Winner, Best Books for Young Adults

2.21 Kim, Helen. **The Long Season of Rain.** Henry Holt, 1996. ISBN 0805047581. 275 pp. 8–12. Fiction.

Junehee Lee lives with her mother, three sisters, and her father's mother in Seoul, Korea. Her father is an infrequent presence in their lives, as he is often gone on trips to America or out with his friends. At eleven years of age, Junehee lives a relatively happy and safe existence. When Pyungsoo, a young boy orphaned by a mudslide, arrives into her home of women, things begin to change dramatically. Junehee slowly learns about the rigid rules governing women in Korean society. She struggles to make sense of it all while watching her mother slowly crumble under the weight of social mores. This book offers an intriguing glimpse into traditional Korean culture and gender roles. (EA)

2.22 Kurtz, Jane. **The Storyteller's Beads.** Illustrated by Michael Bryant. Gulliver / Harcourt, 1998. ISBN 0152010742. 128 pp. 9–12. Fiction.

Intermediate grade readers will find this powerful story set in Ethiopia during a time of famine to be very enlightening. Based in fact, the story follows two girls who become refugees in the 1980s during the Israeli airlifts. Sahay's family has been violently killed, and Rahel is blind. After overcoming many prejudices and difficulties, they realize they must help each other in order to flee their country. In a hopeful conclusion, the author leaves the reader with a compassionate portrayal of the bond of friendship in the time of strife. (MP)

Notable Social Studies Trade Books for Young People, Notable Books for a Global Society

2.23 McGuigan, Mary Ann. **Where You Belong.** Atheneum, 1997. ISBN 0689812507. 171 pp. 10–14. Fiction.

The year is 1963, and Fiona is thirteen and on her own. Her mother has just been evicted from their Bronx apartment and her father is an alcoholic who may fly into a drunken rage at any minute. Just when Fiona feels she does not know where she belongs, Yolanda stumbles back into her life. Irish American Fiona and African American Yolanda had been unlikely friends in school. The girls spend an adventure-packed day together and realize that despite what everyone says, racial differences cannot undermine their friendship. (ER)

2.24   Mead, Alice. **Junebug and the Reverend.** Douglas & McIntyre, 1998. ISBN 0374339651. 186 pp. Fiction. 9–12. Fiction.

Mead realistically describes the hardships Junebug faces, including the divorce of his parents, moving, adjusting to a new school, dealing with bullies, and making friends. Junebug, only ten years old, seems much older because of his responsibility and solid values. Although Junebug feels that adjustment to his new life is complicated, he does not realize that his personality has such a positive impact on everyone he meets. Trust and friendship are what glue the story together. (CMH)

Notable Social Studies Trade Books for Young People

2.25   Meyer, Carolyn. **Jubilee Journey.** Harcourt Brace, 1998. ISBN 01520137776. 181 pp. 10–18. Fiction.

This sequel to *White Lilacs* is like riding a time machine from the past into the present. Spunky Rose Lee Jefferson, the central character of *White Lilacs,* is now eighty-seven years old and known to all as Mama Rose. Her great-granddaughter, the biracial Emily Rose, has come with her family from Connecticut to Texas to join in the Juneteenth Diamond Jubilee celebration. This family from the North finds life in a small Texas town dangerous and difficult to understand. Racial issues that were of no consequence in their Connecticut community become startlingly apparent in Dillon, Texas. There are other unexpected controversies in the African American community as well. In this charged atmosphere, Mama Rose hopes one of her great-grandchildren will be able to accept the Jefferson family legacy. Emily Rose, the only daughter of the only daughter of the only daughter of Mama Rose, must be the one to carry their heritage into the future. (CK)

Notable Social Studies Trade Books for Young People, Notable Books for a Global Society, Best Books for Young Adults

2.26 Mowry, Jess. **Ghost Train.** Henry Holt, 1996. ISBN 080504440X. 164 pp. 9 and up. Fiction.

Remi, a recent immigrant from Haiti, relocates with his mother and father to Oakland, California. Here he befriends his neighbor Niya, an African American girl, and the two develop a trusting relationship as Remi becomes accustomed to life as a teenager in America. Remi, who is sensitive to the supernatural, struggles to understand his encounters with a "ghost train" that roars past his bedroom window at 3:13 each morning. Remi and Niya share an adventure as they search for answers about this unusual phenomenon. Together they ultimately solve a murder mystery of long ago. This intriguing tale of the paranormal is one the reader will not want to put down until the last page. (SSG)

Quick Pick for Young Adults

2.27 Naidoo, Beverly. **No Turning Back: A Novel of South Africa.** HarperCollins, 1997. ISBN 0060275057 (Trade). ISBN 0060275065 (library binding). 160 pp. 8–12. Fiction.

Children of grades three to seven will be entranced by this story of South Africa after apartheid. Jabu, a twelve-year-old boy, runs away from an abusive stepfather and becomes a child of the streets. He learns to survive with the help of a "gang" of boys and then is able to find work with a White shopkeeper. Not long after, the prejudice of the man and his son causes Jabu to run off again. Through the help of a city shelter in Johannesburg, he is reunited with his mother. This realistic third novel by Naidoo follows her other strong stories of apartheid, *Journey to Jo'burg* (1986) and *Chain of Fire* (1990). (MP)

Notable Social Studies Trade Books for Young People

2.28 Namioka, Lensey. **Yang the Second and Her Secret Admirers.** Little Brown, 1998. ISBN 0316597317. 128 pp. 8–11. Fiction.

Readers have enjoyed Namioka's two previous novels about the Yang family's struggle to adjust to life in America. In this novel, the youngest son and daughter, Yingtao and Yingmei, are well on their way to acculturation, but their older sister, Yinglan, is desperately clinging to China and her life there. Yingtao and Yingmei are concerned that she is lonely and unhappy, and after watching Shakespeare's *Much Ado about Nothing*, the two concoct a plan to find a boyfriend for Yinglan. The plan backfires, but the results are positive as Yinglan begins to strike a balance between her old and new cultures. (BK)

2.29 Nye, Naomi Shihab. **Habibi.** Simon & Schuster, 1997. ISBN 0689801491. 259 pp. 11–18. Fiction.

Using a whimsical but serious style, Nye tells of a thirteen-year-old American girl named Liyana, who moves with her Palestinian father and American mother to the Palestinian West Bank. Liyana's many quirky observations of neighbors, food, animals, and boys are fun to read, but her problems of cultural adaptation and of coming of age in the midst of the Israeli occupation also make for powerful content. The events move along energetically and Liyana quickly works her way into the reader's heart. This lyrical and frank book written from a Palestinian American perspective raises difficult issues without descending into polemic, and marks a watershed in juvenile literature about the contemporary Middle East. (KL)

Jane Addams Book Award for Longer Books, ALA Notable Books for Children, Notable Books for a Global Society

2.30 Pevsner, Stella, and Fay Tang. **Sing for Your Father, Su Phan.** Clarion, 1997. ISBN 039582267X. 107 pp. 9–12. Fiction.

This is the story of Su Phan's recollections of life in Vietnam during the war. Now living in the United States, she is able to reflect upon childhood memories and relive the painful and touching experiences of growing up in Vietnam. She writes about what it was like to go from being rich to poor, and to struggle to make ends meet. Not only does she live through the devastation of losing her home and all of her possessions, but she also lives through the humiliation of schoolmates teasing her about a father who refuses to accept the communistic ways and who is put in jail for many years because of those beliefs. Su Phan eventually quits school to help her family sell food to make ends meet. Her lost childhood and experiences growing up with a bitter grandmother and a naive mother make for a compelling story about the impact of war. (SKA)

2.31 Pierson Ellison, Suzanne. **Best of Enemies.** Rising Moon / Northland, 1998. ISBN 0873587146. 12 and up. 200 pp. Fiction.

With a title that might seem like an oxymoron, this story places people of three different cultures—Navajo, New Mexican, and Texan—in a battle. It is a battle of accepting each other's differences in order to survive in the desert. Pierson Ellison maintains a consistent view of each culture, only to make readers realize later that cultural differences must be overcome when the goal is survival. The three young adults take a risk by trusting each other in a difficult situation, but in the end they also create a strong bond of shared camaraderie. (CMH)

2.32 Pinkney, Andrea Davis. **Raven in a Dove House.** Gulliver / Harcourt Brace, 1998. ISBN 0152014616. 208 pp. 5–8. Fiction.

It is August again, and twelve-year-old Nell knows it's time to spend another month in upstate New York with her aunt Ursa and cousin Foley. While Nell enjoys her time spent in Modine with her aunt and cousin, this year she cannot help but feel that her father sent her away so he could spend some time alone with his girlfriend. Despite herself Nell takes pleasure in her cousin's crazy antics and his friend Slade's amorous attention. Things turn dangerous when Foley asks her to hide a pistol he has obtained illegally, saying "this is family helping family." When tragedy strikes Nell is forced to grow up and come to some tough decisions about the truth and about family. (EA)

2.33 Reeve, Kirk. **Lolo and Red-Legs.** Rising Moon / Northland, 1998. ISBN 0873586832. 111 pp. 7–10. Fiction.

Set in East Los Angeles days before summer vacation is over, eleven-year-old Isidoro "Lolo" Garcia discovers, lures, and captures a Mexican red-leg tarantula, which he makes his pet. Lolo's adventures with Red-Legs enable him to understand his stereotypes, explore new relationships, and conquer his fears. Education, curiosity, and trust win out over the threat of gangs and violence. Peppered with Spanish phrases and words, Reeve's story allows readers to visit the barrio life of a young Latino boy, his friends, and his family. (CW)

2.34 Salisbury, Graham. **Shark Bait.** Delacorte, 1997. ISBN 0385322372. 151 pp. 12 and up. Fiction.

Eric, also known as Mokes, is a Hawaiian teenager who likes to hang out with his friends. Mokes finds the fact that his father is the chief of police of their town to be a major inconvenience in his life, especially around his friends. Trouble comes when his friends want to see the gun that Moke's father uses and stores at home. This story takes an unusual look at life in Hawaii, which may be unfamiliar to many students. This is a book to be enjoyed particularly by reluctant readers, because of its fast pace and first-person narrative style. (SA)

2.35 Soto, Gary. **Off and Running.** Delacorte, 1996. ISBN 0385321813. 136 pp. 9–12. Fiction.

Fifth grader Miata Ramirez and her friend Anna are running for president and vice president of the class against Rudy Herrera and Alex. The girls' platform includes planting flowers and beautifying the school, but the boys' pledge to have more ice cream and recess brings strong competition for the positions. The book consists of chapters that show the happy lives of the girls and their interactions with the boys. The goodwill of all the children wins out in the end. (RH)

2.36 Vanasse, Deb. **A Distant Enemy.** Lodestar, 1997. ISBN 0525675493. 179 pp. Fiction.

Half White, half Yup'ik Eskimo, Joseph detests his whiteness and his White (*kass'aq*) father who abandoned his family and deserted their Alaskan village. Joseph's Yup'ik grandfather and his new *kass'aq* high-school English teacher try to help, but his anger at the White intruders drives him to vandalism, betrayal, and near self-destruction. This narrative competently harnesses the fury that at times punctuates adolescence, and couples it with the added tensions that are felt when an enraged young man juggles identities within two distinct cultures. (GG)

2.37 Woodson, Jacqueline. **The House You Pass on the Way.** Delacorte, 1997. ISBN 0385321899 128 pp. 12 and up. Fiction.

Staggerlee, a fourteen-year-old girl, is comfortable with her interracial family but is lonely and shunned by her peers, mainly because her mother is White. But Staggerlee also has a secret. In sixth grade she kissed another girl and liked it. Now rejected by that friend, she wonders if she is gay. A cousin, Trout, whom she has never met before, comes to visit, and the two girls find they are mutually attracted. Seeing an opportunity to share her feelings with someone else, Staggerlee begins to confront her own developing identity. Later Trout writes, telling Staggerlee about a boyfriend she really likes; Staggerlee is devastated, but Trout reminds her they are only fourteen and do not know yet who they will become. This rich, multifaceted novel raises issues of teenagers' self-confidence, sexuality, and the uncertain future they face. (LS)

2.38 Woodson, Jacqueline. **If You Come Softly.** Putnam, 1998. ISBN 0399231129. 181 pp. 12 and up. Fiction.

Jeremiah's family was broken apart when his successful father left his mother for their mutual friend. His mother is depressed and his father is remote. Ellie's parents are surgeons, distant and unable to understand the complexity of her life. Jeremiah is African American and Ellie is Jewish, but this difference does not matter to either of them. Although they seem to come from different worlds, they create a private universe where they understand each other completely. Then, almost too quickly, tragedy tears what they have to pieces. Poetically narrated by both teenagers, this book deals with issues of race and class, violence and death. (CK)

Notable Books for a Global Society, Best Books for Young Adults

2.39 Yee, Paul. **Breakaway.** Groundwood / Douglas & McIntyre, 1994. ISBN 0888992890 144 pp. 11 and up. Fiction.

Born and raised in Canada by Chinese parents, Kwok lives a life constantly divided between two different worlds. His family lives and works on a farm while most of the other Chinese families live in town. To make matters even more difficult, he is a good soccer player but is denied a spot on the travel team because of his Chinese heritage. He is given the opportunity to play for the Chinese "town kids" team, but feels that he is a foreigner there as well. Kwok wrestles with his identity and searches for a place to belong while confronting racism and prejudice. His family adds to the struggle as well, as his mother encourages him to get a good education so that he can be a good citizen while his father tries to ensure that Kwok never forgets his heritage. (CH)

Best Books for Young Adults

2.40 Yep, Laurence. **The Case of the Goblin Pearls.** HarperCollins, 1997. ISBN 006024445 (trade). ISBN 0060244461 (library binding). 160 pp. 10–13. Fiction.

In this first installment of the "Chinatown Mystery" series, the acclaimed author of young adult novels introduces readers to San Francisco's newest Chinatown detectives. The two main characters are Lily, age twelve, and her famous movie star aunt, Tiger Lil, who combine forces to solve the mystery of priceless pearls missing from the New Year's Day parade. Humor flows throughout the book, and although sometimes the dialogue may not seem serious enough, the information Lily discovers about her Chinese American roots is heartwarming. (MP)

2.41 Yep, Laurence. **The Cook's Family.** Putnam, 1998. ISBN 0399229078. 184 pp. 9–12. Fiction.

In this sequel to *Ribbons*, Robin's family seems to be falling apart due to the job stresses and quarreling of her White father and Chinese mother. Then, on an outing in San Francisco's Chinatown, she and her grandmother are asked by a waiter to pretend to be the long-lost relatives of a forlorn and lonely cook. They hesitantly oblige, but Robin finds that this game offers her a sense of her Chinese heritage, a stronger relationship with her grandmother, and an escape from the family tensions. This sensitively told story has an unlikely premise, but it is based on a true incident. (KYR & ER)

3 History and Historical Fiction

History

3.1 Bial, Raymond. **The Strength of These Arms: Life in the Slave Quarters.** Houghton Mifflin, 1997. ISBN 0395773946. 48 pp. 8–12. Nonfiction.

This photo essay serves as an introduction to the daily life of slaves in the United States. Especially striking are the contrasts drawn between the luxury of the masters and the poverty of the slaves. Through photographs, text, and the slaves' own words, Bial depicts their work, housing, family life, diet, religion, and recreation. He includes the horrors and injustices of slavery while emphasizing the strength and dignity with which the slaves resisted their oppressors and preserved their African heritage while adapting to life in a new country. A bibliography and books for further reading are included. (SG)

Notable Social Studies Trade Books for Young People

3.2 Cooper, Michael L. **The Double V Campaign: African Americans and World War II.** Lodestar, 1998. ISBN 0525675620. 82 pp. 9–12. Nonfiction.

This book recounts how African Americans fought two wars during World War II, one against enemy dictators and the other against racial discrimination on the home front. This dual struggle became known as the "Double V Campaign." A vivid account of the two reactivated Black Infantry divisions, the Ninety-second in Europe and the Ninety-third in the Pacific, describes the difficulties they encountered in training, on the battlefield, and in confronting the racial power structure of the military. Photographs, maps, a "gallery of firsts," and a chronology of significant events complement the text. (LD)

3.3 Cooper, Michael L. **Hell Fighters: African American Soldiers in World War I.** Lodestar, 1997. ISBN 0525675345. 96 pp. 12 and up. Nonfiction.

Hell Fighters is the story of the Fifteenth New York Infantry, a group of African American men who were poorly trained, largely uneducated, and unprepared for combat during World War I. This group came to be known as the Hell Fighters because of the severity of the situations they were placed in while fighting in Europe. The efforts of these men were not recognized by many of their White countrymen, even though they fought diligently and received honors in Europe for their gallant efforts. *Hell Fighters* presents the combined struggles of African Americans for acceptance as soldiers in combat as well as recognition as men and citizens at home in America. (CH)

3.4   Fisher, Leonard Everett. **Anasazi.** Atheneum, 1997. ISBN 0689807376. 32 pp. 5–9. Nonfiction.

Fisher draws from clues of archeological remains and theories about the Anasazi civilization to piece together a history of this mysterious culture. The Anasazi flourished in the Four Corners area of the American Southwest, but suddenly vanished from the area around 1300. Illustrated in moody sepia-toned pictures, the text describes the evolution of their housing construction, basketry and pottery, farming and migration. Included is an interesting timeline of parallel events in other parts of the world. (KYR)

3.5   Fleischner, Jennifer. **The Dred Scott Case: Testing the Right to Live Free.** Millbrook, 1997. ISBN 0761300058. 64 pp. 9–12. Nonfiction.

The author relates the story of Dred Scott and the details of the Supreme Court case decision in which arguments for and against slavery were confronted. The introduction relates the story of the court decision. The text then reverts to the past, building the background for the dilemma this country faced in the pre–Civil War era as a result of the conflict caused by slavery. The author gives an accurate account of the political dilemma, as well as details of Scott's early life and what happened to him after the trial. The intriguing text is enhanced by the illustrations and reproductions of pertinent articles. The book includes a bibliography, a list for further reading, and a chronology. (SSG)

3.6   Haskins, Jim. **The Harlem Renaissance.** Millbrook, 1996. ISBN: 1562945653. 192 pp. 12 and up. Nonfiction.

Haskins makes great use of photographs and sketches of events surrounding the years between 1916 and 1940. The Harlem Renaissance was a period of U.S. history when African Americans were recognized for their intellect and creativity and their culture was celebrated. Haskins takes the reader through the Great Migration, the Great Depression, and the onset of World War II. He explains how the economics of America and racial segregation helped bring about the end of the Harlem Renaissance. Haskins also shares many biographical sketches of African American artists, composers, musicians, singers, and writers. He balances well-known historical information with little-known tidbits of African American history to maintain the interest of the reader. (CH)

3.7   Katz, William Loren. **Black Legacy: A History of New York's African Americans.** Atheneum, 1997. ISBN 0689319134. 250 pp. 12 and up. Nonfiction.

Black Legacy is a comprehensive history spanning almost four hundred years. Well written and interesting, this painstakingly detailed account of African Americans in New York links the African sailors and language translators in the early 1600s, through the African American role in the Civil War, to Marcus Garvey, Malcolm X, and David Dinkins. Following African Americans through the growth and history of New York City allows the reader to draw parallels to other populations of African Americans in different cities during the same historical periods. Katz has compiled an enormous amount of research and presents the information clearly. His book becomes an accessible and important textbook. (CW)

3.8   King, Casey, and Linda Barrett Osborne. **Oh, Freedom! Kids Talk about the Civil Rights Movement with the People Who Made It Happen.** Photographs by Joe Brooks. Knopf, 1997. ISBN 0679858563. 138 pp. 9–13. Nonfiction.

With an inspirational foreword by civil rights activist Rosa Parks, King and Osborne divide this account of the civil rights struggle into three parts—"Life Under Segregation," "The Movement to End Legalized Segregation," and "The Movement Shifts: The Struggle to End Poverty and Discrimination." Each part is preceded by background information, and contains interviews with people who lived during the specified historical period. Children of all races and walks of life conduct interviews with family, friends, and others about their involvement in or reaction to selected historical events. Black-and-white photographs appear on almost every page, adding realism and context to the interviews. An extensive bibliography and an index are provided. (JHC)

3.9   Koslow, Philip. **Asante: The Gold Coast.** Chelsea House, 1996. ISBN 079103139X. 64 pp. 10 and up. Nonfiction.

From a twelve-book series entitled "The Kingdoms of Africa," the author draws upon *objets d'art,* artifacts, travel journals of European visitors, and colonial records to provide a rich history of the kingdom of Asante without reference to its colonial national boundaries. The book has lush photographs of gold jewelry and masks, maps, photo portraits, and oral histories, and contains a glossary, bibliography, index, and chronology. (KL)

3.10   Marrin, Albert. **Empires Lost and Won: The Spanish Heritage in the Southwest.** Atheneum, 1997. ISBN 0689804148. 216 pp. 10 and up. Nonfiction.

Full of maps, visuals, and primary source documents, Marrin's book recounts the history of the U.S. Southwest through the eyes and stories of the Spanish conquistadors, missionaries, and soldiers. Gold and God were the original Spanish settlers' primary concerns, yet slowly their priorities changed to land and power. However, gold and God were never far from the thoughts of the explorers. From the travels of Cabeza de Vaca across Mexico to the conquest of the Pueblo Indians to the Alamo, readers are confronted with the rich Spanish/Mexican history of North America. (CW)

3.11   Myers, Walter Dean. *Amistad:* **The Long Road to Freedom.** Dutton, 1997. ISBN 0525459707. 100 pp. 8 and up. Nonfiction.

This book relates the story of the *Amistad* rebellion, in which captive Africans took over a slave ship, were captured, and eventually won their freedom and returned to their African home. The book is written simply but powerfully, with plenty of dates and facts but with a "child's eye view" as well. It contains a timeline, extensive bibliographic citations, historical photos of the people and places, quotations from the trials, and personal information about the main characters. This book can be successfully used in conjunction with the movie by the same name as an American history project for a single student or a whole class. (KL)

Notable Books for a Global Society.

3.12 Philip, Neil, editor. **In a Sacred Manner I Live.** Clarion, 1997. ISBN 0395849810. 93 pp. 12 and up. Nonfiction.

This Native American anthology compiles many rarely seen photographs of Native Americans from the past and present, as well as speeches and interviews of prominent Native Americans concerning their thoughts and beliefs about the world. Some of the famous speeches of Native Americans such as Chief Seattle, Black Elk, Sitting Bull, Geronimo, and others are collected in this book, many supplemented with additional useful information about the speaker. This anthology conveys the compassion these people have for their world in a way most readers can understand. This is a beautiful book that adults as well as children can read to get a better understanding of the beliefs and lives of Native Americans, both in history and in contemporary America. (SA)

Notable Children's Trade Books in the Field of Social Studies, ALA Notable Books for Children, Best Books for Young Adults

3.13 Smith, John David. **Black Voices from Reconstruction, 1865–1877.** Millbrook, 1996. ISBN 1562945831. 174 pp. 12 and up. Nonfiction.

The story of the twelve-year period after the Civil War known as Reconstruction has been told many times, but seldom from the African American perspective. Original source documents, photographs, and drawings are included in a narrative from the point of view of former slaves. At times the text is somewhat dry, but powerful quotes and stories about the search for family members, the desire for land, food, and shelter, the struggle to vote, and the growth of the Ku Klux Klan make for very interesting reading. The social injustices endured by the freed slaves comes through in this well-researched text. (LD)

3.14 Viola, Herman J., editor. **It Is a Good Day to Die: Indian Eyewitnesses Tell the Story of the Battle of the Little Bighorn.** Crown, 1998. ISBN 0517709120. 101 pp. 9–12. Nonfiction.

In this collection of eyewitness reports, Native Americans tell their story of what happened during the Battle of the Little Bighorn (known to the Plains Indians as the Battle of the Greasy Grass). These recollections, taken from thirteen Native Americans including Sitting Bull and Antelope Woman, share the events leading up to Custer's attack and his dramatic defeat. A historical chronology, introduction, endnotes, maps, and archival photographs help to build the context of this exciting story. (KW)

Notable Social Studies Trade Books for Young People

Historical Fiction

3.15   Appelbaum, Diana. **Cocoa Ice.** Illustrated by Holly Meade. Orchard, 1997. ISBN 0531330400. 56 pp. 4–8. Historical fiction.

With bright, colorful illustrations, this picture book story set in the 1800s presents similar events as seen through the eyes of two young girls who live worlds apart. In Santo Domingo, one girl waits for the high-rigged schooner to bring ice, which she will mix with the cocoa her family grows to create a delectable chocolate ice. In Maine, another girl awaits the same schooner to bring cocoa to mix with the ice her family sells to create her own chocolate ice cream. (MR)

3.16   Bosse, Malcolm. **Tusk and Stone.** Front Street, 1995. ISBN 1886910014. 244 pp. 9–12. Historical fiction.

In this story set in seventh century India, a horrible turn of events leaves Arjun, a young boy born into the highly esteemed Brahmin order, totally stripped of his birthright, and witness to the kidnapping of his younger sister and murder of his uncle. He is traded off and begins a new life as a *mahout*, an elephant driver, in the army. Despite his hardships he manages to finds success in all that he does; but first and foremost on his mind is his desire to find his younger sister. The story is captivating, particularly in portraying the internal fortitude of Arjun in the face of great misfortunes. (SA)

3.17   Bruchac, Joseph. **Children of the Longhouse.** Dial, 1996. ISBN 0803717946. 154 pp. 9–12. Historical fiction.

In this novel set in the late fifteenth century, eleven-year-old Ohkwa'ri and his twin sister Otsi:stia are Mohawk Indians living in what is now part of New York State. Ohkwa'ri incurs the wrath of four older boys when he reports to the tribal elders their plans to violate the League of Peace of the Iroquois Nation. When the entire tribe participates in a game of *tekwaarathon* (known today as lacrosse), Ohkwa'ri faces the older boys in peace and earns their respect. Joseph Bruchac paints a fine picture of traditional Mohawk life, the League of Iroquois Nations, and the important role of women in this league. He easily connects past to present in the afterword, providing information about recent attempts by the Mohawk to reclaim some of their lost tribal lands. (BK)

3.18 Bruchac, Joseph. **The Arrow over the Door.** Illustrated by James Watling. Dial, 1998. ISBN 0803720785. 96 pp. 9–12. Historical fiction.

In alternating chapters, fourteen-year-old Samuel Russell wrestles with his Quaker family's belief in pacifism when he feels they are in danger from Loyalists and Indians. Stands Straight, an Abenaki Indian boy whose parents and siblings were killed by American colonists, is on a scouting mission with his uncle who is trying to decide whether to help fight for the British. When their lives intersect, both boys are profoundly changed. This story is based on an actual incident in 1777, and the author's note tells of extensive research and changes that were necessary in order to be historically accurate. In spite of the superb theme of peace, the book is somewhat heavy-handed in attempting to dispel stereotypes. (LS)

Notable Social Studies Trade Books for Young People

3.19 Bunting, Eve. **So Far from the Sea.** Illustrated by Chris K. Soentpiet. Clarion, 1998. ISBN 0395720958. 30 pp. 9–12. Historical fiction.

On this day, Laura Iwasaki and her family will visit her grandfather's grave at the Manzanar War Relocation Camp for the last time before they move to Massachusetts. In a tender, heart-wrenching story, Laura's father remembers the barracks and life behind the wire fence when he was taken from his home with his family. Readers will have difficulty keeping the tears out of their eyes as they are taken back in time through Chris K. Soentpiet's brilliant and sensitive illustrations in this picture book. (KW)

Notable Books for a Global Society

3.20 Chambers, Veronica. *Amistad* **Rising: The Story of Freedom.** Edited by Shelly Bowen. Illustrated by Paul Lee. Harcourt Brace, 1998. ISBN 0152018034. 8–12. Unpaged. Historical fiction.

In 1839 Joseph Cinqué, a young African man, is kidnapped into slavery and taken from Africa on the ship *Amistad.* The fictional story of Cinqué is based on real historical accounts of the revolt of captive Africans on the *Amistad.* Cinqué interacts with John Quincy Adams as the former President argues in defense of the enslaved Africans in the 1841 court case. Children will appreciate this deeply thoughtful story with soft, dark, acrylic illustrations. (MP)

Notable Social Studies Trade Books for Young People

3.21 Collier, Mary Jo, and Peter Collier. **The King's Giraffe.** Illustrated by Stéphane Poulin. Simon & Schuster, 1996. ISBN 0689806795. 40 pp. 5–9. Historical fiction.

In 1826, when the pasha of Egypt decides to send his prized giraffe as a gift to King Charles of France (to reciprocate for France's gift of a printing press), he also sends his stable boy, Abdul, to tend the animal on the long voyage. The lushly whimsical oil paintings show details of life in nineteenth-century France and help make the text-heavy story come alive, as we follow the unusual twosome on their procession from Marseilles to Paris. Throughout the six-week journey, citizens of France greeted the first giraffe ever to set foot in France with enthusiastic affection, which only intensified during the animal's eighteen-year residence at the Royal Menagerie. This vignette of nineteenth-century French history would have been stronger with the inclusion of source notes. The final illustration (showing the Eiffel Tower topped off with the head of a giraffe) is misleading, as the tower was built some forty years after the giraffe died. (SM)

3.22 Connelly, Bernardine. **Follow the Drinking Gourd: A Story of the Underground Railroad.** Illustrated by Yvonne Buchanan. Rabbit Ears / Simon & Schuster, 1997. ISBN 0689802420 (Book and CD edition). 40 pp. 5–8. Historical fiction.

This exquisite and compelling audio production of Bernardine Connelly's story of a slave family's escape on the Underground Railroad combines the talents of actor Morgan Freeman with guitarist/singer Taj Mahal. Freeman gives an understated, yet poignant reading, and Taj Mahal's bluesy instrumental accompaniments and vocals add to the drama of the story. This version differs from other retellings by offering more information on Peg Leg Joe and the use of pepper to deter dogs from human scent. A wonderful addition with a powerful and important message about courage and American history. (KYR)

3.23 Crook, Connie Brummel. **Maple Moon.** Illustrated by Scott Cameron. Stoddart Kids, 1997. ISBN 0773730176. 32 pp. 4–8. Historical fiction.

There are many different stories of how maple syrup was discovered. In this picture book version, Crook introduces the reader to Rides the Wind, an eight-year old boy with a crippled leg, who, with the help of Red Squirrel, discovers the sweet sap that eventually becomes maple syrup and helps to save his tribe from starvation during the bitterly cold winter. The bold illustrations give a very serious tone to the story and the possible hardships of the Missisauga Indians. (MR)

3.24 Curtis, Christopher Paul. **The Watsons Go to Birmingham—1963.** Delacorte, 1995. ISBN 0385321759. 210 pp. 11 and up. Historical fiction.

Nine-year-old Kenny Watson narrates this story of the Watsons, a middle-class African American family living in Flint, Michigan, in 1963. Kenny provides a glimpse of a warm, caring, and fun-loving family. When Kenny's parents determine that his thirteen-year-old brother Byron is evolving from a contrary adolescent into a juvenile delinquent, they decide he should spend some time with his grandmother in Birmingham, Alabama. The Watsons arrive in Birmingham as the Civil Rights movement is reaching its stride, and the author deftly weaves an actual tragedy of the period—the bombing of the Sixteenth Avenue Baptist Church—into the lives of these fictional characters. This tragedy is made more horrifying when it touches the lives of this fine family. (BK)

Newbery Honor Book, Coretta Scott King Author Honor Book

3.25 Dalkey, Kara. **Little Sister.** Harcourt, 1996. ISBN 0140386319. 208 pp. 9–12. Historical fiction.

Thirteen-year-old Mitsuko tells of her sheltered, naive existence, which is shattered when her older sister's husband is murdered. Grief-stricken by the loss, Mitsuko's sister is left numb, as if her soul is dead even though she is still physically alive. To help her sister find her soul, Mitsuko embarks on a journey and evokes supernatural powers. The story takes place in the imperial court of twelfth-century Japan. The author provides a glossary of Japanese history, religion, and mythology to assist readers who are not familiar with them. (MS)

3.26   Duncklee, John. **Quest for the Eagle Feather.** Rising Moon / Northland, 1997. ISBN 0873586689. 85 pp. 7–10. Historical fiction.

Quiet Water is actually an Anglo boy named John Butler. Native Americans raised him after his family's wagon train, heading west, lost him in a storm. Quiet Water is coming of age and needs to prove himself in order to join the Clan of the Eagle. The elders of the village have doubts that Quiet Water will ever truly be one of them, and Quiet Water himself struggles with that same question. Quietly reflecting on his future, Quiet Water and his two best friends head for the Sacred Mountain to see the eagle, find an eagle feather, and gain the wisdom of the eagle in order to become men. A gift from his Indian father before their trip saves their lives, and the ordeal proves to the elders where Quiet Water's heart and loyalty lie. (CW)

3.27   Durrant, Lynda. **The Beaded Moccasins: The Story of Mary Campbell.** Clarion, 1998. ISBN 0395853982. 183 pp. 9–12. Historical fiction.

Twelve-year-old Mary Campbell is kidnapped from her family farm in Pennsylvania by the Delaware Indians in 1759. At first defiant and petulant, she comes to love and respect the Native Americans. Students will find this an engrossing read based on a true story, and teachers will find that they will be able to have enriching discussions based on colonial–Native American conflicts. (KW)

Notable Social Studies Trade Books for Young People

3.28   Hearne, Betsy Gould. **Listening for Leroy.** McElderry / Simon & Schuster, 1998. ISBN 0689822189. 224 pp. 9–12. Historical fiction.

In rural Alabama in the 1950s, Alice has no one to talk to but Leroy, the African American farmhand. When Alice's father objects to Leroy being beaten by bullies, the town continues to tolerate the acts of racism. The family moves to Tennessee without Leroy, but it is Leroy's "whispers in Alice's ear" that continue to nurture and support her spirit. (KW)

Notable Social Studies Trade Books for Young People

3.29   Holt, Kimberly Willis. **Mister and Me.** Illustrated by Leonard Jenkins. Putnam, 1998. ISBN 039923215X. 74 pp. 9–12. Historical fiction.

Eleven-year-old Jolene Jasmine Johnson barely remembers her father, who died when she was three years old. Yet Jolene resents Mr. Leroy Redfield's romantic interest in her mother. Jolene wishes to preserve the fading memory of her father as well as maintain the close family structure she has with her mother and grandfather. Tall, dark Leroy Redfield, or "Mister" as Jolene boldly calls him, will be a major intrusion in their life if her mother considers marriage. This warm story of African American family and community relationships is set in a small Louisiana sawmill town in 1940. Leonard Jenkins's full-page, black-and-white illustrations nicely complement the first-person narrative. (JC)

3.30   Lee, Milly. **Nim and the War Effort.** Illustrated by Yangsook Choi. Foster / Farrar, Straus and Giroux, 1997. ISBN 0374355231. 40 pp. 4–10. Historical fiction.

It is 1943 and Nim, who lives in San Francisco's Chinatown, hopes to win her school's paper drive contest for the war effort. Her determination and resourcefulness help her overcome the racism of her closest competitor—who thinks the winner should be American, "not some Chinese smarty-pants"—and prove that Chinese Americans can be as patriotic as anyone else. Especially touching in this story is the relationship between Nim and her grandfather. The richly-toned illustrations include simple, well-chosen details of Nim's daily life and surroundings, including a family meal, neighborhood stores and storekeepers, and the Ancestral Hall room in her home. They work smoothly with the text to recreate this particular period and place in U.S. history. (KYR & SJ)

Notable Books for Children, Notable Social Studies Trade Books for Young People, Notable Books for a Global Society, IRA Children's Book Award

3.31 Lorbiecki, Marybeth. **Sister Anne's Hands.** Illustrated by K. Wendy Popp. Dial, 1998. ISBN 00803720386. 34 pp. 8–12. Historical fiction.

Sister Anne's Hands relates the transition of a small town in the 1960s through the eyes of a second-grader named Anna. Her teacher, Sister Anne, is the first woman of color many in the town will know. Anna at first shrinks from the touch of those hands, and her teacher is confronted with racism from the first day. Rather than become angry at the children, Sister Anne shows them the colors of hatred that exist toward African Americans through pictures of suffering and segregation. Her message is one of opening hearts, and she gives Anna and her classmates another chance. Some parents pull their children from the school; others watch their children learn to write and subtract, and learn of Sojourner Truth and Dr. Martin Luther King Jr. Popp's illustrations, rendered in pastels, softly reveal the emotion of the children and the love of the teacher they know as Sister Anne. (JY)

Notable Children's Books in the Language Arts

3.32 Matcheck, Diane. **The Sacrifice.** Farrar, Straus and Giroux. 1998. ISBN 0374363781. 198 pp. 12 and up. Historical fiction.

This is an unusual story, set in the 1700s, of a Native American girl who lives in the area now known as Yellowstone National Park. An interesting turn of events leads her to believe that she, not her twin brother, is destined to become the Great One of the Apsaalookas. Throughout the story, her wild determination is tested and refined as she encounters and kills a grizzly bear, and is captured by a young Pawnee Indian and groomed to become a sacrifice for his people. This book offers a realistic look at what life was like for Native Americans in the 1700s. The female character's strong determination helps her to succeed in many of the encounters she faces. It is a captivating story that many girls as well as boys will enjoy. (SA)

Best Books for Young Adults

3.33 McKissack, Patricia C. **Ma Dear's Aprons.** Illustrated by Floyd Cooper. Atheneum, 1997. ISBN 0689810512. 32 pp. 3–8. Historical fiction.

Young David Earl's mother ties on a different apron each day of the week, depending upon what chores await her that day.

Domestic work in the early 1900s, especially in the segregated South, was difficult and tedious, and Ma Dear has to work long hours to support herself and her son. The depiction of life before modern household conveniences will be eye-opening to many children. However, this story, inspired by the author's own great-grandmother, is ultimately about the security that comes from family and home. The soft mistiness of the oil-wash paintings spread across facing pages lends an air of nostalgia as well as intimacy. And the depiction of the American flag and a regimental sword above the fireplace that honor David's father, who "died fighting out west," might provoke discussions of the roles Black soldiers played in American history. (SM)

Notable Social Studies Trade Books for Young People, Notable Books for a Global Society

3.34 McKissack, Patricia C. **Run Away Home.** Scholastic, 1997. ISBN 0590467514. 160 pp. 9–12. Historical fiction.

In a fictional story based on true events, acclaimed author Patricia McKissack tells the story of a young African American girl who befriends an Apache boy who escapes from the train that is taking him to a reservation. In spite of their differences, Sarah Jane and Sky find many things to agree on—Mama's corn pudding, corn-bread, and molasses. But Sarah Jane must then face the decision whether to turn Sky in. With tight plotting and lively dialogue, this book is a nice introduction to some aspects of African American history. (KW)

Notable Social Studies Trade Books for Young People

3.35 Medearis, Angela Shelf. **Rum-a-Tum-Tum.** Illustrated by James E. Ransome. Holiday House, 1997. ISBN 0823411435. 30 pp. 4–8. Historical fiction.

In the early 1900s a young girl from New Orleans is delighted to wake up to the calls of the street vendors outside her window. Their rhythmic voices entice her outside to the markets on her street. There she finds fruits, vegetables, and things from the sea. She listens to her neighborhood come alive with a sing-song verse. A parade goes by and she struts along with the jazz band. James E. Ransome's illustrations are bright with the colors of the fruits in the market and the spirit of this great city. (ER)

3.36   Namioka, Lensey. **Den of the White Fox.** Harcourt, 1997. ISBN 0152012826. 256 pp. 11 and up. Historical fiction.

Our heroes Matsuzo and Zenta are back in another *ronin* adventure in sixteenth-century feudal Japan. This time, they are lured by the legend of a white fox that brings them to a village and draws them into an adventure involving mysteries of martial arts, rebellion, wit, and intrigue. Young adults will enjoy the return of the heroes as well as the flavor of feudal Japan. (KW)

Notable Social Studies Trade Books for Young People

3.37   Park, Francis, and Ginger Park. **My Freedom Trip.** Illustrated by Debra Reid Jenkins. Boyds Mills, 1998. ISBN 1563974681. 32 pp. 5–9. Historical fiction.

Soo is a young Korean schoolgirl when her father leaves North Korea in the middle of the night to seek the "freedom land." His guide comes back for Soo and leads her on a journey over a mountain and through the woods. When a soldier stops them the guide pleads for her freedom, and Soo is allowed to reunite with her father across the river. The Korean War prevents Soo from ever seeing her mother again. The fact that this is based on a true story only heightens the drama of this story. (KW)

IRA Children's Book Award, Notable Books for a Global Society

3.38   Pelgrom, Els. **The Acorn Eaters.** Farrar, Straus and Giroux, 1997. ISBN 0374300291. 204 pp. 5–8. Historical fiction.

The conclusion of the bloody civil war in Spain has left the peasants of Andalusia living in a state of extreme poverty. Curro, an intelligent and crafty eight-year-old, leaves school to work at a local monastery as a swineherd. Each evening he sneaks into the hills behind the monastery to search for *bellotas,* acorn-like nuts, to help feed his starving family. The danger lies in getting caught, because everything surrounding the monastery belongs to the monks, and a peasant would be sorely punished if discovered. As Curro matures he sees the world for the way it truly is, filled with both good and bad people who do not necessarily come from the same caste. (EA)

3.39   Reeder, Carolyn. **Across the Lines.** Atheneum, 1997. ISBN 0689811330. 219 pp. 8–12. Historical fiction.

This is a story told in two voices: Edward, son of a plantation owner, and Simon, his slave companion. The Civil War has erupted. Edward's family believes that they will be safe in Riverview, their plantation, but they are forced to flee when the Union troops advance dangerously close. In the panic to leave, Edward and Simon are separated. Edward's family flees to St. Petersburg. Simon escapes and ends up working for the Union soldiers. (SF)

Notable Social Studies Trade Books for Young People

3.40 Rice, James. **Vaqueros.** Translated by Ana Smith. Pelican, 1998. ISBN 1565543092. 32 pp. 7–12. Historical fiction.

Chi Chi, a talking chihuaha, tells the story of the *vaqueros,* or Native American herdsmen, in this historically based bilingual book. The story covers the period from the Spanish conquest of the New World in the 1500s through the time period following the Civil War. Chi Chi relates the various skills the vaqueros learned over time to control the cattle and describes how their attire changed over the years. In the end, the reader learns that the vaqueros passed their skills on to the Anglo youths, who later came to be known as cowboys. Double-page full-color illustrations complement the text. (ED)

3.41 Robinet, Harriette Gillem. **Forty Acres and Maybe a Mule.** Atheneum, 1998. ISBN 068982078X. 132 pp. 9–12. Historical fiction.

During Reconstruction, twelve-year-old Pascal, his older brother Gideon, and another child named Nelly embark on a journey for freedom and the promised forty acres and a mule. Their joy is short-lived, however, when just a few months after they have planted cotton and built a house, their land is given over to Whites and their school is burned. Although the subject matter is compelling, students may find the writing heavy-handed at times. (KW)

Notable Social Studies Trade Books for Young People, Scott O'Dell Award for Historical Fiction

3.42 Robinet, Harriette Gillem. **The Twins, the Pirates, and the Battle of New Orleans.** Atheneum, 1997. ISBN 0689812086. 138 pp. 8–12. Historical fiction.

Pierre and Andrew are twelve-year-old escaped slaves. Their father Jacques, a free man, cleverly slips into the plantation of the cruel Marquis de Ville to free them. Jacques leaves them in a hidden treehouse in a Louisiana swamp while he goes to free the twins' mother and sister. When Jacques does not return, the twins realize that if their mother and sister are to be freed, it will be up to them. Their adventure leads them to encounters with pirates, the British redcoats, and the American army. (SF)

3.43   Robinet, Harriette Gillem. **Washington City Is Burning.** Atheneum, 1996. ISBN 0689807732. 149 pp. 8–12. Historical fiction.

Virginia is a house slave for President James Madison and Miss Dolly, the First Lady, at their summer retreat. She is summoned to work at the White House by Miss Dolly and the president's coachman, Tobias. Tobias has heard rumors of Virginia's bravery and chooses her to help serve in a conspiracy to free slaves. Virginia's young age serves as an advantage as she can get away with doing things that don't cause suspicion. On the other hand, she does not yet fully understand her mission, and makes mistakes along the way, Set in the year 1814, author Robinet allows the reader to experience an important slice of American history through the voice of a twelve-year-old child. (CW)

3.44   Robinson, Aminah Brenda Lynn. **A Street Called Home.** Harcourt Brace, 1997. ISBN 0152014659. Unpaged. 7–12. Historical fiction.

This accordion-style book unfolds to create Mt. Vernon Avenue, a street in Poindexter Village in Columbus, Ohio. The street became home to many African Americans, including the author's grandparents, when they migrated north. The illustrations teem with the life of this self-sufficient neighborhood. Ten cutout flaps invite the reader to look more closely at some of the lively characters living there. The Vegetable Man or the Chickenfoot Woman can feed you something good to eat, Dr. Kickapoo carries his cures in tinted-glass bottles, and the Cameraman will shoot pictures for ten cents a shot. Pulled out to its full eight feet in length, this two-sided street seems to come alive with color and action. (KB)

Notable Social Studies Trade Books for Young People

3.45 Rosenberg, Liz. **Grandmother and the Runaway Shadow.** Illustrated by Beth Peck. Harcourt Brace, 1996. ISBN 0152009485. 32 pp. 5–8. Historical fiction.

On a voyage to the United States, a young woman is accompanied by her shadow, which is with her every step of the way. From the moment she falls to her knees to kiss the ground when she finally reaches her destination, to the many late nights working at her lonely sewing job, her shadow is always there. It is even there for her first dance with the man who will later become her husband. The somber illustrations of this picture book help depict not only the harsh realities of immigration, but also the woman's bond with her shadow and how it keeps her from being lonely in her new country. (MR)

3.46 Rumford, James. **The Cloudmakers.** Houghton Mifflin, 1996. ISBN 0395765056. 32 pp. 5–9. Historical fiction.

This imaginative story blends history and legend to explain how papermaking spread throughout the world. Set in the year 751 during a war between the Arabs and Chinese, an unemployed grandfather and his grandson are captured by the Sultan of Samarkand. They barter for their freedom by claiming to make clouds, in reality impressing their captors with the process of papermaking. Watercolor illustrations bring to life a distant time and place where two different cultures shared knowledge with each other. A historical note follows the story. (KYR)

3.47 Sanders, Scott Russell. **A Place Called Freedom.** Illustrated by Thomas B. Allen. Atheneum, 1997. ISBN 0689804709. Unpaged. 8–11. Historical fiction.

This is the tale of a town called Freedom. In 1832, Joshua Starman and his family are freed from slavery. Seeking land and opportunity, they walk to Indiana, following the river, or "drinking gourd," along the way. Mama teaches her children to read and write while Papa works the land and finds success as a farmer. Soon, African Americans begin pouring in to this welcoming town, and Freedom is established. Lovely illustrations and eloquent wording make this story of slavery and freedom come to life. (SS)

Notable Social Studies Trade Books for Young People

3.48 Santiago, Chiori. **Home to Medicine Mountain.** Illustrated by Judith Lowry. Children's Book Press, 1998. ISBN 0892391553. 30 pp. 6–10. Historical fiction.

In the 1930s, Native American children were separated from their families and sent to live at government-run residential schools to "unlearn their Indian ways." Although the government paid for the boys to go to school hundreds of miles from their homes, it did not always pay to send them home for summer vacation. Lowry tells the story of how her father and Uncle Stanley find their way home by train one summer. Lowry's beautiful illustrations perfectly capture the rigidity of the school and contrast it with the magic and comfort of home. (KW)

ALA Notable Books for Children

3.49 Smalls, Irene. **A Strawbeater's Thanksgiving.** Illustrated by Melodye Benson Rosales. Little Brown, 1998. ISBN 0316798665. 30 pp. 8–12. Historical fiction.

This slave narrative describes a celebration on the plantations. The owners give the slaves a night to celebrate the harvest. They all gather and shuck the corn that is piled "mountainous" high. Their festive dinner is lavish and generous portions are served. Who is the strawbeater? It is not someone who beats straw, but a musician who stands behind a fiddler, reaches around, and beats on the strings like a drum. Rosales beautifully portrays the diversity among the African American people as well the richness of their shared traditions. (CMH)

3.50 Thomas, Joyce Carol. **I Have Heard of a Land.** Illustrated by Floyd Cooper. Joanna Cotler / HarperCollins, 1998. ISBN 0060234776. ISBN 0060234784 (library binding) 7–11. Historical fiction.

In the late 1880s thousands of pioneers, many of them former slaves, raced to the Oklahoma Territory to stake a claim for land. The female narrator describes what it was like to move to untamed territory and turn it into a home. The lyrical text is beautifully complemented by the soft, earthy colors of Floyd Cooper's illustrations. The author includes a historical note at the end giving personal details of her family, including her great-grandmother, who was among the pioneers who participated in this race. (MP)

Coretta Scott King Illustrator Honor, Notable Books for Children, Notable Social Studies Trade Books for Young People

3.51 Thomas, Dawn C. Gill. **Kai: A Mission for Her Village, Africa, 1440.** Illustrated by Vanessa Holly. Simon & Schuster, 1996. ISBN 0689809867. 65 pp. Historical fiction.

Unlike the rest of the girls in the Yoruba village of Ife, Kai is not afraid to compete with the boys. She runs faster than they do, and longs to become a sculptor of masks. The women in Ife are forbidden to learn this craft, so Kai must practice her art in hiding. A diseased yam crop threatens to send her village into starvation. The Oni, the ruler of Ife, decides that Kai and her lazy sister Jamila must journey to another village to ask for help. Kai is initially disappointed that her best friend Aisha was not chosen to accompany her. Along the way Kai learns that her sister has many more abilities than she ever suspected. Soon the sisters grow to love and depend on one another. Upon reaching the village Kai learns that the women there are revered artists, and she suspects that the Oni knew of her secret passion all along. (EA)

3.52 Trottier, Maxine. **The Walking Stick.** Illustrated by Annouchka Gravel Galouchko. Stoddart Kids, Toronto. ISBN 0773731016. 22 pp. 8–12. Historical fiction.

A father's walking stick is the centerpiece of this lyrical tale about a Vietnamese family. A young boy named Van first finds the teak stick by a Buddhist temple. His uncle, a Buddhist monk, tells Van that the stick will "watch over you . . . and bring you safely home." His treasured stick stays with him through marriage, war, and escape to America where Van raises his family. Through his grandchild, Lynn, the walking stick finds its way back to Vietnam. Striking images abound in the colorful, expressive illustrations. (KYR)

3.53 Van Steenwyk, Elizabeth. **My Name Is York.** Illustrated by Bill Farnsworth. Northland, 1997. ISBN 0873586506. 32 pp. 6–8. Historical fiction.

This is an interesting account of the journey of Meriwether Lewis and William Clark to discover a trade route to the Pacific Ocean in

1803. York, a slave owned by Clark who accompanied the group, narrates the story. Throughout the expedition, York tells of many of the adventures the group has had and of some of the people they met, but throughout the year his desire to be a free man is always on his mind. The descriptive passages of this historical journey are fascinating and complement the main narrative. Although York is the central character, the lack of background information about his life could make it difficult for some readers to relate to his innermost desire to become a free man. (SA)

Notable Social Studies Trade Books for Young People

3.54 Waters, Kate. **Tapenum's Day.** Photographs by Russ Kendall. Scholastic, 1996. ISBN 0590202375. 40 pp. 9–12. Historical fiction.

In 1620 Tapenum, a young Wampanoag boy, is disappointed at not being selected for training as a *pniese,* a warrior counselor. He decides to dedicate himself to intense training in hopes of making it into the next group. The story follows him through his first day of training, as it takes the reader on a journey of his village and the surrounding area. This fictional story makes use of historical information, and is supplemented by photographs taken at the Plimouth Plantation historical site in Massachusetts. Additional background information on the Wampanoag and a glossary of terms are included. This book is a companion to *Sarah Morton's Day* (1989) and *Samuel Eaton's Day* (1993), both also by Waters and Kendall. (CC)

3.55 Whelan, Gloria. **The Indian School.** Illustrated by Gabriela Dellosso. HarperCollins, 1996. ISBN 0060270772. 89 pp. 8–10. Historical fiction.

Two characters collide in culture and circumstance until they are drawn together by crisis. After the death of her parents, eleven-year-old Lucy is sent to live with her aunt and uncle, headmasters of a mission school for Native Americans. Raven and her brother, Star Face, are left at the school by their father, who promises to return for them in the spring when he has money to feed them. Immediately there is conflict between Aunt Emma, who believes Native Americans should change their ways, and Raven, who refuses to change. Although befriended by Lucy, Raven runs away from the confines of the mission school, and returns only when she learns of her brother's frightening illness. It is only then, as Aunt Emma and Raven work together to save Star Face, that their hands communicate through an unspoken language. Throughout the novel Lucy attempts to heal her own pain and tries to understand why so much change must come from the Native Americans and so little from the White man. Black-and-white sketches throughout the novel draw the reader into the text. (JY)

3.56 Wilson, Diane Lee. **I Rode a Horse of Milk White Jade.** Orchard, 1998. ISBN 0531300242 (trade). ISBN 0531330249 (library binding). 232 pp. 9–12. Historical fiction.

The story opens with a grandmother and granddaughter waiting for a special white mare to give birth. While they wait, the grandmother, Oyuna, tells the magical story of her youth. The setting is thirteenth-century Mongolia, and Oyuna is accidentally crippled after being stepped on by a horse. Considered bad luck by many in her clan, she eventually runs away with Kublai Khan's army. Accompanied by her aging white mare, whose presence invokes mysterious powers, Oyuna faces many challenges. The characters are realistically drawn, as are the many details of the land, customs, and general way of life. Through flashbacks, the author succeeds in building suspense and keeping the reader interested in Oyuna's often treacherous life journey. This story maintains a good balance between magical and historical elements. The adventuresome young heroine is sure to appeal to a contemporary audience. A glossary of Mongolian words is included. (SJ)

Best Books for Young Adults

3.57 Wisler, G. Clifton. **Caleb's Choice.** Lodestar, 1996. ISBN 0525675264. 154 pp. 9–12. Historical fiction.

When Caleb Dalaney's family loses its fortune in 1858, he has to leave his private school and privileged life to live with his grandmother in northern Texas. People there are divided about the Fugitive Slave Law that makes it a crime to help a runaway slave. Caleb struggles with this decision when a runaway slave rescues him from drowning and nurses him back to health. The moral struggle of this young boy, set in the context of the Underground Railroad in Texas, provides a story of a sort not often told about this time in history. This work of historical fiction is fast-paced and has a strong character development. (LD)

3.58 Wolff, Virginia Euwer. **Bat 6.** Scholastic, 1998. ISBN 0590897993. 230 pp. 9–12. Historical fiction.

In the small town of Bear Creek Ridge, Oregon, at the fiftieth annual sixth-grade softball game, something horrible happens. Shirley, whose father was killed at Pearl Harbor, slams her elbow into the face of Aki, a Japanese American whose family has just returned three years after the end of World War II. Although the adults cannot talk about why Aki's family had to "go away," the girls of the two teams raise the issue among themselves. Through first-person narrations of the twenty-one girls, a montage is created in which the subjects of racial prejudice and the internment of Japanese Americans are addressed. (KW)

Jane Addams Children's Book Award Winner for Longer Book, ALA Notable Books for Children

3.59 Wyeth, Sharon Dennis. **Once on This River.** Knopf, 1998. ISBN 0679883509. 150 pp. 10–14. Historical fiction.

In 1760, Monday and her mother are traveling by ship to the American colonies, in hopes of rescuing her uncle, a free man, who has been unjustly sold into slavery. Even as these two passengers are on a journey to free a man from enslavement, below the deck the ship's human cargo is headed for a life of slavery. When the ship is boarded by pirates, Monday is saved from becoming part of the cargo by the intervention of the ship's captain. The precarious condition of freedom for Africans is chillingly described in this superbly crafted book, which reads like a thriller but informs like the best of young adult historical fiction.

3.60 Yee, Paul. **Ghost Train.** Paintings by Harvey Chan. Groundwood, 1996. ISBN 0888992572. Unpaged. 8–12. Historical fiction.

Left behind in China while her father goes to Canada to find work, Choon-yi survives by painting and selling her pictures in the market. When her father asks her to join him, Choon-yi painfully discovers on her arrival that her father has died while helping to build the railroad. In a dream her father asks her to paint a "fire car," through which Choon-yi comes to understand what her father and the other men have died for, and their souls are able to travel home. This ghostly yet affirming tale is complemented by the superb oil paintings of Harvey Chan. (KW)

4 Ceremonies and Celebrations

4.1 Bernhard, Emery. **Happy New Year.** Illustrated by Durga Bernhard. Lodestar, 1996. ISBN 0525675329. 32 pp. 6–9. Nonfiction.

The celebration of the new year, as practiced across a variety of cultures and in different times, is described in this book. Celebrations from the United States, Bali, West Africa, Nigeria, China, Japan, and India are included, along with religious observances of Jewish, Islamic, Buddhist, and Iroquois families. Bold, colorful illustrations are accompanied by simple, informative text that provides authenticity to the explanations of events. A glossary of terms is appended. See also *Happy New Year! / Kung-hsi fa ts'ai!* by Demi (**4.2**), and *Celebrating Chinese New Year* by Diane Hoyt-Goldsmith (**4.5**). (CC)

4.2 Demi. **Happy New Year! / Kung-hsi fa-ts'ai!** Crown, 1997. ISBN 0517709589. 32 pp. 4–8. Nonfiction.

A holiday that many children have heard of, but may not know much about, is Chinese New Year. Demi's beautiful book is filled with information about this holiday. The illustrations are whimsical and also very informative. This jewel of a book also includes beautiful Chinese writings, a simple chart of the lunar calendar, a detailed description of the Chinese Zodiac, and much more. Demi's books are always a treat for the eyes, and this book is no exception. The beautiful cover and detailed illustrations fit perfectly with the gaiety of the Chinese New Year. See also *Happy New Year* by Emery Bernhard (**4.1**), and *Celebrating Chinese New Year* by Diane Hoyt-Goldsmith (**4.5**). (SA)

4.3 Ghazi, Suhaib Hamid. **Ramadan.** Illustrated by Omar Rayyan. Holiday House, 1996. ISBN 0823412547. 32 pp. 6–12. Nonfiction.

Watercolor paintings depict Hakeem, a young Muslim boy, working his way through the month of Ramadan. The focus is on the role of Ramadan in the tenets of Islam more than it is on the boy, but his presence in the paintings and in the explanations helps keeps young readers interested. The conversational tone and focus on the experiences of young Muslims, including those who struggle to observe the practices of Islam in non-Muslim countries, helps build awareness of Islam for young American readers. The book nicely sketches the sense of joy as well as solidarity Muslims feel in the month of fasting and feasting. A glossary of Arabic words and phrases used in the text is included at the end of the book. See also *Magid Fasts for Ramadan* by Mary Matthews (**4.14**). (KL and CP)

4.4   Grier, Ella. **Seven Days of Kwanzaa: A Holiday Step Book.** Illustrated by John Ward. Viking, 1997. ISBN 0670873276. 20 pp. 5–8. Nonfiction.

Progressively wider pages edged with colorful borders inspired by Kente cloth create a step effect, and vividly rendered illustrations enhance this overview of the seven-day cultural holiday celebrated by African Americans. Each day's guiding principle and symbol is presented, followed by a chant, song, or recitation. (Original sources are not identified.) Although interesting particulars such as simple recipes are included, the lack of more details about the holiday itself make this book one that is best used as a companion to other books about this holiday. See also *The Children's Book of Kwanzaa* by Dolores Johnson (**4.7**). (SM)

4.5   Hoyt-Goldsmith, Diane. **Celebrating Chinese New Year.** Holiday House, 1998. ISBN 0823413934. 32 pp. 9–12. Nonfiction.

This book is about how a Chinese American boy named Ryan celebrates Chinese New Year with his family in San Francisco. The celebration, portrayed in colorful photographs, is documented over a two-week period. Preparations, including cleaning the house and preparing traditional foods such as *chee goo,* shark fin soup, and black bean and garlic lobster tails, are chronicled, as well as the actual festivities that follow. The customs of honoring the ancestors, wearing the color red for good luck, and performing the Lion Dance are also shared in the colorful pictorials. This story depicts the rich blend of Chinese and U.S. traditions within this family. See also *Happy New Year! / Kung-hsi fa-ts'ai!* by Demi (**4.2**), and *Happy New Year* by Emery Bernhard (**4.1**). (SKA)

Notable Social Studies Trade Books for Young People

4.6   Hoyt-Goldsmith, Diane. **Potlatch: A Tsimshian Celebration.** Photography by Lawrence Migdale. Holiday House, 1997. ISBN: 0823412903. 32 pp. 9–11. Nonfiction.

David Boxley, the thirteen-year-old biracial boy of Metlakatia, Alaska, first introduced to readers in *Totem Pole,* participates in a modern *potlatch.* Throughout he explains the Tsimshian celebration to readers, both in historical and contemporary contexts. This photo essay is accurate, informative, and filled with the history and traditional art of southeast Alaska. (LS)

4.7   Johnson, Dolores. **The Children's Book of Kwanzaa: A Guide to Celebrating the Holiday.** Atheneum, 1996. ISBN 068980864X. 160 pp. 9–12. Nonfiction.

Engagingly written and comprehensive, this book about the Kwanzaa holiday is a great addition to any home or school library. The first part of the book narrates a history of Africans and African Americans, biographies of leading figures who illustrate the seven principles of Kwanzaa, and discussions of the seven principles and symbols. The rest of the book provides detailed directions for crafts, gift-making, and recipes. Illustrations are linoleum block prints and black-and-white drawings. Johnson invites everyone to celebrate this relatively new holiday and to be creative in making it one's own. See also *Seven Days of Kwanzaa* by Ella Grier (**4.4**). (KYR)

4.8   Johnston, Tony. **Day of the Dead.** Illustrated by Jeanette Winter. Harcourt Brace, 1997. ISBN 0152228632. 48 pp. 5–8. Fiction.

The anticipation of the celebration for the Day of the Dead, *el Día de los Muertos,* is almost too much to bear for the children in a small town in Mexico. The text and illustrations vividly evoke the sounds and smells of the preparation. The children are continually told to wait—*espérense*—until at last the family gathers to go out. The celebration honoring *los abuelos,* or deceased grandparents, continues well into the night. Finally, after leaving marigolds on the graves, the families make the return walk home, lit by candlelight. The intensely colored illustrations are set within black borders that are decorated with details from the pictures. See also *A Gift for Abuelita: Celebrating the Day of the Dead / Un regalo para Abuelita: En celebracíon del Día de los Muertos* by Nancy Luenn (**4.13**). (CC)

4.9 Kindersley, Barnabas, and Anabel Kindersley. **Children Just Like Me: Celebrations!** DK, 1997. ISBN 0789420279. 64 pp. 9–12. Nonfiction.

Divided into chapters by the seasons, this book depicts twenty-five different celebrations around the world, described by the children who enjoy them the most. The celebrations are described, as are the clothing that is worn, the food that is eaten, and the places where these events take place. The fabulous photographs by the authors convey a great deal of information about each of these celebrations and how important they are to each culture. (MR)

Notable Social Studies Trade Books for Young People

4.10 King, Elizabeth. **Quinceañera: Celebrating Fifteen.** Dutton, 1998. ISBN 0525456384. 40 pp. 10–15. Nonfiction.

Come along and enjoy the coming-of-age celebration called *Quinceañera*. Cindy Chavez, a Salvadoran American girl, and Suzi Prieto, a Mexican American girl, share their hopes and dreams as they prepare for their big day. This book gives us an opportunity to learn about the history of this rite of passage and how two modern families celebrate the occasion. The detailed color photographs tell their own story of excitement, anticipation, and joy. (ER)

4.11 Livingston, Myra Cohn. **Festivals.** Illustrated by Leonard Everett Fisher. Holiday House, 1996. ISBN 0823412172. 32 pp. 4–8. Poetry.

Festivals is a unique collection of poems celebrating fourteen festivals observed around the world, including Chinese New Year, Las Posadas, Kwanzaa, and Ramadan. A glossary at the end briefly describes the purpose of each festival and the time of year it occurs. Each poem shares the significance of a different celebration and is brought to life by brilliant illustrations. (MS)

4.12 Luenn, Nancy. **Celebrations of Lights.** Illustrated by Mark Bender. Atheneum, 1998. ISBN 068931986. 32 pp. 4–8. Nonfiction.

For thousands of years, lights have played a significant role in celebrations and festivals around the world. Twelve holidays are presented in this book, some of which may be very familiar to the reader and others which may be new. This informational text provides glimpses of the history behind each celebration in the form of a story. The illustrations beautifully portray people and settings from each country celebrating with lights. (MS)

4.13 Luenn, Nancy. **A Gift for Abuelita: Celebrating the Day of the Dead / Un regalo para Abuelita: En celebracíon del Día de los Muertos.** Illustrated by Robert Chapman. Rising Moon / Northland, 1998. ISBN 0873586683. 32 pp. 4–8. Fiction.

This beautifully illustrated book is written in both English and Spanish. The illustrations are made with hand-crafted molds and cast paper, and colorfully depict the everyday activities that Rosita did together with her grandmother before she died. Rosita misses her grandmother very much, and decides to show her love for her on the traditional Mexican holiday, the Day of the Dead. As she braids the cord, she remembers what she loves about her grandmother and is comforted. While this story illuminates a cultural tradition, non-Christian children may have some difficulty relating to the religious imagery and scenes in a graveyard. See also *Day of the Dead* by Tony Johnston (**4.8**). (RH)

Notable Books for a Global Society

4.14 Matthews, Mary. **Magid Fasts for Ramadan.** Illustrated by E. B. Lewis. Clarion, 1996. ISBN 0395665892. 48 pp. 5–9. Fiction.

Magid, an Egyptian boy of eight, tries to fast secretly during Ramadan even though he is under the recommended age. His twelve-year-old sister Aisha is fasting for the first time, and wishes she were not. Desperately wanting to join in this important family custom, Magid fasts during the day by pouring his lemonade in the river and feeding his sandwich to the geese. In the end their grandfather finds a happy compromise for both. The colorful watercolors show the interior of a modest contemporary Egyptian home as well as many careful details of dress and decoration, and portray the family at prayer, breaking the fast, and lighting Ramadan lanterns. Getting inside the head of a young believer who wishes to sacrifice his comforts at an early age is bound to be an interesting challenge for the average American child. See also *Ramadan* by Suhaib Hamid Ghazi (**4.3**). (KL and MR)

4.15 Medearis, Angela Shelf. **Poppa's Itchy Christmas.** Illustrated by John Ward. Holiday House, 1998. ISBN 0823412989. 32 pp. 4–8. Fiction.

George, who lives with his grandfather (Poppa) and Grandma Tiny, wakes up one Christmas morning eager to open his presents. One box reveals a long rainbow-colored scarf, and the next gift is worse: red wool underwear. However, his next present is a pair of ice skates and he is overjoyed. After chopping wood, George goes skating and falls through the ice, but is saved by the garments that he initially disliked. This story of an African American family set in the rural south includes rich details to portray warm family relationships and holiday traditions. (KYR)

4.16   Milich, Melissa. **Miz Fannie Mae's Fine New Easter Hat.** Illustrated by Yong Chen. Little Brown, 1997. ISBN 0316571598. 32 pp. 5–8. Fiction.

Easter is approaching and Tandy and her father travel to the city to buy a new Easter hat for Mama. Mama loves the hat covered with flowers, fruit, and speckled eggs, but thinks it is too expensive and must go back. Tandy's father gets up Easter Sunday morning to deliver milk and wears Mama's new Easter hat instead of his cap. When he returns home, he tells her the hat is worn and cannot go back to the shop. During Easter service, the four bird's eggs on the brim of Mama's hat begin to hatch. The preacher declares it a miracle and everyone follows the family home to watch the birds hatch. Mama places the hat in a tree at home and the family is rewarded with beautiful music from the birds all spring and summer. The illustrations in this book help the reader connect to the family and reflect the warmth of the family relationships. (CH)

4.17   Morris, Ann. **Light the Candle! Bang the Drum!** Illustrated by Peter Linenthal. Dutton, 1997. ISBN 0525456392. 32 pp. 4–8. Nonfiction.

The celebration of holidays around the world is the theme of this book. Children will learn about twenty-four different holidays, some well known in the United States and some less familiar. This informational text celebrates diversity as it presents festivals around the world chronologically throughout the calendar year. It provides a brief introduction to various celebrations and can serve as an excellent tool to encourage students to explore each holiday more closely. A "Notes" section includes a little more information on each celebration presented. Bright and vibrant illustrations depict the central theme of this book: "celebrations." (MS)

4.18 Slate, Joseph. **The Secret Stars.** Illustrated by Felipe Davalos. Marshall Cavendish, 1998. ISBN 0761450270. 32 pp. 6–10. Fiction.

Snuggled in their grandmother's bed on Three Kings Night, Pepe and Sila worry that the kings will lose their way in the icy darkness of New Mexico. As they imagine a morning without toys, their grandmother reassures them in a tour of magical dreams. Rolled in her comforting quilt, they soar together into the night and discover a hidden world of stars. Grandmother captures the mystery of the holiday and quietly soothes the children to sleep. They awake the next morning to find the glory of the Three Kings' gifts. (SS)

Pura Belpré Award Honor Book for Illustration

4.19 Smalls, Irene. **Irene Jennie and the Christmas Masquerade: The Johnkankus.** Illustrated by Melodye Rosales. Little Brown, 1996. ISBN 0316798789. 32 pp. 4–8. Historical fiction.

The Johnkankus was a Christmastime celebration observed by White and Black communities along the North Carolina coast during the eighteenth and nineteenth centuries. It provides the backdrop for the story of a young slave girl, Irene Jennie, who is sad because her parents were lent out to another plantation during Christmas. She prays for their return, but finds comfort in the music, acrobats, and costumes of the Johnkankus parade. Expressive, photorealistic paintings capture the emotions, actions, and costumes of the characters. A note about the history of the Johnkankus is included. (KYR)

4.20 Smalls, Irene. **Jenny Reen and the Jack Muh Lantern.** Illustrated by Keinyo White. Atheneum, 1996. ISBN 0689318758. 32 pp. 5–10. Historical fiction.

A Halloween ghost story told in Ebonic dialect and compiled from several historical sources from the time of slavery, this book tells of a young girl's extraordinary encounter. Jenny Reen, who loses her way while running an errand for her mother, is almost destroyed by a "googly google-eyed monster." Fortunately she knows how to break its spell, and escapes back to her loving extended family. This is a great Halloween read-aloud from a lesser-known American tradition. Bright oil-paint bleeds and alternating black-and-white type create an intense effect. (KL)

Notable Books for a Global Society

4.21   Wesley, Valerie. **Freedom's Gifts: A Juneteenth Story.** Illustrated by Sharon Wilson. Simon & Schuster. 1997. ISBN 0689802692. 32 pp. 8 and up. Historical fiction.

Oral tradition and the advice of an elder settle the differences between two preadolescent cousins in this story that documents the origin of Juneteenth. June 19, 1865, was the day when Black slaves in Texas learned they were free—two years after the Emancipation Proclamation was signed. Lillie, who is from New York, feels that her lifestyle is superior to June's, whose freedom is restricted in Texas by laws of discrimination. It takes intervention from Aunt Marshall, an ex-slave, to remind the girls, "You all have freedom's gifts, and can't nobody take them away." Set in 1943, the book is a reminder of the evolution of freedom for African Americans in the U.S. In 1979, Juneteenth was made a Texas state holiday. Wilson's muted pastel illustrations help support the powerful text. (JHC)

Notable Social Studies Trade Books for Young People

5 Biographies and Autobiographies

5.1 Ada, Alma Flor. **Under the Royal Palms: A Childhood in Cuba.**
Atheneum, 1998. ISBN 0689806310. 80 pp. 9–12. Memoir.

Alma Flor Ada shares stories of growing up in Camagey, Cuba, in
this companion piece to *Where the Flame Trees Bloom.* Readers will
be entranced by the stories of Alma's closely-knit family, such as
when her grandfather sacrifices his wealth for his sick wife. Both
heart-wrenching and humorous stories capture this amazing life
in Cuba. Dramatically illustrated by black-and-white photographs, this book may be more appealing to adults than children.
(KW)

*Pura Belpré Medal Winner for Narrative, Notable Social Studies Trade
Books for Young People*

5.2 Bruchac, Joseph. **Bowman's Store: A Journey to Myself.** Dial,
1997. ISBN 0803719973. 320 pp. 12 and up. Memoir.

In this moving memoir interlaced with legends from his Native
American Abenaki heritage, Joseph Bruchac tells the story of his
life. "Sonny" Bruchac lives with his grandparents in the Adiron-
dack foothills of upstate New York, and experiences a life filled
with passion and prejudice. Complemented by starkly moving
black-and-white photographs, this book will become a personal
favorite of older teenagers, especially those who are experiencing
their own identity struggles. (KW)

Notable Social Studies Trade Books for Young People

5.3 Dingle, Derek T. **First in the Field: Baseball Hero Jackie
Robinson.** Hyperion, 1998. ISBN 0786803487 (trade). ISBN
0786822899 (library binding). 48 pp. 8–12. Biography.

This is the story of the struggle and achievements of Jackie
Robinson, the first African American to play baseball in the major
leagues. Each of the book's five sections highlights an important
part of Robinson's life: his youth, his time spent in the army, playing in baseball's Negro leagues, breaking into the major leagues,
and leading the Brooklyn Dodgers to the World Series. Robinson's

personal integrity and athletic achievements are described in the context of the larger civil rights movement. Numerous photographs, many of which are action images from Robinson's long baseball career, provide visual context and support the text. Also included are a chronology titled "Milestones in Black Sports" and a selected bibliography. The author offers both a detailed record of Jackie Robinson's life and a sense of the man's intense personal style. (SJ)

Notable Social Studies Trade Books for Young People, IRA Children's Book Award

5.4   Duggleby, John. **Story Painter: The Life of Jacob Lawrence.** Illustrated by Jacob Lawrence. Chronicle, 1998. ISBN 0811820823. 55 pp. 9–12. Biography.

Story Painter tells the fascinating story of African American artist Jacob Lawrence, who was born in 1917. Coming of age during the Harlem Renaissance, Lawrence is filled with the desire to learn more about his people's struggles and is determined to depict these struggles as well as his own through art. Complemented by his own distinguished and vibrant art as well as a few photographs, this glorious biography will help unfamiliar readers understand this magnificent artist and his work. (KW)

Notable Social Studies Trade Books for Young People

5.5   Finlayson, Reggie. **Colin Powell: The People's Hero.** Lerner, 1996. ISBN 0822528916. 64 pp. 9–12. Biography.

This book narrates the life of General Colin Powell, from childhood through his career accomplishments. Included in the text are vivid descriptions of Powell's military career and his political contributions to the United States government. Throughout the book the reader will find direct quotations from Powell's speeches and essays. Included as well are ample black-and-white and color photographs with captions. (CP)

5.6   Freedman, Russell. **The Life and Death of Crazy Horse.** Illustrated by Amos Bad Heart Bull. Holiday House, 1996. ISBN 0823412199. 166 pp. 12 and up. Biography.

This fine biography of the Oglala Sioux warrior traces the life of the shy young boy who became a great leader and who, in the face of overwhelming odds, continued to fight for the rights of his people and to preserve their way of life. As in his other biographies, Freedman provides more than a chronicle of the events of an individual's life. He explores the clash of cultures that led to the Indian Wars, provides a balanced account of the prejudice and misunderstanding that resulted in such devastating battles as Little Bighorn, and paints a portrait of a courageous leader who fought for his beliefs. The pictographs by Amos Bad Heart Bull, a cousin of Crazy Horse, were drawn in the 1890s from the personal accounts of witnesses to Sioux history, and add authenticity to this biography. (BK)

NCTE Orbis Pictus Honor Book, ALA Notable Books for Children, Notable Books for a Global Society, Notable Social Studies Trade Books for Young People

5.7 Gollub, Matthew. **Cool Melons—Turn to Frogs! The Life and Poems of Issa.** Illustrated by Kazuko G. Stone and Keiko Smith. Lee & Low, 1998. ISBN 1880000717. Unpaged. 8–12. Biography.

In this biography, perfectly complemented by graceful haiku poetry and soft watercolors, readers are introduced to Issa, an eighteenth-century Japanese writer of over twenty thousand haiku poems. With hardships reminiscent of a fairy tale (wicked stepmother, being sent away as a teenager), Issa's life casts a haunting shadow around his haikus. The kanji on the edges of the pages add to the fragile beauty of this book. Readers may also find the background notes informative and inspirational. (KW)

ALA Notable Books for Children, Notable Books for a Global Society, Notable Social Studies Trade Books for Young People

5.8 Hansen, Joyce. **Women of Hope: African Americans Who Made a Difference.** Scholastic, 1998. ISBN 0590939734. 32 pp. 9–12. Biography.

Through stunning black-and-white portraits and inspirational biographies, readers—especially young African Americans—will find themselves inspired and wanting to know more, read more, and accomplish more. Although the biographies tend to be brief, they highlight each woman's greatest accomplishments and contributions to history. This book may be especially helpful as a springboard for students to consider whom they admire most and whom they would like to know more about. (KW)

Notable Social Studies Trade Books for Young People

5.9   Hart, Philip S. **Up in the Air: The Story of Bessie Coleman.**
Carolrhoda, 1996. ISBN 0876149786. 80 pp. 8 and up. Biography.

The story of this determined and feisty aviator, the first African
American woman to obtain a pilot's license, will inspire any
reader. Her story is told in an easy-to-read, informal style, with
touching photo portraits, newspaper clippings, and quotes from
those who knew and loved her. She is portrayed with all her
strengths and weaknesses, making her all the more endearing.
The book accomplishes much to restore another great African
American woman to her rightful historical prominence. Her
tragic death in an accident related to the inferior conditions she
was forced to endure every day makes the story all the more
affecting. (KL)

5.10   Hurmence, Belinda. **Slavery Time When I Was Chillun.** Putnam,
1997. ISBN 0399230483. 96 pp. 12 and up. Biography.

The author has compiled selected slave narratives collected
through the Federal Writers' Project of the 1930s. The stories are
seen through the eyes of men and women who were children
when slavery came to an end in 1865. From the innocence of children's games, to the accounts of brutal mistreatment, to stories
that describe what it was like when the slaves were finally freed,
these narratives offer vivid firsthand accounts of history, and are
accompanied by photographs of life in the South that add to the
sense of realism. (MP)

Notable Books for a Global Society

5.11   Igus, Toyomi. **Going Back Home: An Artist Returns to the
South.** Illustrated by Michele Wood. Children's Book Press, 1996.
ISBN 0892391375. Unpaged. 9–12. Memoir.

After a personal journey down South to see where her ancestors
lived, artist Michele Wood propels herself back in time and imagines the struggles and hardships that her sharecropping ancestors
endured. Through detailed and finely patterned art, Wood shares
the struggles and triumphs of her family and their community.
Readers may find the beautiful and complex paintings more inviting than the heavy-handed historical text accompanying them.
(KW)

Notable Books for a Global Society

5.12   Jaffe, Nina. **A Voice for the People: The Life and Work of Harold Courlander.** Henry Holt, 1997. ISBN 08050344447. 144 pp. 12 and up. Biography.

This biography chronicles the fascinating life of folklorist Harold Courlander, who crisscrossed the globe collecting songs, chants, and folk stories from African Americans, Africans, Haitians, Eastern Indians, and Native Americans. It covers a period of over sixty years with a backdrop of critical events in American history such as the Great Depression, the Dust Bowl, World Wars I and II, and the civil rights movement. The actual text of several of Courlander's folktales are included in the book. (SF)

5.13   Jiang, Ji-Li. **Red Scarf Girl: A Memoir of the Cultural Revolution.** HarperCollins, 1997. ISBN 0060275855 (trade). ISBN 0060275863 (library binding). 285 pp. 12 and up. Memoir.

In this moving memoir, Ji-Li Jiang shares her memories of life during the Chinese Cultural Revolution. Jiang chronicles her profound transformation from a self-absorbed teenager to a conscientious adult, as she struggles against the intrusions of government into her own life during this tumultuous time in history. While the emotions conjured by this novel can be painful, its detailed, seamless narrative provides an enlightening experience. (SS)

ALA Notable Books for Children, Notable Social Studies Trade Books for Young People, Best Books for Young Adults

5.14   Johnson, Dinah. **All around Town: The Photographs of Richard Samuel Roberts.** Henry Holt, 1998. ISBN 0805054561. 32 pp. 5 and up. Biography.

This handsome book contains a diverse collection of the work of Richard Samuel Roberts, an African American photographer who took some ten thousand photos over a fifteen-year period during the 1920s and 1930s. Roberts was a self-taught photographer from Columbia, South Carolina, whose camera captured the multifaceted lives of African Americans. Portraits of adults and children as well as group photos representing various careers and events are accompanied by uncomplicated text that often invites a response from the reader. The photographs describe this era with a richness that words alone cannot convey. (JHC)

Notable Social Studies Trade Books for Young People

5.15 Krull, Kathleen. **Wilma Unlimited: How Wilma Rudolph Became the World's Fastest Woman.** Illustrated by David Diaz. Harcourt Brace, 1996. ISBN 0152012672. 40 pp. 9–12. Biography.

The life and accomplishments of Wilma Rudolph are brought to life in this biography. Wilma's struggles began at birth, when she weighed only slightly more than four pounds. Then, at age five, she was diagnosed with polio, a crippling and life-threatening disease in the 1940s. Wilma persevered and at the age of twelve was not only walking again but mailed her leg brace back to the hospital. Wilma went on to become a star basketball player in high school, attended Tennessee State University on a full athletic scholarship, and, in 1960, represented the United States in the Olympics as a runner, winning three gold medals. Acrylic, watercolor, and gouache paintings placed on sepia photographed backgrounds provide a visually striking accompaniment to the powerful text. (CC)

Jane Addams Award for Picture Book, ALA Notable Books for Children

5.16 Lester, Julius. **Black Cowboy, Wild Horses: A True Story.** Illustrated by Jerry Pinkney. Dial, 1998. ISBN 0803717873. 32 pp. 6–10. Biography.

Bob Lemmons, a former slave turned cowboy, possessed the uncanny ability to bring in a herd of wild horses all by himself. In this true story, Julius Lester takes the reader along as Lemmons tracks a herd of wild mustangs. We watch as he goes through the process of masking his human scent—effectively becoming one of the horses—and eventually subduing the stallion leading the herd. Jerry Pinkney's illustrations effectively capture the beauty of the plains and the solitude and freedom of a cowboy's life in this tribute to a great African American cowboy. The author's and illustrator's notes at the end of the biography provide interesting background on the subject and a history of the story itself. (BK)

Notable Social Studies Trade Books for Young People

5.17 Littlesugar, Amy. **Jonkonnu: A Story from the Sketchbook of Winslow Homer.** Illustrated by Ian Schoenherr. Philomel, 1997. ISBN 0399228314. 32 pp. 4–8. Biography.

This is a touching story set on the United States' one-hundredth birthday, in 1876. The painter Winslow Homer is seen making sketches of African Americans in a town in Virginia where freed-men and freedwomen are not welcome. Through a White girl named Cilla who is curious about Homer and his sketches, the reader hears about the holiday Jonkonnu, which was celebrated on that day by Black Americans who were not allowed to cele-brate their independence on Independence Day. Although Winslow Homer is a famed artist, this is one facet of him that may be unfamiliar to many. He captured the lives of former slaves with dignity and with sadness for an independence they had yet to receive. (SA)

5.18 Lowery, Linda. **Wilma Mankiller.** Illustrated by Janice Lee Porter. Carolrhoda, 1996. ISBN 0876148801. 56 pp. 7–9. Biography.

This biography for early readers weaves together the story of a contemporary political figure with the history of the Cherokee Nation and the infamous Trail of Tears exodus of 1883. When young Wilma's family moves from Oklahoma to California with the government's promise of a house and a job in San Francisco, she comforts herself with thoughts of home and of the courage shown by her ancestors when they, too, had to find new homes. When she returns to Oklahoma as an adult, her job with the Cherokee Nation eventually leads to her election as Deputy Chief and later, Chief of the Nation. An appended timeline outlines details of her life not covered in the book. (SM)

5.19 Lyons, Mary E. **Catching the Fire: Philip Simmons, Blacksmith.** Houghton Mifflin, 1997. ISBN 0395720338. 48 pp. 8–12. Biography.

This biography of Philip Simmons begins when he leaves his grandparents' home on Daniel Island at the age of eight to live with his mother in Charleston and to attend the new school for African American children there. When he is eleven, Philip falls in love with blacksmithing. Through hard work, determination, and a love for his occupation, he overcomes obstacles to become a master blacksmith and a recognized artist in his field. Simmons' own words are used throughout the book, giving this biography the feel of a personal memoir. Many color photographs feature his wrought iron gates, fences, and railings. Included are an index, notes, a bibliography, and a list of books for further reading. (SG)

5.20   Lyons, Mary E. **Painting Dreams: Minnie Evans, Visionary Artist.** Illustrated by Minnie Evans. Houghton Mifflin, 1996. ISBN 039572032X. 48 pp. 6–12. Biography.

At age forty-three, Minnie Evans, a poor southern African American woman, painted her first painting, based on the nightly dream epics she had been having since childhood. She quit school after the fifth grade, married at sixteen, and raised three sons, all the while continuing to have extraordinary visions and dreams. In 1935, the year her mother died, she started to draw, and never stopped. This book is not only a biography of Evans and a gallery of her strange and affecting works (most paintings are full of staring eyes, swirls, paisley designs, and odd landscapes, all in bright colors), but also a penetrating social history of the period and the place from which this very unusual woman emerged. The many quotations by Minnie, taken from taped interviews by the author, neither idealize nor oversimplify her, and show how strong the art impulse can be. (KL)

5.21   Lyons, Mary E. **Talking with Tebe: Clementine Hunter, Memory Artist.** Illustrated by Clementine Hunter. Houghton Mifflin, 1998. ISBN 0395720311. 48 pp. 6–12. Biography.

Self-taught Louisiana Creole artist Clementine Hunter had an indomitable spirit. Born in 1886 on a plantation, she spent seventy years working for the owners, but also painting the everyday life around her in a bright, flat, opaque style. This remarkable woman, who lived independently to the age of 101, is suitably celebrated in this collection of her art and interviews. Details about the difficult conditions she had to endure and struggle against throughout her life make her tale all the more remarkable. The editor does an outstanding job at piecing together a life told through both oral history and paint, making for a captivating biography. (KL)

5.22   Marrin, Albert. **Plains Warrior: Chief Quanah Parker and the Comanches.** Atheneum / Simon & Schuster, 1996. ISBN 0689800819. 200 pp. 9–12. Biography.

This captivating biography of Quanah Parker skillfully weaves together the stories of the Comanche tribe with the life of one of their most famous chiefs. The illustrations are thoughtfully placed throughout the text. This absorbing text is easily read, and different chapters can be used independently for different purposes; the chapter notes and bibliography provide the reader with valuable resources as well. Quotes, maps, informative anecdotes, and photographs bring a vividness and reality to this period in U.S. history, and provide insight into the lives of the people Quanah Parker led. Quanah Parker's mother, a White settler, was kidnapped and subsequently adopted into the tribe. She later married a Comanche chief and had three children, the eldest being Quanah. Quanah Parker was known as the last great Comanche chief, and it is through his life story that the reader glimpses the tragedy and triumph of the Comanche in a world created and dominated by the White man. (SSG)

5.23 Mathis, Sharon Bell. **Running Girl: The Diary of Ebonee Rose.** Browndeer / Harcourt Brace, 1997. ISBN 0152006745. 60 pp. 8 and up. Fiction with biographical vignettes.

This interesting and heart-warming book is about Ebonee Rose, a runner who is very passionate about her sport. Through a diary format, the reader shares Ebonee's thoughts and fears on a journey of hard work, passion, friendship, and triumph, as she prepares to run in the All-City Track Meet. Interspersed throughout her diary are factual vignettes honoring the famous female African American runners who have inspired her. Although the book focuses on Ebonee Rose as a girl who is proud of herself and of her heritage as an African American and a female runner, this is also a very engaging photo-essay about female African American runners throughout history. It also serves as a great lesson on perseverance and believing in oneself. (SA and CMH)

5.24 McKissack, Patricia C., and Fredrick L. McKissack. **Young, Black, and Determined: A Biography of Lorraine Hansberry.** Holiday House, 1998. ISBN 0823413004. 160 pp. 12 and up. Biography.

In this involving and intelligently written biography of playwright Lorraine Hansberry, we meet a child who grew up in an intellectual atmosphere where distinguished people like Paul Robeson, Langston Hughes, and Jesse Owens were entertained in her house. Her parents also made her aware of the tensions of racism that divided U.S. society, and raised her to "advance the cause of African American equality through intelligent and articulate leadership." The McKissacks' biography provides a window into the fascinating life and times of Hansberry as well as an in-depth treatment of her most well-known play, *A Raisin in the Sun*. The book includes a bibliography and a timeline. (LS)

Best Book for Young Adults

5.25   Medearis, Angela Shelf. **Princess of the Press: The Story of Ida B. Wells-Barnett.** Lodestar, 1997. ISBN 0525674934. 48 pp. 7–10. Biography.

Drawing heavily from the diaries of Ida B. Wells-Barnett and a biography written by Wells-Barnett's daughter Alfreda, Medearis deftly chronicles the life of this courageous woman. Responsible for the care of her younger siblings at an early age, Wells-Barnett began teaching at age fourteen, and later became a writer, news-paper owner, and an unrelenting crusader against the barbaric lynching of African Americans. In addition, she was involved in the women's club movement, women's suffrage, and state poli-tics. Several photographs of the Barnett family are included as well as a bibliography and an index. (JHC)

5.26   Mochizuki, Ken. **Passage to Freedom: The Sugihara Story.** Illus-trated by Dom Lee. Lee & Low, 1997. ISBN 1880000490. Unpaged. 8–12. Biography.

Can one person make a difference? This story tackles this ques-tion, as well as ideas about bravery, honor, and justice, as Ken Mochizuki tells Hiroki Sugihara's story of how his father hand-wrote hundreds of visas to save the lives of ten thousand Polish Jewish refugees, in defiance of the Japanese government's poli-cies. Dom Lee's mixed-media illustrations carry both the somber-ness and poignancy of the story. The afterword, written by Hiroki, will leave readers grateful for the courage of the great Sugihara and wanting to know more. (KW)

ALA Notable Books for Children, Notable Children's Books in the Lan-guage Arts, Notable Social Studies Trade Books for Young People, Notable Books for a Global Society

5.27   Morey, Janet, and Wendy Dunn. **Famous Hispanic Americans.** Cobblehill, 1996. ISBN 052565190X. 208 pp. 12 and up. Biography.

Fourteen prominent Hispanic Americans are featured in this book. Included are people who have made contributions in edu-cation, entertainment, sports, politics, the arts, and business.

Among those included are Gloria Estefan, Matt Rodriguez, Chicago's police chief, and Jaime Escalante, the educator featured in the 1988 film, *Stand and Deliver*. The stories are inspiring and compelling, as readers see the many diverse contributions Hispanic Americans have made in the United States. The black-and-white illustrations add realism to the stories. (RH)

5.28   Murdoch, David. **Tutankhamun: The Life and Death of a Pharaoh.** Illustrated by Chris Forsey. DK, 1998. ISBN 0789434202. 48 pp. 7 and up. Biography.

This large, attractive book, one of the DK Discovery series, effectively uses double-page spreads, some of which fold open into four-page spreads, to describe the discovery of King Tut's tomb in 1922 and the life and times of the young King before and after his death. The deft layout and design will appeal to today's multimedia-savvy students, with cutaway photos and skillful colored-pencil drawings of the tomb, maps, and dioramas, interspersed with lively text boxes. "Was he murdered?" and "What lay behind the sealed doorway?" are some of the catchy headings for sidebars. This is an ideal book for readers who may be captivated by the attractive presentation, and drawn to take a deeper look. (KL)

5.29   Myers, Walter Dean. **Toussaint L'Ouverture: The Fight for Haiti's Freedom.** Illustrated by Jacob Lawrence. Simon & Schuster, 1996. ISBN 0689801262. 36 pp. 8 and up. Biography.

The text to this biography of the revered liberator of Haiti, Toussaint L'Ouverture, is formed around the forty-one tempera paintings by contemporary African American artist Jacob Lawrence. The paintings, in a dark, evocative *art naif* style reminiscent of Edward Munch woodcuts, were first shown to the public in 1940, and have now been reproduced for this book. The simple text sketches the life and history surrounding Toussaint, presenting a powerful portrait of his courage and leadership. This would be a good entree to Caribbean or Haitian history for elementary children in the middle grades. (KL)

ALA Notable Books for Children

5.30   Orgill, Roxane. **If I Only Had a Horn: Young Louis Armstrong.** Illustrated by Leonard Jenkins. Houghton Mifflin, 1997. ISBN 0395759196. 32 pp. 5–9. Biography.

Culled from various biographical and autobiographical sources, this is the story of the young musician's early love for jazz, especially Joe "King" Oliver's cornet playing. After being sent to the Colored Waifs' Home as punishment for shooting a gun into the air on New Year's Eve, Louis manages to join the Colored Waif's Home Band. After honing his skills first on a tambourine, then a drum, and then a bugle, he is eventually presented with his own cornet. Jenkins's mixed-media illustrations are as energetic as this glimpse into one short period of Armstrong's life. (SM)

Notable Social Studies Trade Books for Young People

5.31   Parks, Rosa, and Jim Haskins. **I Am Rosa Parks.** Illustrated by Wil Clay. Dial, 1997. ISBN 0803712065 (trade). ISBN 0803712073 (library binding). 48 pp. 6–8. Autobiography.

Based on her 1992 autobiography (also coauthored with Jim Haskins), Parks has rewritten her story to make it accessible for younger readers. Well illustrated with color illustrations that closely parallel the text, this is history told in a clear and straightforward manner. Parks explains the concept of segregation, and how she one day refused to give up her seat on the bus to a White person. The subsequent bus boycott and the civil rights movement it helped initiate are presented in an easy-to-understand manner, while personal details, such as Parks's being inspired by a young Martin Luther King Jr., help to fill out the narrative. (SM)

Notable Social Studies Trade Books for Young People

5.32   Pinkney, Andrea Davis. **Bill Pickett: Rodeo-Ridin' Cowboy.** Illustrated by Brian Pinkney. Harcourt Brace, 1996. ISBN 015200100X. Unpaged. 4–8. Biography.

Children will delight in this biography of Bill Pickett, rodeo star and African American cowboy. The son of former slaves, Bill Pickett's achievements include the invention of "bulldogging," which is now one of seven standard rodeo events. Readers will also find the back pages of historical information on black cowboys both interesting and informative. (KW)

ALA Notable Books for Children

5.33 Pinkney, Andrea Davis. **Duke Ellington: The Piano Prince and His Orchestra.** Illustrated by Brian Pinkney. Hyperion, 1998. ISBN 0786801786 (trade). ISBN 0786821507 (library binding). Unpaged. 5–9. Biography.

Written in a hip, sassy style that echoes the life and music of Edward "Duke" Ellington, Andrea Pinkney traces the Duke from his days as a young, recalcitrant piano student to his fame as a world renowned bandleader, musician, and composer. Brian Pinkney's lush, vibrant scratchboard paintings are rhythmic and imaginative, and are nicely integrated into the text. (JC)

Coretta Scott King Illustrator Award Honor, Caldecott Honor Book, Notable Social Studies Trade Books for Young People, ALA Notable Books for Children.

5.34 Potter, Joan, and Constance Claytor. **African Americans Who Were First.** Illustrated with photographs. Cobblehill, 1997. ISBN 0525652469. 128 pp. 9–12. Biography.

This book compiles short biographies of African Americans who were "first" in a variety of fields, from medicine to politics, from sports to the entertainment world. The book is arranged chronologically from Phillis Wheatley's landing in Boston in 1761 (the first African American to publish a book) to Beverly Harvard, the first woman police chief of a big U.S. city (Atlanta). Some are familiar, some are surprising, yet all are interesting in their accomplishments. For example, Daniel Hale Williams was the first person to perform open heart surgery. Unfortunately, Harriet Tubman's accomplishments are minimized as she is mentioned as the first African American woman to appear on a postage stamp! (KYR)

5.35 Rappaport, Doreen. **The Flight of Red Bird: The Life of Zitkala-Ša.** Dial, 1997. ISBN 0803714386. 186 pp. 9–12. Biography.

Zitkala-Ša (Red Bird), born Gertrude Bonnin, shares her struggle of being the child of an American father and Sioux Indian mother. She was sent to a boarding school when she turned eight years old. Upon returning to the reservation at fourteen she did not feel she belonged. Zitkala-Ša went on to become an activist for Native Americans and spent her life helping others understand the social injustice done to her people. Useful resources, including a list of important dates, a glossary, source notes, a bibliography, and an index, are provided at the end of the text. (MS)

Notable Social Studies Trade Books for Young People, Notable Books for a Global Society

5.36   Rohmer, Harriet, editor. **Just Like Me: Stories and Self-Portraits by Fourteen Artists.** Children's Book Press, 1997. ISBN 0892391499. 31 pp. 9–12. Biography.

These are not ordinary self-portraits! In this beautifully compiled book, fourteen extraordinary artists and picture book illustrators present a variety of self-portraits, from the seemingly conventional to the more whimsical and humorous. The artists are of ethnically diverse backgrounds, including Japanese, Chinese, Mexican, Native American, African American, Jewish, and mixed race. Each self-portrait is accompanied by biographical information provided by the artist as well as explanations of the art and what inspired its creation. Readers will be inspired to create their own self-portraits and to reflect on what makes them unique. (KW)

5.37   Ross, Michael Elsohn. **Wildlife Watching with Charles Eastman.** Illustrated by Laurie A. Caple. Carolrhoda, 1997. ISBN 1575050048. 48 pp. 9–12. Biography.

Part of the Naturalist's Apprentice Biographies series, this biography not only compellingly recounts the life of a little-known naturalist but serves as a history of Native Americans in the late 1800s and early 1900s, as well as a nature guide including activities for young naturalists. Hakadah, later known as Charles Eastman, was born a Dakota (called Sioux by the Europeans), became a physician, and later used his childhood experiences to teach children to love and respect nature. Period photographs and illustrations reveal a fascinating man who blended his Native American traditions with the "White man's" science and worldview. (KYR)

5.38   St. George, Judith. **Sacagawea.** Putnam, 1997. ISBN 0399231617. 128 pp. 9–12. Biography.

Drawing from Lewis and Clark's journals and other sources, this well-researched biography documents Sacagawea's contributions to the explorers' famous 5,000-mile journey westward. St. George humanizes her subject by including the imagined thoughts and feelings of this sixteen-year-old pregnant Shoshone girl as she acts as translator, provisioner, and peacemaker to the thirty-three-member "Corps of Discovery." There is plenty for adventure fans to like: grizzly bears, sickness, whitewater rapids, hostile encounters, hunger, and the struggle to survive. Many details about the different Native American cultures they meet along the way add to the realism. A bibliography is included. (KYR)

5.39   St. George, Judith. **To See with the Heart: The Life of Sitting Bull.** Putnam, 1996. ISBN 0399229302. 182 pp. 9–12. Biography.

Sitting Bull began life in 1831 with the name Slow, but it was not long before he was given his father's name after the fourteen-year-old distinguished himself for his bravery during a battle with an enemy tribe. Sitting Bull's heroism would be brought to the test for many years to come when he became the leader of the entire Sioux Nation during the historic encounter with the White men's forces expanding westward into sacred Sioux territory. (SA)

5.40   Savage, Jeff. **Tiger Woods: King of the Course.** Lerner, 1998. ISBN 0822536552. 64 pp. 9–12. Biography.

This book narrates the life story of Tiger Woods from his childhood through his recent golf accomplishments. Included are colorful photographs, a chronology of important events in Woods's life, a glossary of golf terms, and an address to which interested readers may write to Woods. The text is easy to read and includes quotations from both Woods and his family. (CP)

5.41   Schroeder, Alan. **Minty: A Story of Young Harriet Tubman.** Illustrated by Jerry Pinkney. Dial, 1996. ISBN 0803718888 (trade). ISBN 0803718896 (library binding). Unpaged. 8–12. Biography.

This fictionalized story of young Harriet Tubman is based on facts from her life. Tubman, whose childhood nickname was Minty, is depicted as a strong-willed child whose dream of escape to freedom began at a very young age. The physical and psychological cruelties of slavery only strengthen her resolve to be free. Though her mother tries to teach her to accept her fate, her father recognizes her indomitable spirit and teaches her the skills she will need to survive after escaping. An illustrator's note explains the careful research needed to portray authentically Maryland plantation life for both the enslaved and the slave owners, as realized in the two-page colored pencil and watercolor illustrations of this book. (KB)

Coretta Scott King Illustrator Award Winner, ALA Notable Books for Children, Notable Books for a Global Society

5.42 Schroeder, Alan. **Satchmo's Blues.** Illustrated by Floyd Cooper. Doubleday, 1996. 0385320469. Unpaged. 6–10. Biography.

From very early in his life, Louis Armstrong was drawn to places where music was made. There were many opportunities to enjoy music in New Orleans: in jazz halls, at weekend dances, marching with parade bands, singing gospel songs at church, and seeking out street musicians. Driving the story's plot is Louis's single-minded desire to own and learn to play a horn. Although the family struggles with poverty, Louis's mother encourages his musical inclinations. The golden-toned, double-page illustrations follow Louis in his travels around town and back home. They provide a soothing, understated background for Louis's struggles and eventual success. An author's note that follows the story gives a brief history of Louis Armstrong's rise to fame in popular music. (SJ)

5.43 Severance, John B. **Gandhi: Great Soul.** Clarion, 1997. ISBN 039577179X. 144 pp. 8–14. Biography.

This attractive, photo-filled book tells the story of the famed liberator of India and model for nonviolent resistance and purity of mind. Each chapter is full of facts and captivating anecdotes, including Gandhi's countless meetings with many other world leaders, both political and cultural, and many pictures of Gandhi at different stages of life. It is fascinating to see him looking dapper with a full head of hair, and then follow his path toward asceticism. Several of his witty quips to others are included, giving him a more human dimension, and his stubbornness is corroborated as well. Readers will be inspired by the amount one small person could accomplish with the simple power of love, combined with the tools of language and self-sacrifice. (KL)

Notable Social Studies Trade Books for Young People

5.44 Spivak, Dawnine. **Grass Sandals: The Travels of Basho.** Illustrated by Demi. Atheneum, 1997. ISBN 0689807767. Unpaged. 5–10. Biography.

This is an enchanting story of the seventeenth-century Japanese haiku poet Basho and his travels throughout his native country. The haiku poems, presented with Japanese characters that represent words from the verses, add richness to the text. Demi's illustrations are delicate and reflect the quietness of the story. Each double-page spread includes a segment of the story, a painting of Basho on his journey, a haiku poem reflecting the idea of the text, and a word that appears in three forms: a Japanese character, its transliteration, and the English translation. (MP)

Notable Social Studies Trade Books for Young People, Notable Books for a Global Society

5.45 Stewart, Whitney. **Aung San Suu Kyi: Fearless Voice of Burma.** Lerner, 1997. ISBN 082254931X. 128 pp. 9 and up. Biography.

This is the biography of Aung San Suu Kyi, a woman compelled by strong convictions to become a leader in the fight for democracy for her beloved country of Burma. Although she witnessed the turmoil and unrest in her country during her childhood, it was not until she had moved abroad that she began to take a more active role in shaping democracy in Burma. During a visit home, she decided to take up the cause for democracy, as her father had before he was assassinated. She was immediately placed under house arrest and spent over six years continuing her fight from the confines of her home. Learning from the teachings of Martin Luther King Jr. and Gandhi, Aung led the Burma National League for Democracy to governmental victories. This book includes an account of Burma's political history starting from the early 1940s, providing the background information necessary to understand the country's political struggles. (SKA)

Notable Social Studies Trade Books for Young People

5.46 Sullivan, George. **Black Artists in Photography, 1840–1940.** Cobblehill, 1996. ISBN 0525652086. 97 pp. 11 and up. Biography.

This collection of works by various early African American photographers celebrates the contributions of a largely ignored group of artists, including Jules Lion, Augustus Washington, James P. Ball, Addison Scurlock, Cornelius M. Battey, and the Goodridge brothers. Each of these men is placed in the context of his times, further illustrating the relevance and importance of his work. This book is well written with many fine reproductions of these artists' photos, and provides much-needed attention to an often overlooked topic. (LS)

5.47 Tillage, Leon Walter. **Leon's Story.** Illustrated by Susan L. Roth. Farrar, Straus and Giroux, 1997. ISBN 0374343799. 107 pp. 12–18. Autobiography.

This book for older students offers a scorchingly realistic representation of life before the civil rights movement made its powerful impact. Leon's description of the senseless death of his father and the false contrition of the White youth who killed him is an image that will not be easily forgotten by any reader. Throughout the text, which is taken from a speech given at the school where he works as a custodian, Leon's strong voice remains optimistic and forgiving. The graphic realism of this book may make it unsuitable for young children. (CK)

Boston Globe–Horn Book Award Winner, ALA Notable Books for Children, Notable Social Studies Trade Books for Young People, Best Books for Young Adults

5.48 Turk, Ruth. **Ray Charles: Soul Man.** Lerner, 1996. ISBN 082254928X. 112 pp. 10 and up. Biography.

This is a telling biography of Ray Charles, father of soul music. From his childhood in Florida to his fabulous musical career, Ray Charles has proved himself a true musician and an inspiration to many. In his life he has battled blindness, racism, loneliness, and drug addiction, and has come out on top. Black-and-white photographs give visual support to the text. (ER)

A.

B.

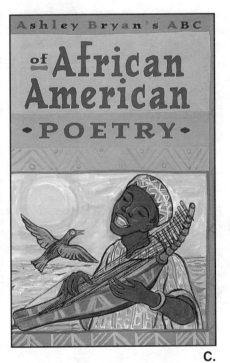

C.

A. *So Far from the Sea* by Eve Bunting; illustrated by Chris K. Soentpiet (**3.19**). **B.** *The Golden Flower: A Taino Myth from Puerto Rico* by Nina Jaffe; illustrated by Enrique O. Sánchez (**8.28**). **C.** *Ashley Bryan's ABC of African American Poetry* by Ashley Bryan (**7.6**).

A.

B.

C.

A. *The Bat Boy and His Violin* by Gavin Curtis; illustrated by E. B. Lewis (**1.17**).
B. *What's the Most Beautiful Thing You Know about Horses?* by Richard Van Camp; illustrated by George Littlechild (**1.94**). **C.** *Miro in the Kingdom of the Sun* by Jane Kurtz; illustrated by David Frampton (**8.36**).

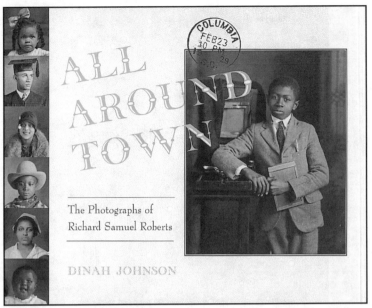

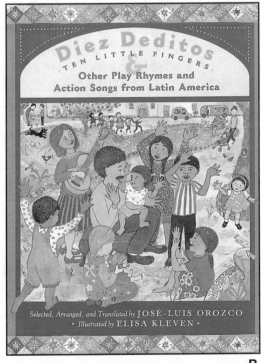

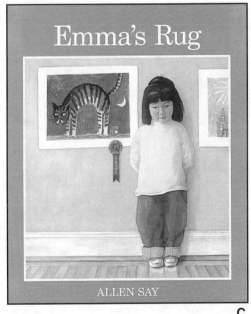

A. *All around Town: The Photographs of Richard Samuel Roberts* by Dinah Johnson (**5.14**). **B.** *Diez Deditos: Ten Little Fingers & Other Play Rhymes and Action Songs from Latin America* by José-Luis Orozco; illustrated by Elisa Kleven (**7.26**). **C.** *Emma's Rug* by Allen Say (**1.77**).

A.

B.

C.

A. *Staying Cool* by Nancy Antle; illustrated by E. B. Lewis (**1.1**). **B.** *Ten Suns: A Chinese Legend* by Eric A. Kimmel; illustrated by YongSheng Xuan (**8.34**). **C.** *Cendrillon: A Caribbean Cinderella* by Robert D. San Souci; illustrated by Brian Pinkney (**8.68**).

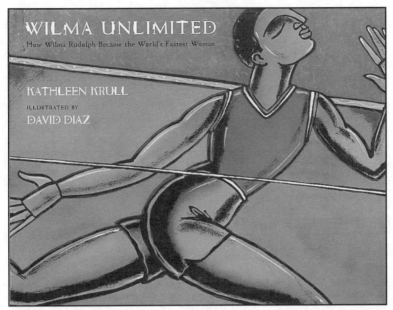

A.

B.

C.

A. *Wilma Unlimited: How Wilma Rudolph Became the World's Fastest Woman* by Kathleen Krull; illustrated by David Diaz (**5.15**). **B.** *Tiktala* by Margaret Shaw-MacKinnon; illustrated by László Gál (**1.81**). **C.** *The Secret Stars* by Joseph Slate; illustrated by Felipe Dávalos (**4.18**).

A.

B.

C.

A. *Running Girl: The Diary of Ebonee Rose* by Sharon Bell Mathis (**5.23**). **B.** *Children Just Like Me: Celebrations!* by Barnabas Kindersley and Anabel Kindersley (**4.9**). **C.** *The Cook's Family* by Laurence Yep (**2.41**).

A.

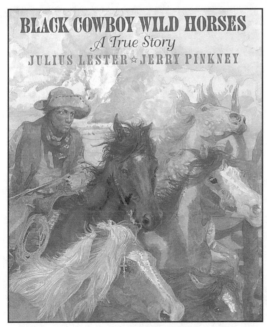

B.

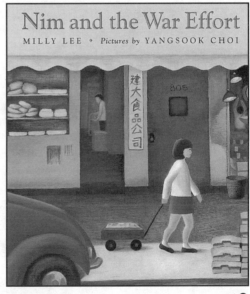

C.

A. *In Rosa's Mexico* by Campbell Geeslin; illustrated by Andrea Arroyo (**1.26**). **B.** *Black Cowboy, Wild Horses: A True Story* by Julius Lester; illustrated by Jerry Pinkney (**5.16**). **C.** *Nim and the War Effort* by Milly Lee; illustrated by Yangsook Choi (**3.30**).

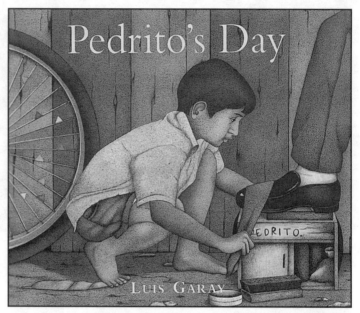

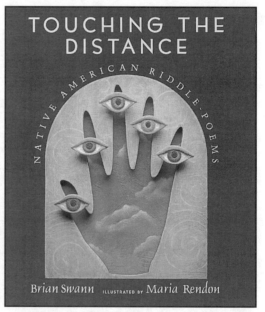

A. *Pedrito's Day* by Luis Garay (**1.24**). **B.** *Duke Ellington: The Piano Prince and His Orchestra* by Andrea Davis Pinkney; illustrated by Brian Pinkney (**5.33**). **C.** *Touching the Distance: Native American Riddle-Poems* by Brian Swann; illustrated by Maria Rendon (**7.32**).

A.

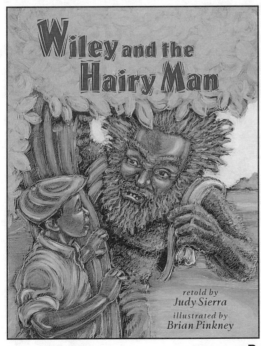

B.

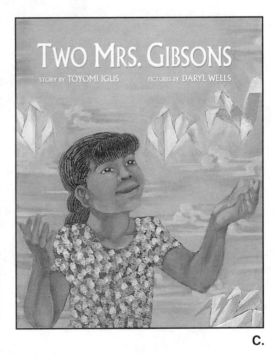

C.

A. *Celebrating Chinese New Year* by Diane Hoyt-Goldsmith; photographs by Lawrence Migdale (**4.5**). **B.** *Wiley and the Hairy Man* by Judy Sierra; illustrated by Brian Pinkney (**8.73**). **C.** *Two Mrs. Gibsons* by Toyomi Igus; illustrated by Daryl Wells (**1.37**).

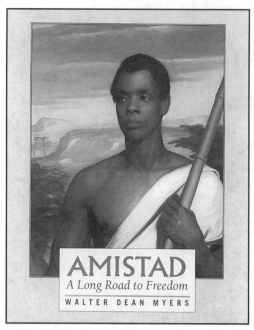

A.

B.

C.

A. *Amistad: A Long Road to Freedom* by Walter Dean Myers (**3.11**). **B.** *Jade and Iron: Latin American Tales from Two Cultures* by Patricia Aldana; illustrated by Luis Garay (**8.4**). **C.** *Satchmo's Blues* by Alan Schroeder; illustrated by Floyd Cooper (**5.42**).

A.

B.

C.

A. *In My Family/En mi familia* by Carmen Lomas Garza (**1.54**). **B.** *Something Beautiful* by Sharon Dennis Wyeth; illustrated by Chris K. Soentpiet (**1.100**) **C.** *Angel to Angel: A Mother's Gift of Love* by Walter Dean Myers (**7.23**).

A.

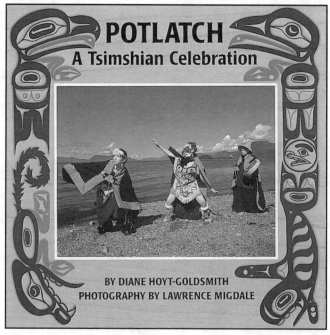

B.

A. *The Paper Dragon* by Marguerite W. Davol; illustrated by Robert Sabuda (**1.18**).
B. *Potlatch: A Tsimshian Celebration* by Diane Hoyt-Goldsmith; photographs by Lawrence Migdale (**4.6**).

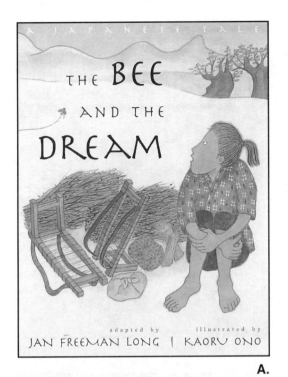

A.

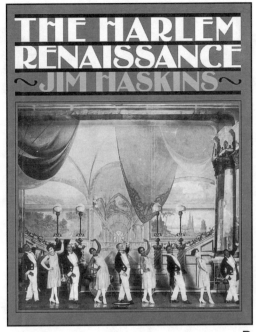

B.

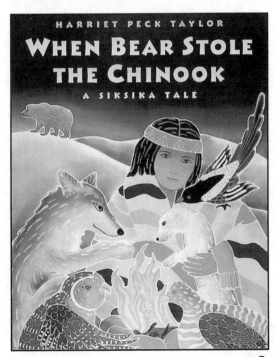

C.

A. *The Bee and the Dream: A Japanese Tale* by Jan Freeman Long; illustrated by Kaoru Ono (**8.39**). **B.** *The Harlem Renaissance* by Jim Haskins (**3.6**). **C.** *When Bear Stole the Chinook: A Siksika Tale* by Harriet Peck Taylor (**8.76**).

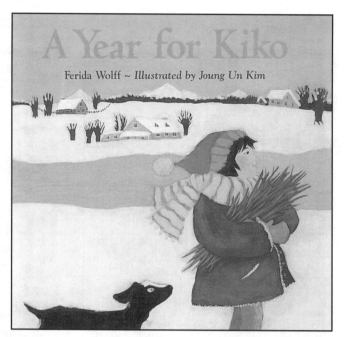

A.

B.

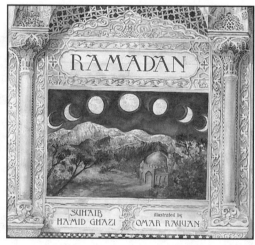

C.

A. *A Year for Kiko* by Ferida Wolff; illustrated by Joung Un Kim (**1.98**). **B.** *A Man Called Raven* by Richard Van Camp; illustrated by George Littlechild (**1.93**). **C.** *Ramadan* by Suhaib Hamid Ghazi; illustrated by Omar Rayyan (**4.3**).

A.

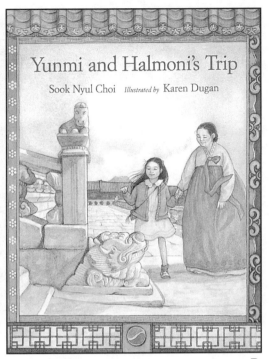

B.

C.

A. *A Girl Named Disaster* by Nancy Farmer (**2.10**). **B.** *Yunmi and Halmoni's Trip* by Sook Nyul Choi; illustrated by Karen Dugan (**1.12**). **C.** *Six Words, Many Turtles, and Three Days in Hong Kong* by Patricia McMahon; photographs by Susan G. Drinker (**6.29**).

A.

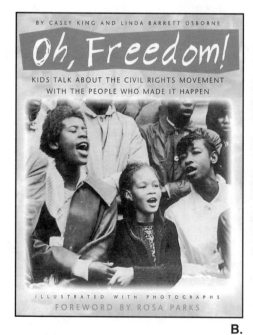

B.

C.

A. *Jalapeño Bagels* by Natasha Wing; illustrated by Robert Casilla (**1.97**).
B. *Oh Freedom! Kids Talk about the Civil Rights Movement with the People Who Made It Happen* by Casey King and Linda Barrett Osborne (**3.8**). C. *Jonkonnu: A Story from the Sketchbook of Winslow Homer* by Amy Littlesugar and Ian Schoenherr (**5.17**).

6 Informational Books

6.1 Ancona, George. **Barrio: Jose's Neighborhood.** Harcourt Brace, 1998. ISBN 0152010491. 48 pp. 6–10. Nonfiction.

In Jose's neighborhood of San Francisco's Mission District, people speak Spanish, English, and even a little Chinese. Readers will enjoy seeing the familiar Halloween festivities gradually transform into a Day of the Dead celebration. Jose also shares aspects of his school, play, and family life that illustrate his cultural heritage. Nicely complemented by photographs, including views of prominent murals in the neighborhood, this book is a good introduction to the Mexican American experience. (KW)

Pura Belpré Award Honor Book for Illustration, Américas Award, Notable Social Studies Trade Books for Young People

6.2 Ancona, George. **Mayeros: A Yucatec Maya Family.** Lothrop, Lee & Shepard, 1997. ISBN 0688134653. 40 pp. 7–12. Nonfiction.

Without any condescension, George Ancona has created a sympathetic portrayal of a contemporary extended Maya family in the Yucatan peninsula of Mexico. Readers follow the family through several days of activities at home, in town, and at the family ranch, as they maintain ancient traditions but also adopt new ways. The captions for the vivid photos are wonderfully sparse, letting faces and activities speak for themselves. The book includes a glossary of Spanish and Yucatec Mayan words along with illustrations from ancient Mayan artifacts that show the continuity of the Mayan culture from ancient times to the present. (DD)

Notable Social Studies Trade Books for Young People

6.3 Ashabranner, Brent. **To Seek a Better World: The Haitian Minority in America.** Photographs by Paul Conkin. Cobblehill / Dutton, 1997. ISBN 0525652191. 84 pp. 10 and up. Nonfiction.

More than thirty years before Haitian "boat people" began washing up on the shores of the United States, thousands of Haitians arrived as legal immigrants. Their stories and pictures are proudly displayed in the pages of this book. Many of these early immigrants were and are professional middle-class tradespeople who left Haiti to escape the brutal regime of Francois Duvalier. The book takes a frank look at how they have adapted to life here and how they look toward the future and a better life for all Haitian immigrants. (EA)

6.4   Bernhard, Emery. **A Ride on Mother's Back.** Illustrated by Durga Bernhard. Gulliver / Harcourt, 1996. ISBN 0152008705. 40 pp. 2–6. Nonfiction.

Daily life from a variety of cultures is viewed through the perspectives of children carried by family members. A Guatemalan mother carries her baby in a shawl tied around her waist while preparing the morning meal. A grandfather in the African rain forest carries his grandson in a sling on his hip while the father searches for honeycombs. On the island of Bali, sisters carry their three-month-old twin brothers in slings hung from their shoulders. In all, twelve cultures are tenderly described through the sights and sounds witnessed by the children. Each full-page gouache painting illustrates a different culture, while the facing page mixes simple explanatory text with patterns and artifacts from the culture. Colorful world maps showing the location of each culture are found on the front and back endpapers. Additional information on each culture is appended. (CC)

6.5   Bial, Raymond. **Cajun Home.** Houghton Mifflin, 1998. ISBN 0395860954. 48 pp. 9–12. Nonfiction.

Who are the Cajuns? Often misunderstood or considered ignorant because of their unusual dialect, the Cajuns are here presented as people known for their generosity, and who possess a unique history and culture. Based on his meticulous research, Bial describes Cajun social customs that date back to 1623. Cajun French text is strategically placed within the text along with definitions. Bial's beautiful photography offers realistic glimpses of this swampy land in Louisiana. This excellent cultural resource book depicts the Cajuns as warm, caring people with strong ties to their communities. (CMH)

6.6   Bonvillain, Nancy. **The Cheyennes: People of the Plains.** Millbrook, 1996. ISBN 0761300155. 64 pp. 8 and up. Nonfiction.

This informational book on the Cheyenne people is a good resource. Included are a glossary, a bibliography, photos and drawings of Cheyenne culture, and even a recipe. The book combines historical information about the Cheyennes with descriptions of contemporary life on the reservation. This book is one in a series of books about Native American people and their cultures. Bonvillain does a brilliant job of communicating the message that each Native American culture is unique. With Bonvillain's brilliant research outdated stereotypes and generalizations about "Indians" are effectively swept away. (CMH)

6.7 Brenner, Barbara, and Julia Takaya. **Chibi: A True Story from Japan.** Illustrated by June Otani. Clarion, 1996. ISBN 0395696232. 63 pp. 4–8. Nonfiction.

In this true story set in Tokyo, Oka-san, a mother duck, finds a place to raise her ducklings. She chooses the Mitsui office park, attracting much attention from people who come to watch the ducklings hatch. A photographer, Mr. Sato, becomes very interested in the lives of the ducks, especially Chibi, one of the new ducklings, who becomes separated from his family during a storm. All turns out well in the end in this perfect read-aloud for young children. This book would make a good companion to *Make Way for Ducklings* by Robert McCloskey. (MP)

6.8 Chin-Lee, Cynthia. **A Is for Asia.** Illustrated by Yumi Heo. Orchard, 1997. ISBN 0531300110 (trade). ISBN 0531330117 (library binding). 32 pp. 4–8. Nonfiction.

This beautifully illustrated book introduces the reader to Asian cultures and languages. For each letter of the alphabet, Chin-Lee includes a piece of information designed to enlighten the reader on such topics as Asian food, clothing, geography, and customs. Many pages also include words spelled in languages native to the people of Asia. This book's text and pictures are truly engaging. (CP)

6.9 Colbert, Jan, and Ann McMillan Harms, editors. **Dear Dr. King: Letters from Today's Children to Dr. Martin Luther King Jr.** Photographs by Ernest C. Withers and Roy Cajero. Hyperion, 1998. ISBN 0786804173. 63 pp. 9–12. Nonfiction.

The editors invited elementary school children from Memphis, Tennessee, to write letters to Dr. Martin Luther King Jr. "posing questions or telling about their own lives and feelings, their perceptions of the past, or dreams for the future." The results are compiled in this attractively formatted book. The text appears in a variety of fonts and arrangements on each page. Rick Cajero captures the hopefulness and wonder of the children in his photos placed throughout the volume. Ernest Withers's captioned photographs depict scenes of the civil rights struggle in the United States during the 1960s. These photos accompany the children's evaluation of social advancements, continuing challenges, and unanswered inquiries that are crucial to the health of a democratic society. (JC)

6.10   Dolphin, Laurie. **Our Journey from Tibet.** Photographs by Nancy Jo Johnson. Dutton, 1997. ISBN 0525455779. 40 pp. 8–12. Nonfiction.

Based on a true story and interviews with a nine-year old Tibetan girl, the author has written a poignant, first-person narrative of Sonam's dangerous journey from Tibet to Dharamsala, India. Sonam's family decides to help their children escape Chinese-occupied Tibet to pursue a traditional Tibetan education in India. Accompanied by her two sisters, her Buddhist monk brother, other children, and a guide, Sonam relates how she hides in salt sacks, fears discovery at checkpoints, fights frostbite, and endures other hardships along her journey. The narration includes many details of Tibetan culture and beliefs. Photographs present stunning images of Tibetan landscapes and dramatize the plight of the Tibetan people. Contains a letter from the Dalai Lama. (KYR)

Notable Social Studies Trade Books for Young People, Notable Books for a Global Society

6.11   Erlbach, Arlene. **Sidewalk Games around the World.** Illustrated by Sharon Lane Holm. Millbrook, 1997. ISBN 0761300082 64 pp. 9–12. Nonfiction.

Readers who enjoy playing games will embrace this book, as they learn games from twenty-six countries around the world. A table of contents outlines the games by country, and a detailed classified index and bibliography at the end of the book are useful resources. A map shows the geographic location of each country and gives brief descriptions of the different countries as well. Each game is outlined with instructions and an illustration of how to play. (MS)

6.12 Finley, Carol. **Art of the Far North: Inuit Sculpture, Drawing, and Printmaking.** Lerner, 1998. ISBN 0822520753. 64 pp. 9–12. Nonfiction.

Part of the Art Around the World series, this splendidly done book offers perhaps the best information to date about the Inuit people and their art. The book contains a brief history of the Inuits, then continues to explain the sculptures, drawing, and prints that reflect the different aspects of the Inuit culture and customs. Students will find the photographs very appealing, and the explanations easy to understand. (KW)

Notable Social Studies Trade Books for Young People

6.13 Fraser, Mary Ann. **A Mission for the People: The Story of la Purisima.** Illustrated by Mary Ann Fraser. Henry Holt, 1998. ISBN 0805050507. 38 pp. 9–12. Nonfiction.

This book relates the history of the Mission la Purisima, once found in what is now the Santa Barbara region of California, as it relates to the native people of the area, the Chumash. The story traces the colonization of the Chumash, the settlement of the area, and the struggles faced by everyone who came into contact with the mission, through short one- to two-page essays. Many of the pages have sidebars with supporting information. Acrylic illustrations of scenes and artifacts accompany the text and provide further insight into daily life at the mission as well as its ultimate abandonment and restoration. The story leaves the reader pondering the importance of remembering one's cultural heritage. A timeline and additional resources are included. (ED and SF)

6.14 Ganeri, Anita. **Religions Explained: A Beginner's Guide to World Faiths.** Henry Holt, 1997. ISBN 080504874X. 69 pp. 8 and up. Nonfiction.

Numerous effective graphics, colorful photos, and design features might seem to reduce even further the ability of a small book to tackle a serious subject such as world religions with any substance, but this book nevertheless does. The book is remarkably even-handed, according the same amount of space and positive tone to all the major world faiths, with a section on new religions and "spirit religions" of traditional cultures. The section on Africa regrettably uses the loaded term "witch doctor," and there is no acknowledgment of millions of atheists, agnostics, and free-thinkers worldwide; but by and large, the book provides an attractive cultural *entrée* to the varieties of belief and practice in the human family. (KL)

6.15   George, Linda. **The Golden Age of Islam.** Benchmark, 1998. ISBN 076140273X. 80 pp. 8–14. Nonfiction.

Here is an informative, balanced book answering frequently asked questions about Islam, covering its history, tenets, practices, and other items that are missing from many other books. Included are discussions of the role of women (with sidebars featuring notable women in Islamic history), the origin of the Shiite–Sunni split, the genesis of the Arabian Nights tales, and a list of English words derived from Arabic. Bright photos on glossy paper stock make the book pleasant for reading or scanning, and a chronology, glossary, and bibliography complete the package. (KL)

6.16   Getz, David. **Frozen Girl.** Illustrated by Peter McCarthy. Henry Holt, 1998. ISBN 0805051538. 72 pp. 9–12. Nonfiction.

When the curled, clothed body of a frozen girl is discovered near the summit of a Peruvian mountain, archaeologists realize that she is a five-hundred-year-old Incan sacrifice. Using direct quotes and suspenseful narrative, Getz spins the story of her discovery and the efforts of archaeologists to prevent thawing and decay while studying her. He includes easily understood, nonromanticized explanations of Inca beliefs and practices of sacrifice, as well as the impact of the Spanish conquest on the Inca civilization. Getz does a masterful job of tracing the lines of inquiry that the scientists pursue in terms that children can easily follow, and does not succumb to the temptation to reach for unsubstantiated answers. This may be unsatisfying to some readers, but it accurately reflects the nature of archaeology and could serve to start interesting discussions in class. Pencil illustrations are interspersed with photos of the mummy, which may prove disturbing to certain readers. A bibliography and index are included. (DD)

Pura Belpré Honor for Illustrations, Notable Social Studies Trade Books for Young People

6.17 Gordon, Ginger. **Anthony Reynoso: Born to Rope.** Photographs by Martha Cooper. Clarion, 1996. ISBN 039571690X. 32 pp. 7–12. Biography.

Nine-year-old Anthony Reynoso shares his experiences of growing up in Arizona in this warm first-person narrative. He relates aspects of his Mexican heritage, including learning to rope and ride in the style of the Mexican rodeo. Experiences at school and at family gatherings further illuminate the cultural life of this young boy. Color photographs also provide a glimpse of the closeness and joy Anthony and his family share. (ED)

6.18 Haskins, James, and Kathleen Benson. **African Beginnings.** Illustrated by Floyd Cooper. Lothrop, Lee & Shepard, 1998. ISBN 0688102565 (trade). ISBN 0688102573 (library binding). 48 pp. 10 and up. Nonfiction.

This beautifully designed picture book for older students gives information on African civilizations, beginning with Nubia (3800 B.C.E.) and continuing to cover eleven cultures. There are sections on dance and music, Islam, slavery, trade with Europeans, art, and religion. A timeline of notable milestones and a bibliography are also included. Floyd Cooper has contributed exceptional oil and wash paintings. The reader can move into each story, seeing the people portrayed authentically in the various cultures. For an older child, this book would be an excellent starting place for research on Africa's rich history. (MP)

Notable Social Studies Trade Books for Young People

6.19 Hopcraft, Xan, and Carol Cawthra Hopcraft. **How It Was with Dooms: A True Story from Africa.** Margaret McElderry / Simon & Schuster, 1997. ISBN 0689810911. Unpaged. 8–11. Nonfiction.

In this scrapbook tale, Carol Hopcraft and her twelve-year-old son Xan recount the wonderful story of Dooms, an abandoned cheetah who became their family's beloved pet. Through Xan's colorful drawings and Carol's breathtaking photographs, readers get to know Dooms in the picturesque African countryside near the Hopcraft home in Nairobi, Kenya. This exciting tale captures a family's love of animals and of one another, but fails to detail the obvious risks of living with a wild animal. (SS)

Notable Social Studies Trade Books for Young People

6.20   Horenstein, Henry. **Baseball in the Barrios.** Gulliver / Harcourt Brace, 1997. ISBN 0152004998. Unpaged. 5–12. Nonfiction.

In this realistic photoessay we meet Hubaldo, a fifth grader from Caracas, Venezuela, who loves baseball. The reader learns not only about the most popular sport in Venezuela but also about the culture of the country and its baseball history. A baseball vocabulary in English and Spanish and a map are located at the end of the book. Children aged five to twelve will greatly enjoy this interesting essay. (MP)

6.21   Hoyt-Goldsmith, Diane. **Buffalo Days.** Photographs by Lawrence Migdale. Holiday House, 1997. ISBN 0823413276. 30 pp. 9–12. Nonfiction.

This photoessay tells the history of the buffalo from the perspective of the Crow Indian tribe. The story begins with an introduction to a young boy and his family at the Crow Reservation in Montana. The text tells the reader about the decline and near extinction of the buffalo and the consequences for the tribe, as well as the tribe's current efforts to maintain buffalo populations. At the end of the book, we are treated to appealing photos of the annual Crow fair and rodeo. (MP)

6.22   Jensen, Vickie. **Carving a Totem Pole.** Henry Holt, 1994. ISBN 0805037543. 32 pp. 8–11. Nonfiction.

Using sepia-toned photographs to complement her text, the author chronicles Nisga'a artist Norman Tait's design and carving of a contemporary totem pole, which becomes the doorway of the Native Education Centre in Vancouver, British Columbia. Each stage in the creation is carefully told, from finding a suitable tree, to designing its story, to the actual carving by Tait and family members, and finally to the traditional raising and celebration of the forty-two-foot pole. The significance of the totem pole to Native American cultures is carefully explained as well. In the foreword Tait himself explains that each totem pole, like the elders of the tribe, tells the stories and legends of the culture. (SM)

6.23   Jones, Bill T., and Susan Kuklin. **Dance.** Photographs by Susan Kuklin. Hyperion, 1998. ISBN 0786803622 (trade). ISBN 0786823070 (library binding). Unpaged. 4–10. Nonfiction.

In this extraordinary book, dancer Bill T. Jones and photographer Susan Kulkin collaborate to portray the ways a dancer uses both mind and body to communicate ideas. The still photographs move across the pages in ways that truly capture the physical movement of dance. The spare text and totally white background allow visual focus to remain on the African American dancer, while the reader is guided toward understanding the dancer's feelings and intentions. One is acutely aware of dance as an expression of the body's seemingly limitless physical possibilities as well as an outlet for personal expression. The book is an irresistible invitation to dance. (SJ)

6.24   King, Martin Luther, Jr., and Coretta Scott King. **I Have a Dream.** Scholastic, 1997. ISBN 0590205161. 40 pp. 4–8. Nonfiction.

This book features Dr. King's words accompanied by illustrations from fifteen Coretta Scott King Award or Honor Book Citation winners. The illustrators describe their work at the end of the text. A biography of King helps illuminate this important speech given in 1963. This book is appropriate for K–8 children who are studying the civil rights movement or Dr. Martin Luther King Jr.'s life. Students will pick up this book over and over whenever they need visual inspiration about a great leader. (MP)

Notable Books for a Global Society, Notable Social Studies Trade Books for Young People

6.25   Libura, Krystyna, Claudia Burr, and Maria Christina Urrutia. **What the Aztecs Told Me.** Groundwood / Douglas & McIntyre, 1994. ISBN 0–88899–305. 32 pp. 10–14. Nonfiction.

This picture book was adapted from a twelve-volume collection of books written by Friar Bernardino do Sahagun, a missionary from Spain, in the sixteenth century. The original collection is called *A General History of the Things in New Spain*. It describes the daily routines, the religious practices (including human sacrifice), and the major gods that the Aztecs worshipped. The illustrations are taken from the original manuscript. A glossary of terms is included at the end of the book. (SF)

6.26   Lucas, Eileen. **Cracking the Wall: The Struggles of the Little Rock Nine.** Illustrated by Mark Anthony. Carolrhoda, 1997. ISBN 0876149905. 48 pp. 8–10. Nonfiction.

This is the story of the desegregation of Central High School in Little Rock, Arkansas, by nine teenagers in 1957. An author's note and afterword carefully frame the incident in its historical context, from the Supreme Court's decision in 1954 against school segregation to the eventually successful integration of the school, as evidenced when the nine African Americans return to the school as adults in 1987. Muted, sometimes menacing illustrations contribute to the somber feeling of the story. (SM)

6.27   McConduit, Denise Walter. **D.J. and the Jazz Fest.** Illustrated by Emile F. Henriquez. Pelican, 1997. ISBN 1565542398. 32 pp. All ages. Nonfiction.

The annual spring New Orleans Jazz Fest is the setting for this informational picture book. Loosely centered around an African American boy reluctant to accompany his mother to the event, this story offers the reader a sampling of the diverse activities usually featured at the festival. Captured in words and through Henriquez's bright, cartoon-like watercolor drawings, the boy and his mother visit booths of handcrafted items and food and watch demonstrations by dance and music performers from many cultures. Unfortunately, jazz itself is given little attention, as only two short pages of text are devoted to the topic. (JHC)

6.28   McKee, Timothy Saunders. **No More Strangers Now: Young Voices from a New South Africa.** Photographs by Anne Blackshaw. Foreword by Archbishop Desmond Mpilo Tutu. DK Ink, 1998. ISBN 0789425246. 112 pp. 12 and up. Nonfiction.

Twelve South African teenagers of different races and backgrounds tell their stories of life under apartheid through stories and photographs. In these first-person interviews they share their hope for a nonbiased government, and discuss the different prejudices and ignominies they have suffered—or inflicted—under apartheid. This would be a delightful accompaniment to Jason and Ettagle Laur's *South Africa: Coming of Age under Apartheid.* (KW)

Notable Social Studies Trade Books for Young People, ALA Notable Books for Children, Best Books for Young Adults

6.29 McMahon, Patricia. **Six Words, Many Turtles, and Three Days in Hong Kong.** Houghton Mifflin, 1997. ISBN 0395686210. 45 pp. 9–12. Nonfiction.

Bright photos illustrate a weekend in the life of Tsz Yan Law, a Chinese girl who lives in Hong Kong with her parents. On this particular weekend she has six English words that she must learn as part of her homework. Her weekend begins at the end of her school day on Friday with doing homework, playing with friends, and eating at McDonald's. Saturday brings an excursion to an amusement park via a train, a ferry, and a bus. On Sunday, the family enjoys *dim sum* at the neighborhood restaurant, a trip to the market, and family visits. Tsz Yan plays with her cousins, helps her grandmother in the kitchen, and enjoys meals with her extended families. The weekend activities end as the family heads home so that Tsz Yan can finish her homework and relive her busy weekend through the six new English words that she has just learned. Through this glimpse into Tsz Yan's life, readers are introduced to Hong Kong, as well as to some Chinese customs and traditions. (SKA)

6.30 McMillan, Bruce. **Salmon Summer.** Houghton Mifflin, 1998. ISBN 0395845440. 32 pp. 4–8. Nonfiction.

This photographic story of salmon is set on Kodiak Island, Alaska. A nine-year-old boy fishes in this wilderness area every year at his family's fishing camp. The reader learns about Aleut heritage and the Russian influences on Kodiak Island. This book is an up-close and personal look at salmon fishing and the care that the Aleut people give to nature and to their environment. A detailed glossary gives information at the end of the text. (MP)

6.31 Millard, Anne. **Pyramids.** Kingfisher, 1996. ISBN 1856976742. 64 pp. 6–10. Nonfiction.

Forty-one of the sixty-four pages in this large, handsome book are devoted to the Egyptian pyramids and the civilization that created them. The large, double-spread paintings depict many people at work in and around the pyramids and include rich, three-dimensional panoramas in a spacious layout. The author has written many books about archeology and uses scientific consultants to ensure accuracy. Beautifully conceived and executed, with attractive typography and layout, this book is sure to appeal to a large group of readers. (KL)

6.32 Onyefulu, Ifeoma. **Grandfather's Work: A Traditional Healer in Nigeria.** Millbrook, 1998. ISBN 0761304126 (library binding). 32 pp. 5–9. Nonfiction.

A young Nigerian boy tells the story of his "magician" grandfather, a traditional healer. The story is broken up into two parts. In the first part we meet other members of the family, including lawyers, doctors, carvers, and a seamstress; in the second part we meet Grandfather, who shows us how he collects plants from the forest and uses them to heal the sick. Beautiful, full-page photographs are a wonderful accompaniment to this straightforward story. (KW)

Notable Social Studies Trade Books for Young People

6.33 Onyefulu, Ifeoma. **Ogbo: Sharing Life in an African Village.** Gulliver Books / Harcourt Brace, 1996. ISBN 015200498X. 32 pp. 9–12. Nonfiction.

Brilliant photographs and simply written text explain the Nigerian custom of the *ogbo*, a village-wide age group. Information is presented through the voice of Obioma, a six-year-old Nigerian girl. Through the *ogbo*, everyone contributes to the life of the village. Even those who move away remain a part of their *ogbo* group and may attend meetings whenever they return for visits. This book presents to readers the work, customs, and recreational activities of contemporary Nigerians. An author's note preceding the text gives additional background information on *ogbo*. (CC)

ALA Notable Books for Children, Notable Books for a Global Society

6.34 Rendon, Marcie R. **Powwow Summer: A Family Celebrates the Circle of Life.** Photographs by Cheryl Walsh Bellville. Carolrhoda, 1996. ISBN 0876149867. 8–10. Nonfiction.

The Downwind family are more commonly known as Anishinabe, Ojibway, or Chippewa. They participate in a contemporary powwow trail each summer, meeting members of various tribes each weekend for a celebration of singing and dancing. Native rituals and customs—both traditional and modern—are explained in some depth in this book, and colorful photographs contribute to the energetic descriptions of the different dances enjoyed by the different members of the family, including the Downwind's foster children. Rendon, identified as a member of the White Earth

Anishinabe tribe, has written a useful description of this Native American tradition, although at times the text and photos are somewhat inconsistent. (SM)

6.35 Sha'ban, Mervet Akram, Galit Fink, and Litsa Boudalika. **If You Could Be My Friend: Letters of Mervet Akram Sha'ban and Galit Fink.** Translated by Alison Landes. Orchard, 1998. ISBN 0531301133. 128 pp. 9–12. Nonfiction.

Friend or foe? The power of friendship is tested between Galit, an Israeli girl, and Mervet, a Palestinian girl, as they correspond through letters from 1988 to 1991. The two girls share their family stories and plan to meet in Jerusalem, despite the political boundaries. An accompanying glossary as well as a historical overview help to fill in the context of the political conflict. (KW)

Notable Social Studies Trade Books for Young People

6.36 Sis, Peter. **Tibet: Through the Red Box.** Farrar, Straus and Giroux, 1998. ISBN 0374375526. Unpaged. 10 and up. Nonfiction.

What is in the magical red box? Peter Sis tells the story of his father's journey to Tibet. With the help of the diaries stored in the red box, he reconstructs the daunting adventure of his father, a documentary filmmaker, who finds himself separated from his crew and caught in a blizzard. Woven within the diary entries are stories from Tibet—stories such as those of "giant fairy beings," or Yetis, who help him to rest and recover. This mysterious journey is complemented by pages from his father's diary, with elaborate images of mountains, mazes, and mandalas. Perhaps more suited for adults who can better understand the gentleness of Tibet, this book will also be savored by the more mature child. (KW)

Caldecott Award Honor Book, ALA Notable Books for Children

6.37 Solá, Michéle. **Angela Weaves a Dream.** Photographs by Jeffrey Jay Foxx. Hyperion, 1997. ISBN 0786800739. 47 pp. 7–12. Nonfiction.

The day of the beginners' weaving contest has arrived in a small town in the Mexican state of Chiapas. Under the tutelage of her grandmother, Angela has woven a sampler based on a vision in a dream. Abundant photos, informative captions, and extensive sidebars explain the process of carding, spinning, and dyeing the wool, threading the backstrap loom, and incorporating the sacred Maya designs of Angela's town. The primary focus of this book is on weaving as a cultural expression and the stories behind the designs, rather than on technical information or the details of Angela's life. A glossary, maps, and background notes are helpful additions. (DD)

6.38   Strom, Yale. **Quilted Landscape: Conversations with Young Immigrants.** Simon & Schuster, 1996. ISBN 0689800746. 80 pp. 9–15. Nonfiction.

Immigrant children tell their families' stories in twenty-six interviews. Small maps show where these children have traveled from and to, black-and-white pictures illustrate their lives here in the United States, and fact columns give the reader some facts about their homelands. In telling of their journeys and the hardships they have endured, including learning new languages, assimilating culturally, and facing prejudices and misunderstanding, these children are given voice to express how far they have come both physically and spiritually. (CW)

6.39   Walgren, Judy. **The Lost Boys of Natinga.** Houghton Mifflin, 1998. ISBN 0395705584. 48 pp. 9–12. Nonfiction.

An ongoing civil war in Sudan has taken more than one million lives and driven more than four million people from their homes into refugee camps. In this photographic essay on life in a camp in Natinga, Africa, the hardships of war, famine, and disease are central themes. The full-color photographs of schools, churches, recreation, and camp life paint a portrait of life in Natinga. A table of contents at the beginning of the book helps readers find specific topics about the camp. (MS)

6.40   Wood, Nancy, editor. **The Serpent's Tongue: Prose, Poetry, and Art of the New Mexico Pueblos.** Dutton, 1997. ISBN 0525455140. 230 pp. 12 and up. Nonfiction.

This elegant anthology gives the reader more than five hundred years of Pueblo culture of the U.S. Southwest. Important scholars, writers, and artists, both from within and without the Pueblo tribe, have contributed to the text. The author has thoroughly researched the material for this volume, which is fully annotated with a bibliography and notes for scholars, plus maps, sketches, and historic photos. Detailed and scholarly, this book is written for young adults or even older researchers. (MP)

Notable Social Studies Trade Books for Young People, Notable Books for a Global Society

Series Books

Series: California Missions

6.41   Abbink, Emily. **Missions of the Monterey Bay Area.** Lerner, 1996. ISBN 0822519283. 76 pp. 9 and up. Nonfiction.

This informative historical interpretation tells of the establishment of the Spanish missions in California and the early encounters between the European and Native American cultures. The text is easily read and the illustrations support the text well. This book is one in a series of six about the twenty-one California missions, organized by geographic region. The text includes a glossary of Spanish terms, maps, charts, informational inserts, and an afterword, as well as reproductions of some beautiful paintings showing the missions and the surrounding areas. Beginning in the time before colonization and moving toward the present, the author conveys the tremendous impact the collision of Spanish and Native American cultures caused, and the consequences that persist to the present day. Highlighting three missions (San Carlos Borromeo de Carmelo, Mission Santa Cruz, and Mission San Juan Bautista), the book examines the people and cultures involved, and the overall impact these missions have had on the Monterey Bay area and its inhabitants. (SSG)

Other titles in the California Missions series

Behrens, June. **Missions of the Central Coast.** Lerner, 1996. ISBN 0822519305.

Brower, Pauline. **Missions of the Inland Valleys.** Lerner, 1996. ISBN 0822519291.

Lemke, Nancy. **Missions of the Southern Coast.** Lerner, 1996. ISBN 0822519259.

MacMillan, Diane. **Missions of the Los Angeles Area.** Lerner, 1996. ISBN 0822519275.

White, Tekla N. **Missions of the San Francisco Bay Area.** Lerner, 1996. ISBN 0822519267.

Series: The World's Children

6.42   Hermes, Jules. **The Children of Bolivia.** Carolrhoda, 1996. ISBN 0876149352. 48 pp. 8–10. Nonfiction.

This book offers a look at the country of Bolivia through the lives of its children. With various children acting as hosts, the reader is shown how the children work, play, and celebrate. The hosts represent different locations and social and economic classes in Bolivia, giving the reader a complete overview of this country. (SF)

6.43   Staub, Frank. **The Children of the Sierra Madre.** Carolrhoda, 1996. ISBN 0876149433. 45 pp. 9–12. Nonfiction.

The full-color photographs and text provide a glimpse of what life is like in the northern region of the Madre Occidental mountains of Mexico, in the area of Barrancas del Cobre. The text includes an overview of the geography and history of the area. The culture and traditions of the Tarahumara Indians are depicted through the daily activities of various children. The daily lives of the *mestizo* and White Mexicans are also briefly covered in this book. The photographs capture the essence of the people of this region in realistic settings. (ED)

6.44   Staub, Frank. **Children of Yucatán.** Carolrhoda, 1996. ISBN 0876149840. 47 pp. 9–12. Nonfiction.

The full-color photographs and text portray the way of life of the modern Mayan people who live throughout the Mexican state of Yucatán. The text includes an overview of the history and architecture of the Mayans. This book captures the customs, traditions, and economic realities in the daily lives of various Mayan children and their families from various cities in the state. Although a realistic sense of Mexican indigenous culture emanates from this book, commonalities with U.S. culture are also revealed. (ED)

Other titles in The World's Children series

> Beirne, Barbara. **Children of the Ecuadorean Highlands.** Carolrhoda, 1996. ISBN 1575050005.

> Kinkade, Sheila. **Children of the Philippines.** Photographs by Elaine Little. Carolrhoda, 1996. ISBN 087614993X.

> Lorbiecki, Marybeth. **Children of Vietnam.** Photographs by Paul P. Rome. Carolrhoda, 1997. ISBN 157505034X.

> Staub, Frank. **Children of Cuba.** Carolrhoda, 1996. ISBN 0876149891.

> Staub, Frank. **Children of Belize.** Carolrhoda, 1997. ISBN 1575050390.

Earlier books in the series

> **Children of China, Children of Egypt, Children of Guatemala, Children of India, Children of Mauritania, Children of Micronesia, Children of Nepal, Grandchildren of the Incas, Grandchildren of the Vikings.**

Series: Colors of . . .

6.45 Littlefield, Holly. **Colors of Japan.** Carolrhoda, 1997. ISBN 0876148852. 24 pp. 4–8. Nonfiction.

Watercolor illustrations show how individual colors can elicit connections to the fascinating facts of a particular country. For example, Littlefield explains how blue symbolizes the waters surrounding Japan. She then relates how important the water is because it provides food and products such as pearls. The name of each color is written in Japanese characters, accompanied by pronunciation cues. This book is a brief introduction to some of the primary facts about Japan. (SKA)

6.46 Olawsky, Lynn Ainsworth. **Colors of Mexico.** Illustrated by Janice Lee Porter. Carolrhoda, 1997. ISBN 0876148860. 24 pp. 4–8. Nonfiction.

A simple introduction to Mexican life and customs, this book discusses the significance of ten different colors for the people and the culture of Mexico. With Spanish translations of the colors described, *Colors of Mexico* features architecture, foods, and holidays, in order to give the reader a basic understanding of our neighbor to the south. Readers will enjoy the splash of each individual color on the page on which it is described. (CP)

Series: Count Your Way

6.47   Haskins, Jim, and Kathleen Benson. **Count Your Way through Brazil.** Illustrated by Liz Brenner Dodson. Carolrhoda, 1996. ISBN 0876148739. ISBN 0876149719 (paperback). 24 pp. 6–9. Nonfiction.

In this title from the *Count Your Way* series, the Portuguese numbers one through ten are used to introduce a variety of facts about Brazil and its culture. Exotic animals, musical instruments, and foods are just some of the subjects this books discusses. This book would be an entertaining supplement to a study of Brazil or South America, but does not contain enough information to give true insight into this culture. The Amazon rain forest is mentioned as an important resource, for example, but nothing is said about its ongoing destruction. (SM)

Series: Endangered People and Places

6.48   Rootes, David. **The Arctic.** Photography by Bryan and Cherry Alexander. Lerner, 1996. ISBN 0822527766. 48 pp. 9–12. Nonfiction.

The purpose of this informational text is to describe Arctic geography and its native people. The book begins with a description of Arctic lands, seasons, and ways its inhabitants have learned to survive the cold. The customs and religion of Arctic people are thoroughly explored next. Following that is a discussion of some contemporary issues facing the land and people of the Arctic. A glossary is included as are colorful, informative photographs. (CP)

Series: Journey between Two Worlds

6.49   Berg, Lois Ann. **An Eritrean Family.** Lerner, 1997. ISBN 0822534053. ISBN 0822597551 (paperback). 64 pp. 8–14. Nonfiction.

An ethnographic narrative paints a portrait of an Eritrean family who barely escaped Ethiopian troops during the Eritrean war of independence, lived in a refugee camp in Sudan, and finally emigrated to the United States. Their story is told through bits of dialogue as they interact with each other and their interviewer in their home in Minnesota. Eritrean culture is introduced through a brief historical survey, maps, and a two-page decorated folktale, along with an index, a pronunciation guide, and a bibliography for further reading. The tale does not mince words and fans of Haile Selassie will not be pleased, but Eritreans—who now have a nation of their own—could only be delighted that their people are depicted in a children's book in the United States with such conscientious, compassionate coverage. Excellent photos decorate every page of the book. (KL)

6.50   Malone, Michael. **A Guatemalan Family.** Lerner, 1996. ISBN 0822534002. 64 pp. 9–12. Nonfiction.

The Mendez family, a Mayan refugee family, emigrated to the United States in order to escape the political turmoil in their native country of Guatemala as a result of a civil war. Their dangerous journey began when the grandfather decided the family should flee the country after being threatened by guerillas. The text honestly reveals both the struggles and joys the family experienced living in Guatemala, leaving their homeland, adjusting to a new culture, and preserving their cultural heritage while raising children born in the United States. The text also provides an overview of Mayan history and the current political situation in Guatemala. Full-color photographs and maps complement the text. (ED)

6.51   Gogol, Sara. **A Mien Family.** Lerner, 1996. ISBN082253407X. 64 pp. 8–14. Nonfiction.

The book follows the life and history of a Mien family in Oregon. The Mien, an ethnic minority who once lived in the highlands of Laos, were caught in the crossfire of the Laotian civil war and the Vietnam War, where they were recruited by the U.S. to fight the Pathet Lao—and lost. The extended family tells of their hair-raising escape from Laos and years in a refugee camp in Thailand, their fear of "people-eating giants" in the United States, and their gradual adjustment to the life in the United States. Mien culture is introduced through many photographs showing traditional dress, food, stories, games, a brief historical survey, a pronunciation guide, and a bibliography. The lively photos and informal nature of the stories the family shares make the reading experience very engaging and personal, and the book reads almost like a combination photo album and scrapbook. (KL)

Other titles in the Journey between Two Worlds series

Archibald, Erika F. **A Sudanese Family.** Lerner, 1997. ISBN 0822597535.

Chicoine, Stephen. **A Liberian Family.** Lerner, 1997. ISBN 0822534118.

Greenberg, Keith Elliott. **An Armenian Family.** Lerner, 1997. ISBN 0822534096.

Greenberg, Keith Elliott. **A Haitian Family.** Lerner, 1998. ISBN 082253410X.

Murphy, Nora. **A Hmong Family.** Lerner, 1997. ISBN 0822534061.

Earlier books in the series

A Bosnian Family, A Kurdish Family, A Nicaraguan Family, A Russian Jewish Family, A Tibetan Family.

Series: We Are Still Here

6.52 Yamane, Linda. **Weaving a California Tradition: A Native American Basketmaker.** Photographs by Duan Aguilar. Lerner, 1997. ISBN 0822526603. 48 pp. 8–11. Nonfiction.

The author Yamane is a member of the Rumisen Ohlone tribe of California and a basketmaker. In this book she tells the story of eleven-year-old Caryl Tex, a Western Mono Indian, who learns from her relatives the art of basketweaving, including how to gather plants, prepare the needed materials, and weave them in the traditional manner of her tribe. Although she is a member of a traditional indigenous culture, this book makes an effort to show that Caryl's life at home, with her family, and at school is in many ways not unlike that of most other girls her age. Both Caryl's contemporary daily life and cultural traditions are woven together with bits of history in this story. The extensive photographs and illustrations make this a beautiful cultural history. (LD)

7 Poetry, Verse, and Song

7.1 Ada, Alma Flor. **Gathering the Sun: An Alphabet in Spanish and English.** Translated by Rosa Zubizarreta. Illustrated by Simón Silva. Lothrop, Lee & Shepard, 1997. ISBN 0688139035. Unpaged. 4–10. Poetry.

An alphabet book, a book of poetry, and a visual extravaganza, this beautiful book is a hearty tribute to Mexican farmworkers whose efforts bring food to so many. The short poems, which appear in both Spanish and English, are laden with images of growing things, family love, and personal pride. The double-page illustrations portray these images in strong, clear tones, offering exceptionally realistic representations of vast fields, wide skies, and sturdy people. For those who are accustomed to seeing foods unloaded from cardboard boxes into supermarket bins, or packaged in plastic, the pictures in this book will provide a striking view of fruits and vegetables before they are harvested. (SJ)

Pura Belpré Honor Book for Illustration, Notable Children's Books in the Language Arts

7.2 Alarcón, Francisco X. **From the Bellybutton of the Moon and Other Summer Poems / Del ombligo de la luna y otros poemas de verano.** Illustrated by Maya Christina Gonzalez. Children's Book Press, 1998. ISBN 0892391537. 31 pp. 5–8. Poetry.

Readers will want to read aloud Francisco X. Alarcón's colorful, whimsical poems in both English and Spanish. Inspired by his childhood memories of Mexico, Alarcón lets us hear his grandmother's stories, feel the tropical sun and wind, learn the keys to the universe, and meet his bilingual dog. Perfectly complemented by Maya Christina Gonzalez's vibrant illustrations, this book of poems will bring readers back again and again. (KW)

Pura Belpré Honor Book for Narrative

7.3 Alarcón, Francisco X. **Laughing Tomatoes and Other Spring Poems / Jitomates risueños y otros poemas de primavera.** Illustrated by Maya Christina Gonzalez. Children's Book Press, 1997. 32 pp. 5–8. Poetry.

These poems are like tomatoes turned inside-out—bright, sweet, and juicy! Francisco X. Alarcón's twenty poems are meant to be read aloud and enjoyed by all. Follow Maya Christina Gonzalez's animated crew of Grandma, four children, and a variety of pets as they bring each poem to life in a celebratation of the first rains of spring, and share their dreams and prayers with readers. (KW)

Pura Belpré Honor Book for Narrative

7.4   Berry, James. **Everywhere Faces Everywhere.** Illustrated by Reynold Ruffins. Simon & Schuster, 1997. ISBN 0689809964. 96 pp. 10–16. Poetry.

Award-winning writer James Berry gives us a collection of forty-six poems that draws on his Jamaican childhood as well as his adult life and work in the United Kingdom. With perceptive and witty observations on a variety of topics, Berry's poems celebrate youth and its dramas, salute nature, explore cultural conflicts, and welcome ethnic diversity and tolerance. As Berry's poems capture so well the festive rhythms and picturesque language of his Caribbean background, they are most effective when read aloud. His poetic styles range from free verse to haikus to dialogue. (KYR)

7.5   Bloom, Valerie. **Fruits: A Caribbean Counting Poem.** Illustrated by David Axtel. Henry Holt, 1997. ISBN 0805051716. 25 pp. 5–7. Poetry.

Two little girls crave the fruits they find in and around their home in the Caribbean. Covertly they nibble, taste, and sample ten different kinds of fruit native to the area, with predictable results. The text is written in dialect that begs to be read aloud, but only after some practice. A glossary is provided to give the reader more information about each fruit. (SF)

7.6   Bryan, Ashley. **Ashley Bryan's ABC of African Poetry.** Illustrated by Ashley Bryan. Jean Karl / Atheneum, 1997. ISBN 0689812094. 32 pp. 4–8. Poetry.

Through the use of beautiful, colored paintings reminiscent of the style of Vincent Van Gogh, Ashley Bryan introduces us to the poetry and spiritual songs of twenty-six African American poets. The poem verses are organized so that a key verse begins with each new letter of the alphabet. Readers are introduced to some familiar and beloved African American poets as well as some less well-known ones. The text provides a brief illustrated introduction to this rich tradition of African poetry. (RF)

Coretta Scott King Illustrator Honor, Notable Social Studies Trade Books for Young People

7.7   Carlson, Lori Marie, editor. **Sol a sol.** Illustrated by Emily Lisker. Henry Holt, 1998. ISBN 080504373X. 32 pp. 5–8. Poetry.

"Sol a sol" means "sunup to sundown," the length of a day. In this poetry collection, a young girl tells us about a day in her life through lively verse. Each poem is written in English and in Spanish and portrays both events and people in her life. Her world includes her mother who "smells like honey," her grandmother, "a sweet sugarcane woman," her grandpa who "plays his old guitar," and her cat, "a free flip of fur." The bold colors of the full-page illustrations enhance the childlike voice of the poems. (CC)

Notable Social Studies Trade Books for Young People

7.8   Charles, Faustin. **A Caribbean Counting Book.** Illustrated by Roberta Arenson. Houghton Mifflin, 1996. ISBN 0395779448. Unpaged. 3–12. Songs and rhymes.

While visiting the Caribbean, author Charles collected some of the many rhymes chanted by young and old alike. In the foreword to this whimsical book, he explains that life in the Caribbean is conducive to song. The temperature, the unique colors and sounds, and the fascinating environment provide ample opportunity for the creation of games and songs. In this counting book he recalls many of these charming rhymes to help children learn their numbers. The pictures, mostly done in collage format, accurately portray life in the Caribbean. (SS)

7.9   Clinton, Catherine, editor. **I, Too, Sing America: Three Centuries of African American Poetry.** Illustrated by Stephen Alcorn. Houghton Mifflin, 1998. ISBN 0395895995. 128 pp. 8 and up. Poetry.

Twenty-five African American poets—twelve men and thirteen women—are represented here, most with a single poem, and none with more than four, for a total of thirty-five poems. The large, glossy pages contain full-page illustrations with a social realism feel, and fabric-like, monochromatic designs. The poets, among whom only four are still living, are presented chronologically, and each has a page of biographical information. Each poem is given its own page, with a facing page of art. Many classic poems of African American literature are included, but the quality of poetry is uneven (the first poet, for example, calls Native Americans "awful creatures" in a poem about a battle in the colonial period). (KL)

Best Books for Young Adults

7.10   Field, Edward, and Knud Rasmussen. **Magic Words.** Illustrated by Stefano Vitale. Gulliver / Harcourt, 1998. ISBN 0152014985. 32 pp. 4–8. Poetry.

The magic of poetry is truly captured by Edward Field's book. This suite of poems, based on the songs and stories of the Netsilik Inuit collected by Knud Rasmussen, is perfect for older children and ideal for reading aloud to younger ones as well. Mysterious metaphors and ancient images are echoed in Stefano Vitale's vibrant illustrations. This book will serve as a wonderful introduction to the Netsilik Inuit myths and culture. (KW)

Notable Social Studies Trade Books for Young People

7.11   Greenfield, Eloise. **Angels.** Illustrated by Jan Spivey Gilchrist. Jump at the Sun / Hyperion, 1998. ISBN 0786804424. Unpaged. 6–10. Poetry.

Jan Spivey Gilchrist's lovely black-and-white illustrations of African American children with parents, brothers, sisters, grandparents, and friends—some of whom are represented as angels—are portrait-like in their expressive rendering of a range of emotions. Eloise Greenfield describes writing the accompanying poems after studying each drawing, attempting to express its meaning in words. Topics of these poems include the anticipation of a baby's birth, a special friendship between a teenager and a younger child, the gift of a bouquet for a daughter's first singing performance, and playing in a backyard treehouse. The poems' attention to detail and rhythmic phrasing assures their appeal as read-alouds. Together, the poems and illustrations offer a celebration of the power of angels in everyday events and in the lives of children. (SJ)

7.12   Grimes, Nikki. **It's Raining Laughter.** Photographs by Myles C. Pinkney. Dial / Penguin, 1997. ISBN 0803720033. 32 pp. 5–8. Poetry.

The substance of a child's life, from mundane objects like drinking glasses, to names, to fights with friends, are raised to a level of significance through the joyful poems of Nikki Grimes. Told from a first-person perspective, a child's voice can be heard in each of the twelve poems. Photographs of African American children in various activities provide radiant images. Many of the photographs that accompany the text appear to be candid rather than posed, adding to the playful nature of the text. (CC)

7.13　Gunning, Monica. **Under the Breadfruit Tree.** Illustrated by Fabricio Vanden Broeck. Wordsong / Boyds Mills, 1998. ISBN 1563975394. 48 pp. 9–12. Poetry.

Through the voice of a young Jamaican girl, Gunning shares glimpses of her Caribbean childhood. Family and friends are portrayed with both love and candor. While each poem stands well on its own, taken as a whole the poems weave a poignant story of her island life. The simple black-and-white scratchboard illustrations by Fabrico Vanden Broeck complement the text. Introductory notes and a glossary of Jamaican words are included. (CC)

7.14　Hathorn, Libby. **Sky Sash So Blue.** Illustrated by Benny Andrews. Simon & Schuster, 1998. ISBN 0689810903. 32 pp. 5–9. Poetry.

Susannah, a young house slave, cherishes the sky blue sash given to her by her mother. Susannah wants her mother to use the blue sash when she makes a wedding dress for Sissy, Susannah's sister. The three female slaves are collecting various scraps of cast-off and used fabric for the dress. Sissy is engaged to John Bee, who will marry her on his next visit to the plantation. Eventually he will be able to purchase Sissy's freedom. When the momentous day of Sissy's emancipation arrives, Susannah surrenders her prized possession to symbolize the tie that binds the family until all are free. Benny Andrews's bold illustrations, consisting of fabric collages, support the poignant, poetic text. (JHC)

7.15　Herrera, Juan Felipe. **Laughing Out Loud, I Fly (A carcajadas yo vuelo): Poems in English and Spanish.** Illustrated by Karen Barbour. Joanne Cotler / HarperCollins, 1998. ISBN 0060276045. 48 pp. 7–11. Poetry.

The author's note at the end of this book informs the reader that these rhythmic poems in two languages were written as a response to Picasso's book of poems *Hunk of Skin*. Like Picasso's paintings, these poems create an overall sensation and are not poems to be read and understood literally. Images from the author's childhood memories simmer together in a delightful wordplay stew. Pale drawings of Mexican folk art images float behind the poems, which are written alternately in English and Spanish on each two-page spread. (KB)

Pura Belpré Honor Book for Narrative

7.16   Ho, Minfong. **Maples in the Mist: Poems for Children from the Tang Dynasty.** Illustrated by Jean Tseng and Mou-Sien Tseng. Lothrop, 1996. ISBN 068812044X. Unpaged. 5–8. Poetry.

The beauty of Chinese watercolor art is often complemented by a poem, delicately scribed in Chinese calligraphy on the edges of the painting. Mingfong Ho brings us the same delicate beauty in her presentation of these children's poems, a collection of Tang poems traditionally taught to children. At times, the resplendency of the detailed watercolor brushwork outshines the simple poetic verses. (KW)

ALA Notable Books for Children, Notable Books for a Global Society

7.17   Hughes, Langston. **Carol of the Brown King: Nativity Poems by Langston Hughes.** Illustrated by Ashley Bryan. Atheneum, 1998. ISBN 0689818777. Unpaged. 5–8. Poetry.

This beautifully illustrated book about Christmas combines a collection of poems written years ago by Langston Hughes with one poem by an anonymous poet. Many of the poems are very rhythmic and will capture the attention of readers and listeners. Although the poems tell the same story of Christmas, they show the many different viewpoints of the people who witnessed the Nativity. Ashley Bryan's illustrations depict Nativity scenes featuring dark-skinned people, using vibrant colors that enhance the sense of celebration. (SA)

7.18   Johnson, Angela. **Daddy Calls Me Man.** Illustrated by Rhonda Mitchell. Orchard, 1997. ISBN 0531300420. 32 pp. 3–6. Poetry.

"Big Shoes," "Spin," "Noah's Moon," and "Baby Sister" are the titles of four short, rhythmic poems narrated by a young African American boy about some significant things in his life. "All I want is big shoes / Tie shoes / Fast shoes / Red and black jump high shoes / Line them up by Daddy's / and call them all our shoes." The artful illustrations are especially compelling in this handsome volume. Each poem is introduced by a full-page painting that represents the colors and the content of the text that follows. For example, an abstract painting of colorful, energetic swirls is the prelude for the poem "Spin." Other, more representational illustrations, in blue, gold, and rich brown, show the boy and his sister twirling around a room. Johnson and Mitchell portray African American family life creatively through text and pictures. (JHC)

7.19 Johnston, Tony. **My Mexico / México mío.** Illustrated by F. John Sierra. Philomel, 1996. ISBN 0399222758. 36 pp. 4–8. Poetry.

Eighteen short poems are presented in both English and Spanish. The colors, tastes, smells, sounds, and life of Mexico come vibrantly alive in this book. Poems celebrate the shaking of the corn in preparation for tortillas, the selling of iguanas in the marketplace, and women weaving by an *ahuehuete* tree. Occasionally a darker side comes through, in the poems of homeless dogs trying to live off the street and a scared mother holding her cold child. There is a heart-wrenching poem about the Aztecs and the traces they have left behind. The pastel-tinted pencil drawings of F. John Sierra help to leave a happy, calm, peaceful feeling with the reader. (RH)

7.20 Lundgren, Mary Beth. **We Sing the City.** Illustrated by Donna Perrone. Clarion, 1997. ISBN 039568188X. 32 pp. 8–12. Poetry.

Throughout this colorful story, children of different ethnic backgrounds come together to celebrate the joy of city living. They delight in the sounds of street life, outdoor concerts, glorious colors, and diverse families. While the author idealizes diversity to a great extent, the poetic language flows nicely. The strong rhythmic beat could be fun for children to chant along with. (SS)

7.21 Merriam, Eve. **The Inner City Mother Goose.** Illustrated by David Diaz. Simon & Schuster, 1996. ISBN 0689806779. 69 pp. 12 and up. Poetry.

The traditional Mother Goose rhymes take on a different emphasis when Eve Merriam writes her version using inner city experiences to express a social and political stance. This version of

Mother Goose rhymes is definitely written for an older audience. First written more than twenty years ago, this book of poems and black-and-white photographs has been updated to include an introduction by poet Nikki Giovanni. The poems still maintain a relevance to life in many inner city communities today. (CH)

7.22   Mora, Pat. **This Big Sky.** Illustrated by Steve Jenkins. Scholastic, 1998. ISBN 059037127. Unpaged. 8–12. Poetry.

In this seamlessly woven collection of poetry, Pat Mora illustrates the vast openness of the U.S. Southwest. She writes of coyotes serenading the skies, urban raccoons scampering here and there, and mountains as still as the night. Through her words she creates a calm sense of beauty, as nature intertwines with the people of the South. The cut-paper collages that accompany the pictures reinforce the excitement of this vast, beautiful landscape. (SS)

Notable Social Studies Trade Books for Young People

7.23   Myers, Walter Dean. **Angel to Angel: A Mother's Gift of Love.** HarperCollins, 1998. ISBN 0060277211. Unpaged. 9 and up. Poetry.

This tender collection of ten poems depicts images of a mother's love. Myers's own mother died when he was two, and he was left with no picture of the two of them together. He wonders if this book serves as that picture. The collection celebrates the special bond between mother and child on pages illustrated with antique sepia-toned photographs and flowing silver motifs. Subjects range from the everyday objects in a love-filled room to a protective grandmother in "Don't Mess with Grandmama and Me." Children and adults alike will find inspiration for writing their own poetry. (KB)

7.24   Myers, Walter Dean. **Harlem.** Illustrated by Christopher Myers. Scholastic Press, 1997. ISBN 0590543407. 12 and up. Poetry.

Walter Dean Myers offers his contribution to the songs about Harlem with his rich, rhythmic poem. Tracing roots back to Ghana and Senegal, Myers invokes a journey of warriors, heroes, blues, dreams, darkness, despair, and hope that moves and gathers energy as it is carried across the backs of children and through fences and street corners but promises never to end. Powerfully complemented by Christopher Myers's collage art, *Harlem* is a poem meant to be read aloud again and again. (KW)

Boston Globe–Horn Book Fiction and Poetry Honor, Caldecott Honor, Coretta Scott King Illustrator Honor, ALA Notable Books for Children, Notable Social Studies Trade Books for Young People, Notable Books for a Global Society, Quick Picks for Young Adults, Best Books for Young Adults

7.25 Nye, Naomi Shihab, editor. **The Space between Our Footsteps: Poems and Paintings from the Middle East.** Simon & Schuster, 1998. ISBN 0689812337. 144 pp. 7 and up. Poetry and art.

This elegant and handsome anthology consists of poems in translation and accompanying paintings by living Middle Eastern poets and artists. Although a dozen nationalities, including Israelis, Turks, and Persians, are represented in the writings, the largest number of contributors are Palestinians, both from within Palestine and from the diaspora. Well-known writers such as Nazim Hikmat and Mahmoud Darwish are featured along with lesser-known and younger poets. The poems touch universal themes and are generally simple, accessible, and fresh. All of the elements, including generous background information on the contributors, an introduction that establishes the context, and an index, work tastefully with the layout and design on thick, glossy paper stock. (KL)

Notable Books for a Global Society

7.26 Orozco, José-Luis. **Diez Deditos: Ten Little Fingers and Other Play Rhymes and Action Songs from Latin America.** Illustrated by Elisa Kleven. Dutton, 1997. ISBN 0525457364. 56 pp. 2–8. Poetry.

This delightful book is packed with action and appeal. It includes thirty participation songs with musical notation for piano and guitar, lyrics in English and Spanish, and pictographs showing corresponding hand/body movements. The songs are Latin American in origin and include both traditional and modern selections about such universal topics as friends, holidays, animals, food, and family. They are easily accessible to a wide range of ages. The joyful illustrations are filled with people, animals, and fanciful creatures who dance, work, eat, and sing their way across the pages. Also included are descriptive background notes about each song as well as a topical index. (SJ)

Notable Social Studies Trade Books for Young People

7.27 Philip, Neil, editor. **Earth Always Endures: Native American Poems.** Photographs by Edward S. Curtis. Viking, 1996. ISBN 0670868736. 93 pp. 9 and up. Poetry.

This book pairs poems and chants from Native American tribes with Edward Curtis's striking, sepia-toned photographs. You get a great sense of history from the beautifully photographed faces of Sioux leaders and Cree children. The poems eloquently tell of the lives that different tribespeople lead. (ER)

7.28 Siegen-Smith, Nikki. **Songs for Survival: Songs and Chants from Tribal Peoples around the World.** Illustrated by Bernard Lodge. Dutton, 1996. ISBN 0525455647. 73 pp. 8 and up. Songs.

This book contains a thoughtful and comprehensive collection of songs and chants from tribal peoples around the world. The delightful songs and chants provide a glimpse into various traditions and beliefs of many different walks of life. Children can learn about the Quechua harvest song from South America and on the next page read about the joy of the Inuits. The illustrations are a wonderful companion to the text and will keep prereaders engaged throughout. (EA)

7.29 Siegen-Smith, Nikki, editor. **Welcome to the World: A Celebration of Birth and Babies from Many Cultures.** Orchard, 1996. ISBN 0531360067. 48 pp. 10 and up. Poetry.

This interesting anthology of poetry celebrates the joy and mystery of pregnancy, childbirth, and childrearing. Poems from well-known and anonymous authors highlight specific cultural traditions as well as universal feelings of delight, fear, exuberance, and frustration. These writers and photographers work together to tell a familiar tale of hope for mothers, fathers, grandparents, friends, and siblings. As many of the photographs are intense, it should be enjoyed by older audiences. (SS)

7.30 Silverman, Jerry. **Just Listen to This Song I'm Singing: African American History through Song.** Millbrook, 1996. ISBN 1562946730. 96 pp. 8 and up. Song.

The idea of teaching U.S. history through the study of our song heritage is a great one. Thirteen songs are provided in sheet music form, along with short chapters describing the connection of the songs to Black historical events. Three of the chapters are centered around the great African American songwriters and composers Scott Joplin, W. C. Handy, and Jelly Roll Morton. Black women are oddly absent from the song choices and historical narratives, which encompass such themes as slave resistance and escape, African American working people, and the modern civil rights movement. (KL)

7.31   Steptoe, Javaka, editor. **In Daddy's Arms I Am Tall: African Americans Celebrating Fathers.** Illustrated by Javaka Steptoe. Lee & Low, 1997. ISBN 1880000318. 32 pp. 9–12. Poetry.

In a magnificent blend of art and verse, Javaka Steptoe (the son of the late illustrator John Steptoe) creates an astonishing vision. The text consists of a collection of short poems that celebrate a father's strength, vision, and dignity, and explore the special bond between father and child. Complemented by ingenious mixed-media collages, the verses are contributed by such acclaimed poets as Angela Johnson and Davida Adedjouma. This is a wonderful book to be shared and treasured by every parent and child. (KW)

Coretta Scott King Illustrator Award Winner, ALA Notable Books for Children

7.32   Swann, Brian. **Touching the Distance: Native American Riddle-Poems.** Illustrated by Maria Rendon. Browndeer / Harcourt Brace, 1998. ISBN 0152008047. Unpaged. 5–9. Poetry.

This book presents fourteen Native American riddle poems, each accompanied by unusual collage illustrations in a double-page format. The pictures provide the clues to the answers of each riddle. Young children will enjoy solving these mysteries, while the Native American connections provide discussion material for an interesting curricular topic. (MP)

Notable Books for a Global Society

7.33   Wong, Janet S. **A Suitcase of Seaweed and Other Poems.** Illustrated by Janet S. Wong. Margaret McElderry / Simon & Schuster, 1996. ISBN 0689807880. 42 pp. 9–12. Poetry.

In beautifully simple verse, Janet Wong writes about her own diverse experiences in Korean, Chinese, and U.S. cultures. Dividing the book into three sections corresponding to these three aspects of her heritage, Wong offers brief biographies of her Korean mother, her Chinese father, and finally her own American self. The biographies are followed by poems reflecting on experiences classified as "Korean," "Chinese," and "American." While each poem in this collection stands alone, certain themes and subjects overlap, and Wong's proud but humorous voice is infused throughout. Readers will laugh out loud as they recognize themselves and their families in these poems. (KW)

7.34 Wood, Douglas. **Northwoods Cradle Song: From a Menominee Lullaby.** Illustrated by Lisa Desimini. Simon & Schuster, 1996. ISBN 0689805039. 22 pp. 4–7. Poetry.

Wood transforms this traditional Menominee poem into a lullaby song that he performs in his *Earthsongs* collection. In the book Wood explains his efforts to adapt the poem in a way that remains true to the spirit of the original, and accurately reflects the culture from which it came. Although the words are in poetic format, it would have been helpful to provide musical notation as well, so parents and others could share his poetry musically with their children. Desimini captures the night with her navy blue pages and beautiful illustrations. Unfortunately, in her quest to give the story universality she creates an amalgam of all Native Americans, thus obscuring the distinctness of the Menonimee culture. (CMH)

7.35 Young, Ed. **Voices of the Heart.** Illustrated by Ed Young. Scholastic, 1998. ISBN 0590501992. 32 pp. 9–12. Poetry.

Acclaimed artist Ed Young brings us another lavishly produced picture book, this time exploring the vast emotions of human experience. With fantastic collages rendering Chinese calligraphy, each page explores one of twenty-six emotions. Readers will perhaps find the pictures more amazing than the accompanying text. While Young's personal reflections on each emotion may be universal, the text can be rather abstract at times, and likely to be better appreciated by more mature readers. (KW)

Notable Social Studies Trade Books for Young People, Notable Books for a Global Society, Notable Children's Books in the Language Arts

8 Folktales, Myths, and Legends

8.1 Aardema, Verna, reteller. **Anansi Does the Impossible: An Ashanti Tale.** Atheneum, 1997. ISBN 068981092. 32 pp. 4–8. Folklore.

Aardema has written another delightful version of an African Ashanti folktale. In this tale, Anansi is again confronted with a challenge which he must use all of his resources to resolve. The trickster, Anansi, along with his clever wife, must perform three daunting tasks in order to buy back all the stories of the world, which the Sky God owns. Anansi must attain for the Sky God a live python, a fairy, and forty-seven stinging hornets. Only by these deeds will the world's stories be secured for all to enjoy. The story is told with simple language that all children will enjoy, and is accompanied by brightly colored collage illustrations that complement and add to the story. (RF)

8.2 Aardema, Verna, reteller. **This for That: A Tonga Tale.** Illustrated by Victoria Chess. Dial, 1997. ISBN 0803715536 (trade). ISBN 0803715544 (library binding). 32 pp. 4–8. Folklore.

Rabbit, lazy and thirsty, drinks from a well dug by Lion and Elephant. Sent away from the well, Rabbit implores help from Ostrich, who finds watery berries for the pair to eat. Later, Rabbit secretly eats the remainder of the berries but blames Ostrich for what she has done. Ostrich reluctantly pays Rabbit with a feather for the berries, and the remainder of the tale involves Rabbit's manipulation of other characters for items that she wants. The tale ends with punishment for Rabbit and justice for the characters whom she has wronged. (CP)

8.3 Ada, Alma Flor. **The Lizard and the Sun / La lagartija y el sol.** Illustrated by Felipe Davalos. Translated by Rosa Zubizarreta. Doubleday, 1997. ISBN 038532121X. 40 pp. 4–8. Folklore.

In a time long ago the sun disappeared and the world was in darkness. Various animals went in search of the sun to no avail. But the lizard continued the search and eventually came upon a glowing rock. The lizard, with the help of the emperor and a woodpecker, found the sun asleep inside the rock. The sun agreed to awaken and return to the sky only if the emperor provided a feast with the finest musicians and dancers. The sun returned as promised, and since then the feast is repeated annually to ensure the sun's place in the sky. Facing pages feature English and Spanish text. The deep colors of the illustrations vividly capture the world in darkness and in light. (CC)

Notable Social Studies Trade Books for Young People

8.4   Aldana, Patricia, editor. **Jade and Iron: Latin American Tales from Two Cultures.** Illustrated by Luis Garay. Translated by Hugh Hazelton. Groundwood, 1996. ISBN 0888992564. 64 pp. 9–12. Folklore.

This unique collection contains fourteen translated tales collected from a number of Latin American storytellers. The collection represents tales that have been passed on by both indigenous people and European settlers of Mexico, Central America, and South America. Many of the native tales provide mythical explanations of origins, such as how separated lovers turned into volcanoes, how a white worm (also know as the Milky Way) came to hold up the sky, and how a possum gave fire to humankind. The tales of European settlers often focus on people's relationships with each other and with nature, and encompass characters such as a powerful enchantress, a seven-colored horse, and wise boy who encounters a foolish thief. Full-page color illustrations accompany each tale and provide bold visual depictions of some of the characters. (ED)

8.5   Bannerman, Helen. **The Story of Little Babaji.** Illustrated by Fred Marcellino. HarperCollins, 1996. ISBN 0062050656. Unpaged. 4–8. Folklore.

If something considered offensive is made over with mostly cosmetic changes, can the result regain the popularity of the original while avoiding controversy? *The Story of Little Babaji* attempts to do just that, as Bannerman resurrects the *Little Black Sambo* story and recasts it in India with Little Babaji, Mamaji, and Papaji. However, the images are not authentic to the people who live where tigers do. The essential story is amusing, although readers may find the African American *Sam and the Tigers* by Julius Lester and illustrated by Jerry Pinkney (another revision of Bannerman's original story; see **8.38**) more culturally sensitive. (KW)

ALA Notable Books for Children

8.6 Ben-Ezer, Ehud. **Hosni the Dreamer: An Arabian Tale.** Illustrated by Uri Shulevitz. Farrar, Straus and Giroux, 1997. ISBN 0374333408. 32 pp. 6–10. Folklore.

Hosni, a shepherd, lives in the Arabian desert and works for a sheikh who wants to bring his camels to market. This is Hosni's big chance to see the city, which he has always dreamed about. When he gets there, he spends all his money on a verse, which ends up saving his life soon after, when the sheikh is killed in an accident. He meets a stranded young woman, Zobeide, and together they visit many cities and eventually fall in love. Illustrations are comic, almost surrealistic depictions of oversized costumes and strange landscapes. This book could be used in conjunction with *Jack and the Beanstalk* tales, since it deals with a similar theme of a foolish purchase proving to be very valuable. (KL)

Notable Social Studies Trade Books for Young People

8.7 Berry, James. **First Palm Trees: An Anancy Spiderman Story.** Illustrated by Greg Couch. Simon & Schuster, 1997. ISBN 0689810601. 40 pp. 5–8. Folklore.

The king offers a reward to whoever can get the first palm trees to grow on his land, and greedy Anancy is determined to get the reward. He immediately runs to Sun-Spirit to enlist his help. Sun-Spirit points out that "My work makes other works work. And other works make my work also work." Anancy is not happy about sharing the reward but realizes he must enlist the help of all the spirits—Sun, Water, Earth, and Air—to reach his goal. James Berry's original West Indian tale stresses the themes of teamwork and cooperation. Greg Couch's illustrations show the human Anancy with long arms and legs and flowing robes in constant motion, suggesting the movement of a spider's eight legs. The three pairs of glasses Anancy wears on his head, along with his own eyes, cleverly suggest a spider's eight eyes. The rhythmic, melodious text makes this an ideal read aloud. (BK)

Notable Social Studies Trade Books for Young People

8.8 Bierhorst, John, editor. **The Deetkatoo: Native American Stories about Little People.** Illustrated by Ron Hilbert Coy. Morrow, 1998. ISBN 0688148379. 153 pp. 9–12. Folklore.

Renowned folklorist John Bierhorst includes twenty-two tales of little people from fourteen different Native American cultures, including the Aztecs, Inuits, and Mayans. The collection is scholarly yet down-to-earth, with extensive notes, a guide to the tribes, and a bibliography for teachers. The illustrations are black-and-white scratchboard. Children will enjoy hearing or reading the stories. (MP)

8.9 Climo, Shirley, reteller. **The Little Red Ant and the Great Big Crumb.** Illustrated by Francisco X. Mora. Clarion, 1995. ISBN 0395707323. 40 pp. 5–9. Folklore.

Little Red Ant finds a cake crumb. Unfortunately, he is too small to carry it home. He approaches stronger animals to help him, and each animal that he finds is stronger than the previous one. They all refuse to help him, however. Finally, he encounters someone whom all the animals fear. It is this encounter that lets him know who the strongest creature really is. (SF)

8.10 Dabcovich, Lydia, reteller. **The Polar Bear Son: An Inuit Tale.** Illustrated by Lydia Dabcovich. Clarion, 1997. ISBN 0395727669. 37 pp. 8–11. Folklore.

This story is an adaptation of the original *The Bear Story.* The coldness of the Arctic landscape is captured in the illustrations' muted gray and white colors. Although the colors are chilling, the reader feels the warmth of the lonely old woman when she encounters the orphaned polar bear cub and takes him home to care for him. Kunikdjuaq, the polar bear son, in turn takes care of the old woman by providing her with food. The village men are jealous of the bear's instinctive hunting habits that bring the old woman an overabundance of food, and they plan to kill him. After pleading with the men to no avail, the old woman regretfully sends her polar bear son across the ice to safety. This story shows that love between humans and animals is powerful when great care is taken to respect and preserve the relationship. (CMH)

Notable Social Studies Trade Books for Young People

8.11 Day, Noreha Yussof. **Kancil and the Crocodiles.** Illustrated by Britta Teckentrup. Simon & Schuster, 1996. ISBN 0689809549. Unpaged. 4–8. Folklore.

This funny and thought-provoking tale from Malaysia with colorful illustrations is about Kancil, a mouse deer, and her best friend Kura-Kura, a turtle. Kancil comes up with a clever idea to get to the other side of the river by tricking the fearsome crocodiles. All goes well for the two as they laugh at the crocodiles for being so gullible, until Kancil remembers that they must eventually get back to the other side of the river. This is a thoroughly enjoyable trickster tale with artwork that effectively conveys the tropical serenity of the story. (SA)

8.12 Delacre, Lulu, reteller. **Golden Tales: Myths, Legends, and Folktales from Latin America.** Scholastic, 1996. ISBN 059048186X. 73 pp. 9–12. Folklore.

Twelve classic tales from Latin America are faithfully retold, bringing cultures, literature, and history together in one volume. The artwork complements the text well, and children will be fascinated by stories that are probably unfamiliar to them. The *pourquoi* tales, legends of the *conquistadores,* and other folklore date from the 1400s. The author's introduction and notes are particularly useful for further understanding these tales and the cultures from which they come. (MP)

8.13 Demi, reteller. **The Dragon's Tale: And Other Animal Fables of the Chinese Zodiac.** Illustrated by Demi. Henry Holt, 1996. ISBN 0805034463. 32 pp. 4–8. Folklore.

Demi employs the animals of the Chinese zodiac to create a gorgeously illustrated book and to retell fables with fortune-cookie-like messages. Each two-page spread has a story within a wide border on the left page and accompanying images on the right. The stories are brief but witty and entertaining, and each is followed by its appropriate moral. Demi also shares some of her painting secrets, including descriptions of traditional ingredients she uses in her paints such as cinnabar and azurite, and special tools such as a single mouse hair she uses for delicate work. Background information about the zodiac and story sources are not provided, however. (KYR)

8.14　Demi. **One Grain of Rice: A Mathematical Folktale.** Illustrated by Demi. Scholastic, 1997. ISBN 059093998X. Unpaged. 8–11. Folklore.

In India there once lived a raja who thought he was wise and fair. Every year he kept nearly all the land's rice for himself. A village girl named Rani devises a clever plan when she is offered a reward for her honesty: she requests only one grain of rice, with the provision that her allotment of rice be doubled each day for thirty days. The mathematical lesson is richly illustrated with larger and larger animals delivering rice—and more and more rice! Teachers will appreciate the multiple uses of this book within the curriculum. (MP)

Notable Social Studies Trade Books for Young People, Notable Books for a Global Society

8.15　Diakité, Baba Wagué, reteller. **The Hunterman and the Crocodile.** Illustrated by Baba Wagué Diakité. Scholastic, 1997. ISBN 0590898280. Unpaged. 4–8. Folklore.

This West African folktale, in which a man does not honor all the animals of the forest and subsequently learns a lesson of the need to live in harmony with nature, is richly illustrated with the author's ceramic-tile paintings. Children will appreciate the humorous lesson and will enjoy this delightful new folktale about Africa. (MP)

Coretta Scott King Illustrator Honor Book, ALA Notable Books for Children, Notable Social Studies Trade Books for Young People

8.16　Doucet, Sharon Arms, reteller. **Why Lapin's Ears Are Long and Other Tales from the Louisiana Bayou.** Illustrated by David Cattrow. Orchard, 1997. ISBN 0531300412 (trade). ISBN 0531330419 (library binding). 64 pp. 4–8. Folklore.

Complete with a glossary and wonderfully imaginative illustrations, this book tells three Cajun tales of Lapin, a mischievous rabbit, including one that explains why his ears are long and his tail is short. The book includes an introduction to the stories that serves to foreshadow the fun and energy that the reader will encounter. Interwoven dialogue gives each character depth and color. These fables are suited for both independent reading and reading aloud. (CP)

8.17 Ehlert, Lois, reteller. **Cuckoo: A Mexican Folktale / Cucu: Un cuento folklorico mexicano.** Illustrated by Lois Ehlert. Translated by Gloria De Aragon Andujar. Harcourt, 1997. 40 pp. 5–8. Folklore.

You can't judge a bird by its feathers. In this bilingual retelling of an old Mexican tale, Cucu, a cuckoo bird with a golden voice, behaves selfishly at first but becomes the hero in the end. While the other birds assume that she would be useless, Cucu saves seeds and sacrifices her voice in exchange. The fable cleverly explains how the cuckoo bird has lost its feathers and song. The vibrant Mexican art coupled with this clever tale make for an enjoyable experience throughout. (KW)

Notable Social Studies Trade Books for Young People, Notable Trade Books in the Language Arts

8.18 French, Fiona. **Lord of the Animals: A Miwok Indian Creation Myth.** Illustrated by Fiona French. Millbrook, 1997. ISBN 0761301127. 32 pp. 4–8. Mythology.

In this intriguing Native American tale, Coyote gathers animals from all around the world in order to determine who should become the ruler. Naturally, each animal tells Coyote that the leader of all animals should have the particular unique feature that he or she possesses. Because of the ensuing chaos, Coyote tells each animal to fashion a leader out of mud. The animals fall asleep during their task, however, and crafty Coyote creates man with various features from each animal, including Coyote's cunning nature. (CP)

Notable Social Studies Trade Books for Young People

8.19 Ganeri, Anita. **Out of the Ark: Stories from the World's Religions.** Illustrated by Jackie Morris. Harcourt Brace, 1996. ISBN 0152009434 104 pp. 9–12. Mythology.

This is a collection of stories from the many religions of the world. The stories are categorized in the table of contents with topics including creation, animals, birth, courtship, marriage, war, pestilence, persecution, and the lives of religious leaders. At the end of the book the author provides a "religious fact file" that gives some brief information about each religion presented in the text, including when and where it began, its founders, places of worship, holy books, and festivals. Each story in this text is beautifully illustrated in bright watercolors. (MS)

8.20   Gavin, Jamila. **Children Just Like Me: Our Favorite Stories from around the World.** Illustrated by Amanda Hall. Photographs by Barnabas Kindersley. DK, 1997. ISBN 0789414864. 48 pp. 4–8. Folklore.

Set in ten different countries, this book presents famous folktales told throughout time, along with a wide range of information about the cultures from which they originate. For each country a child is introduced and his or her surroundings described. There are also explanations on each page of how each folktale fits into each culture. Whether it be similarities in homes, hobbies, or food they eat, the stories are somehow tied into the lives of the children from that country. The bold photographs and illustrations give a clear view of what life is like in different areas of the world. (MR)

Notable Social Studies Trade Books for Young People

8.21   Greene, Ellin, reteller. **Ling-Li and Phoenix Fairy: A Chinese Folktale.** Illustrated by Zong-Shou Wang. Clarion, 1996. ISBN 0395715288. 32 pp. 9–11. Folklore.

In this retelling of a classic Chinese folktale, Ling-Li is a poor but clever young woman who weaves an extraordinarily beautiful cloth for her wedding robe. Ling-Li will not trade her robe with the jealous Golden Flower, who then steals it, only to have it stolen from her by a flock of magpies. Ling-Li captures the magpies, who bring her to the Phoenix Fairy. The robe is returned along with a blessing for Ling-Li's marriage. This tale typifies Chinese values of hard work, rising above difficulty, and resourcefulness, and is also typical in its use of fantasy and magic. (KYR)

8.22   Greger, C. Shana. **Cry of the Benu Bird: An Egyptian Creation Story.** Illustrated by C. Shana Greger. Houghton Mifflin, 1996. ISBN 0395735734. 32 pp. 6–10. Mythology.

The author combines elements of three separate groups of Egyptian myths from the earliest written sources, and weaves them into a unique creation story. Like other creation myths, it does not make much sense as a story; mainly it introduces a cast of characters who will later interact with humans in complex ways. The illustrations are phantasmagoric—sometimes like Chagall, sometimes like early Hindu paintings—and wrap around the text in interesting ways. (KL)

8.23 Hamilton, Virginia, reteller. **A Ring of Tricksters: Animal Tales from America, the West Indies, and Africa.** Illustrated by Barry Moser. Scholastic, 1997. ISBN 0590473743. 123 pp. 8–12. Folklore.

Virginia Hamilton once again brings us another collection of tales from the Black diaspora, specifically from the United States, the West Indies, and Africa. The lyrical language that Hamilton is reknowned for will again delight readers, who will be enchanted by the familiar Bruh Rabbit and Anansi, and will also get to know Africa's Cunnie Rabbit and Hare. Complemented by Moser's vivid watercolors, this book will quickly become a family favorite. (KW)

Notable Social Studies Trade Books for Young People, Notable Books for a Global Society

8.24 Hamilton, Virginia, reteller. **When Birds Could Talk and Bats Could Sing: The Adventures of Bruh Sparrow, Sis Wren and Their Friends.** Illustrated by Barry Moser. Scholastic, 1996. ISBN 0590473727. 5–9. 63 pp. Folklore.

Virginia Hamilton brings us another collection of fables and stories from the U.S. South, featuring bold buzzards, sly sparrows, and hilarious hummingbirds. Although the dialect has been eliminated, Hamilton continues to bring us the cadence that makes these stories a perfect selection to be read aloud. The layout of the book, from the large binding to the vivid watercolor pictures, makes this a sweet selection to be read aloud at night, and parents will surely want their children to discuss the morals presented at the end of each tale. (KW)

ALA Notable Books for Children

8.25 Han, Oki S., and Stephanie Haboush Plunkett, retellers. **Kongi and Potgi: A Cinderella Story from Korea.** Illustrated by Oki S. Han. Dial, 1996. ISBN 0803715714 (trade). ISBN 0803715722 (library binding). 30 pp. 4–8. Folklore.

In this version of the Cinderella tale, Kongi is the lovely, uncomplaining daughter, and Potgi is the pampered stepsister. Although Kongi's stepmother assigns her impossible tasks, they are performed for her by magical beings who may embody the spirit of her dead mother. This retelling ends with a more forgiving conclusion for the repentant Potgi and her mother. Colorful, whimsical illustrations depict the landscapes, homes, furnishings, dress,

and customs of the Korean culture. This story offers enough varia-
tion to make interesting comparisons with other versions. (KYR)

8.26   Hickox, Rebecca. **The Golden Sandal: A Middle Eastern Cin-
       derella Story.** Illustrated by Will Hillenbrand. Holiday House,
       1998. ISBN 0823413314. 32 pp. 5–10. Folklore.

       This Iraqi Cinderella is named Maha. She is mistreated by a step-
       mother, but instead of a fairy godmother, a magic red fish protects
       her. Her Prince Charming is not royalty but a merchant's brother-
       in-law who falls in love with her after finding her slipper in a
       stream. This book is full of details, including the *henna* ceremony
       of Muslim weddings and life in a fishing village. The semifanciful
       watercolors are especially strong in showing emotions through
       facial features of the characters. (KL)

8.27   Hickox, Rebecca. **Zorro and Quwi.** Illustrated by Kim Howard.
       Delacorte, 1997. ISBN 0385321228. Unpaged. 4–7. Folklore.

       In this trickster tale, a clever guinea pig outsmarts a fox who is
       determined to eat him. In each episode the guinea pig manages to
       get the fox into progressively more humorous situations, leading
       to a side-splitting final episode. Spanish words are used through-
       out the text of the story. This adaptation of a Peruvian folk tale is
       sure to stand up to multiple rereadings. (SF)

8.28   Jaffe, Nina. **The Golden Flower.** Illustrated by Enrique O.
       Sánchez. Simon & Schuster, 1996. ISBN 0689804695. Unpaged.
       4–8. Mythology.

       This Taino myth tells how the island of Puerto Rico came to be. At
       the beginning of time, Earth was all desert. Then one day a boy
       finds a seed. He finds seeds each day until he has a sackful. He
       plants his seeds at the top of the mountain, and from the seeds a
       beautiful forest grows. The forest has one mysterious plant that is
       big, round, and golden like the sun. This plant plays a critical role
       in the formation of the island of Puerto Rico. (SF)

       Pura Belpré Honor for Illustration

8.29   Jaffe, Nina, and Steve Zeitlin, retellers. **The Cow of No Color.**
       Illustrated by Whitney Sherman. Henry Holt, 1998. ISBN
       0805037365. 162 pp. 10–16. Folklore.

This book is perfect for a middle school multicultural unit. These folktales from around the world span history, from the first century C.E. to the present. The stories are grouped in sections by topic: "Poetic Justice," "Bringing Wrongdoers to Justice," "Matters of Guilt and Innocence," "Forgiveness and Mercy," "Settling Disputes," "Deciding Ownership," "Cosmic Justice," and "You're It! The Playground and Beyond." Each tale is divided into two parts. First, the stem of the original tale is told and the reader is invited to propose a solution. Then the original ending of the tale is presented along with an explanation of the logic leading the storyteller to the solution to the problem. Unlike Aesop's fables, these stories do not present simple morals, but rather teach something profound about human nature and culture. (CK)

Notable Social Studies Trade Books for Young People

8.30 Jendresen, Erik, and Alberto Villoldo. **The First Story Ever Told.** Illustrated by Yoshi. Simon & Schuster, 1996. ISBN 0689805152. 32 pp. 6–9. Folklore.

In this creation tale inspired by the legends of the Incas, an explorer finds an old map in a museum and realizes he has the directions to Vilcabamba, the lost city of gold that lies somewhere in the mountains of Peru. He sets out on his quest, but one night, in a dream, Grandmother Fire tells him the "first story ever told." He wakes from his dream with the knowledge that the lost city of gold is more a state of being than a physical place. The story-within-a-story structure adds sophistication to the tale, and Yoshi's illustrations evoke a mystical feeling. The author's note provides background on the Incas. (BK)

8.31 Keams, Geri, reteller. **Snail Girl Brings Water: A Navajo Story.** Illustrated by Richard Ziehler-Martin. Rising Moon, 1998. ISBN 087358662X. 32 pp. 5–8. Folklore.

In this folktale, the People went to a new world to find a home, but the ocean water was salty and they could not drink without getting sick. First Woman declared that someone had to crawl back through the hole to find some fresh water. First Woman, Otter, and Beaver, and then Frog and Turtle, were sent to fill the water bottle with fresh water. Turtle was artistic and created a shell armor with seashells. Frog's eyes were bulging under the weight of the bottles. They still needed fresh water, so Snail Girl volunteered, even though no one believed she could do it. She collected enough fresh water to fill the water bottle and begin her journey home. But there was a hole in the bottom of the bottle, and when Snail Girl discovered the water bottle was empty, she cried herself to sleep. First Woman found the fresh water and sang her magic song that turned the small drops of fresh pure water into a river. Snail Girl was honored in a ceremony and given the beautiful water bottle to carry on her back as a symbol of her great journey and as a message to everyone that pure water is precious and should be maintained. (CH)

8.32 Kessler, Cristina. **Konte Chameleon Fine, Fine, Fine! A West African Folk Tale.** Illustrated by Christian Epanya. Boyds Mills, 1997. ISBN 156397181X. 32 pp. 4–8. Folklore.

Konte Chameleon is convinced that he is sick because when he sits on a red orchid, he turns red, and when he sits on a banana, he turns yellow. He seeks a cure from Dr. Jalloh, and with further experimentation, they discover the nature of Konte's condition and how it will help him hunt for food and hide from enemies. Kessler uses a repetitive, sound-effect language throughout that at times interferes with the story. The illustrations are vivid and colorful, although Konte's body proportions are not consistent throughout. (KYR)

8.33 Kherdian, David, reteller. **The Golden Bracelet.** Illustrated by Nonny Hogrogian. Holiday House, 1998. ISBN 0823413624. 32 pp. 5–10. Folklore.

A great Armenian story has been told in two new books within one year. This tale and *A Weave of Words* (**8.70**) are two retellings of the same folktale. In this version the prince is named "Haig" and the monster is a sorcerer named "Zilnago." The prince admires a common woman who will marry him only if he learns a useful trade, and this later saves both his life and that of his faithful servant, Vartan. It would be hard to invent a tale from scratch with more contemporary resonance and zestful appeal. The two books together could be used in a unit on narrative styles and artistic renderings of stories, especially for the early grades. The illustrations are flat, bright, colorful, and surrounded by illuminated borders, like Persian miniatures. (KL)

8.34 Kimmel, Eric A., reteller. **Ten Suns: A Chinese Legend.** Illustrated by YongSheng Xuan. Holiday House, 1998. ISBN 0823413179. 32 pp. 4–8. Folklore.

This beautifully illustrated Chinese legend tells of Di Jun, his wife Xi He, and their ten sons. Each morning Xi He travels across the sky with a different son in order to bring light to Earth below. The boys grow bored with their task and decide that they will all travel across the sky together. The result is devastating heat to the planet. When the people of Earth plead with Di Jun and Xe He for help, they send Hu Yi, the Archer of Heaven, to shoot each of the sons. Di Jun realizes, however, that one son must be saved and sends a messenger to steal one of Hu Yi's arrows. As a result, one son brings light to Earth each day while the other sons, now crows, watch the sun rise each day. (CP)

Notable Social Studies Trade Books for Young People

8.35 Krishnaswami, Uma, reteller. **The Broken Tusk: Stories of the Hindu God Ganesha.** Illustrated by Maniam Selven. Linnet, 1996. ISBN 0208024425. 99 pp. 9–12. Mythology

The elephant-headed Hindu god Ganesha is the central character in this collection of seventeen stories. Topics of these stories range from how Ganesha got his elephant head, to why Ganesha never married, to how gods, kings, demons, and humans coexist in the world. A brief explanation of Hindu mythology is useful, as is a section of guides for teachers and storytellers at the end of the book. A pronunciation guide, a list of characters with descriptions, a glossary, and a bibliography further help the reader. Black-and-white drawings of Ganesha can be found throughout the book. (MS)

8.36 Kurtz, Jane, reteller. **Miro in the Kingdom of the Sun.** Illustrated by David Frampton. Houghton Mifflin, 1996. ISBN 0395691818. 29 pp. 4–8. Folklore.

As the prince grows weaker over time, it is known that only the water from the lake at *pachap cuchun cuchun* can save him. In this Incan folktale, Miro finds herself trying to save the prince, a feat no one else has been able to accomplish, and rescue her brothers as well. She must travel high and low through many dangers to fill the golden flask with water. The woodcuts that illustrate this folktale seem appropriate to depict the time and circumstances of this story; their bold, strong colors convey the extraordinary task of this very ordinary girl. (MR)

8.37 Kurtz, Jane. **Trouble.** Illustrated by Durga Bernhard. Gulliver / Harcourt Brace, 1997. ISBN 0152002197. 30 pp. 5–8. Folklore.

Teklah is a well-intentioned goatherd whose zest for adventure brings trouble to those around him. When his father makes a *gebeta* board for him, it is with the hope that the game will keep his son from further mischief. Teklah soon loses his *gebeta* to a group of traders attempting to build a fire. He receives a bone-handled knife in its place and soon embarks upon a series of adventures, each time giving a stranger a much-needed item in exchange for an object that pleases Teklah even more. The satisfying conclusion brings Teklah back home with yet another *gebeta* board and two extremely well-fed goats, while his father is none the wiser. (SM)

8.38 Lester, Julius, reteller. **Sam and the Tigers.** Illustrated by Jerry Pinkney. Dial, 1996. ISBN 0803720289. 34 pp. 4–8. Folklore.

In the magical place called Sam-sam-sa-mara, there lives a boy named Sam. On his first day of school Sam heads off in his fine new clothes. He runs into a tiger on the way, and Sam bargains with the tiger to take his brand-new red coat instead of eating him. Sam proceeds to run into many tigers, trading them pieces of his new clothing for his life. He cries about his lost clothing as the tigers argue about which is the best dressed. The tigers begin to chase each other around a tree, shedding the clothing and eventually turning into a pool of butter. This story is a delightful retelling of *Little Black Sambo,* written in an African American storytelling style by Julius Lester. Jerry Pinkney's watercolors colorfully depict the story of *Sam and the Tigers.* (ER)

ALA Notable Books for Children

8.39 Long, Jan Freeman, reteller. **The Bee and the Dream: A Japanese Tale.** Illustrated by Kaoru Ono. Dutton, 1996. ISBN 0525452877. 40 pp. 6–9. Folklore.

This traditional tale begins and ends with two old Japanese sayings. The first one is quizzical: "When you see a bee fly from someone's nose, good fortune will be yours." The second one deals with fate: "If good fortune is meant for you, no matter what happens, it will be yours." What happens in the middle is a pleasure to read. The honorable and persevering hero, Tasuke, must follow his convictions and embark on an adventurous journey to seek his fortune. Expressive, humorous illustrations by one of Japan's leading illustrators complement the text. (KYR)

8.40 MacDonald, Margaret Read, reteller. **The Girl Who Wore Too Much.** Translated by Supaporn Vathanaprida. Illustrated by Yvonne Lebrun Davis. August House Little Folk, 1998. ISBN 0874835038. Unpaged. 5–8. Folklore.

The author retells this Thai story about a young girl who is so spoiled that she only thinks about her clothes and how she looks every day. When she cannot decide which items to wear to a dance, she decides to wear them all. She learns that trying to impress friends does not always enable one to keep friends. The text is written in both Thai and English and the book has brightly colored illustrations. (MP)

Notable Social Studies Trade Books for Young People

8.41 McCaughrean, Geraldine, reteller. **The Golden Hoard: Myths and Legends of the World.** Illustrated by Bee Willey. Margaret McElderry / Simon & Schuster, 1995. ISBN 0689807414. 130 pp. 9–12. Folklore.

This anthology of myths and legends shares the stories of our ancestors on how the world came to be. In this brightly illustrated text, twenty-two tales from around the world are retold. The tales honor many voices and the author has attempted to "preserve the pleasure each story gave to its original audience." A brief explanation of each story can be found at the end of the book. (MS)

8.42 McCaughrean, Geraldine, reteller. **The Silver Treasure.** Illustrated by Bee Willey. Margaret McElderry, 1996. ISBN 0689813328. 130 pp. 9–12. Folklore.

McCaughrean retells twenty-three folktales from a wide range of cultures. Familiar tales such as "The Tower of Babel," "Saint Christopher," and "Rip Van Winkle" are included, along with lesser known myths and legends from the Middle East, South America, and Africa. Willey's mixed-media artwork complements the text. The rich language of the retellings makes them ideal for reading aloud. Limited information regarding the cultural aspects of the stories is appended. (CC)

8.43   McDermott, Gerald, reteller. **The Voyage of Osiris: A Myth of Ancient Egypt.** Illustrated by Gerald McDermott. Harcourt Brace, 1997. ISBN 0152002162. 32 pp. 6–10. Folklore.

Retelling a five-thousand-year-old myth with minimal words and his characteristic iridescent mosaic paintings, McDermott recounts the death and resurrection of Osiris as god of the underworld, culminating in the sentence, "Now we will all journey from this earth to live again in the realm of Osiris." This is a great book to draw emergent readers into the basic beliefs of the ancient Egyptians and why preparations for death were so elaborate and meaningful. (KL)

8.44   Malotki, Ekkehart, reteller. **The Magic Hummingbird: A Hopi Folktale.** Translated by Ekkehart Malotki. Illustrated by Michael Lacapa. Kiva, 1996. ISBN 1885772041. Unpaged. 5–9. Folklore.

This Hopi folktale tells the story of two abandoned children who are helped by a sunflower stalk shaped like a hummingbird that magically comes to life. The bird helps solve the drought problem and rain is restored to the land. Through the children's interactions with the bird, the reader learns about the world of the Hopi. The calm, serene Hopi world is based on harmony of nature's elements. As an authentic example of Hopi oral literature, this story should appeal to children aged five to nine. (MP)

8.45   Mama, Raouf, reteller. **Why Goats Smell Bad and Other Stories from Benin.** Illustrated by Imna Arroyo. Linnet, 1998. ISBN 0208024697. 128 pp. 9 and up. Folklore.

This text contains a collection of twenty tales from the West African republic of Benin. These folktales are full of rich detail about kings and queens, orphans, talking animals, sages, fools, tricksters, contests, journeys, transformations, twists, and lessons to be learned. At the end of each tale the author briefly explains the cultural beliefs underlying it. The tales convey a message that soundly warns against hatred, envy, greed, pride, egotism, and deceitfulness. (MS)

8.46   Marston, Elsa. **The Fox Maiden.** Illustrated by Tatsuro Kiuchi. Simon & Schuster, 1996. ISBN 0689801076. 32 pp. 6–12. Folklore.

Based on a Japanese folktale, this haunting, poignant story centers around a mountain fox who is able to change into a woman. The curious young fox becomes a woman and enters a village, operating under the name Yuri. The author and illustrator deftly sketch Yuri's longing to express her fox nature and to run free, which she finally does, escaping to the woods with a chicken she has stolen. She returns to the village and again finds life there stifling, but begins to fall in love with a man, thus intensifying her predicament. After another trip to the woods and back, the magic does not work right; she is condemned by the villagers when a fox tail is seen dragging along below her kimono. The doomed lovers must run away with dogs at their heels, and Yuri returns to the forest forever, a sadder fox. This tale could be used in conjunction with Hans Christian Andersen's *The Little Mermaid*, which has a similar charm and complexity—and a similarly sad ending. Also, if carefully done, the book could be used to illustrate the conflicts felt by immigrants who are pulled between cultures. (KL)

8.47 Martin, Rafe. **The Eagle's Gift.** Illustrated by Tatsuro Kiuchi. Putnam, 1997. ISBN 039922923X. 32 pp. 8–12. Folklore.

Marten is the youngest of three sons of an Inuit couple. It is through him that the reader is taken on a magical journey into the land of the eagle, where Mother Eagle asks for his help to teach the gift of joy to his people. The message, explained at the end of the book, tells people not to forget that sharing happy times with others is as much a part of living as is striving for personal goals. (SA)

8.48 Martin, Rafe. **Mysterious Tales of Japan.** Illustrated by Tatsuro Kiuchi. Putnam, 1996. ISBN 03992267X. 74 pp. 9–12. Folklore.

This is a wonderful collection of tales of mysterious and unexplainable events and experiences. The stories will keep you intrigued and wondering whether or not these accounts could really be true. The soft, hazy illustrations add to the mysterious aura of the tales. (SKA)

Notable Social Studies Trade Books for Young People, ALA Notable Books for Children, Notable Books for a Global Society

8.49 Matthews, Andrew, reteller. **Marduk the Mighty and Other Stories of Creation.** Illustrated by Sheila Moxley. Milbrook, 1996. ISBN 0761302042. 96 pp. 9–12. Folklore.

A collection of creation stories from various cultures are presented in this text. Matthews explains that this book is about beginnings and endings. Posing the central question of where the world came from, he then presents answers from a variety of different people around the world. A section called "Who's Who?" at the end of the book serves as a glossary of the characters from all the stories. Vibrant illustrations capture the central theme of each tale. (MS)

8.50   Max, Jill, editor. **Spider Spins a Story: Fourteen Legends from Native America.** Illustrated by Robert Annesley, Benjamin Harjo, Michael Lacapa, S. D. Nelson, Redwing T. Nez, and Baje Whitethorne. Rising Moon, 1997. ISBN 0873586115. 72 pp. 8–12. Folklore.

The spider is an important creature to many Native American tribes. Here is a collection of fourteen legends about the spider from different tribes in the United States. The stories are fascinating and beautifully illustrated, and each legend begins with a short introduction about the tribe from which the story comes. As the stories unfold, the reader cannot help but look at spiders with a newfound respect. Each legend is endorsed by the tribe from which it originates. The illustrations have been created by Native American artists. Both of these facts add authenticity to this anthology of Native American culture. (SA)

8.51   Mayo, Margaret, reteller. **When the World Was Young: Creation and Pourquoi Tales.** Illustrated by Louise Brierley. Simon & Schuster, 1996. ISBN 0689808674. 77 pp. 9–12. Folklore.

Ten *pourquoi* tales, stories created to answer questions about our world, are retold by Mayo. Each story comes from a different culture and answers a significant question such as why children come in all different colors, how the sun was made, and why the sea is salty. Brierley's watercolor illustrations, richly colored and softly textured, provide a visual harmony to the text. A brief introduction on creation and *pourquoi* tales precedes the text. Valuable source notes on each tale are appended. (CC)

8.52   Mike, Jan M., reteller. **Gift of the Nile: An Ancient Egyptian Legend.** Illustrated by Charles Reasoner. Troll, 1996. ISBN 0816728135. 32 pp. 6–10. Folklore.

This heartwarming story of friendship and women's equality, reconstructed from a 3,500-year-old papyrus, tells of Mutemwia, a palace musician under Pharaoh Senefru, whose refreshing candor pleases the Pharaoh beyond all else. She tells him she misses her freedom, but he delays granting it to her. However, when they venture out on the Nile (in a boat rowed by twenty women, with Mutemwia at the bow, singing), a golden lotus given her by the Pharaoh falls into the water and Mutemwia tries in vain to fetch the flower back. The Pharaoh realizes that the best way to love her is to give her freedom and some land of her own. The themes that freedom, not bondage, builds loyalty, and that honesty is better than flattery make good discussion topics. The stylized faceless figures in the paintings give the feel of a patina on an old fresco. (KL)

8.53 Mollel, Tololwa M. **Ananse's Feast: An Ashanti Tale.** Illustrated by Andrew Glass. Clarion, 1997. ISBN 0395674026. 31 pp. 4–8. Folklore.

During a drought, selfish Ananse the spider has hoarded food for himself. Just as he is ready to dine on his feast all by himself, his friend Akye the Turtle pays him a visit. Unable to turn away his friend, Ananse invites him in, but connives to have Akye leave several times while Ananse gradually eats all the food. Later, Akye turns the tables on Ananse, and the spider is the one sent away hungry. The comical, colorful illustrations are a feast for the eyes and enhance this folktale's rich characterizations and humorous storyline. (KYR)

8.54 Mollel, Tololwa M. **Dume's Roar.** Illustrated by Kathy Blankley Roman. Stoddart Kids, 1998. ISBN 0773730036. 32 pp. 4–8. Folklore.

In this African folktale, the animals decide to pick a king. When Kobe, the tortoise, volunteers for the job, the other animals laugh at his offer. Dume, the lion, roars a loud, fierce roar and proclaims that he should be king. The mighty roar, sharp claws, and large teeth are sufficient to convince the other animals to agree with him. When Dume immediately begins to abuse his power as king, it takes the clever Kobe to not only save all the animals, but also to teach Dume to be a wise leader. (SF)

8.55 Mollel, Tololwa M. **Kitoto the Mighty.** Illustrated by Kristi Frost. Stoddart Kids, 1998. ISBN 0773730193. 30 pp. 5–9. Folklore.

This is one of many folktales that carry the theme of seeking the most powerful being. Mollel's version is about self-preservation, unlike many versions that speak of romance. The tale conveys a message that strengths are often hidden, and that "the weakest proves to be the most powerful being." Children will enjoy this African folktale with familiar objects: the sun, animals, water, hawks, and mice. Frost's illustrations use a warm color palette and are filled with fantastic images. Her interpretation of the topography of Africa lends a sense of immediacy. (CMH)

8.56　Mollel, Tololwa M. **Shadow Dance.** Illustrated by Donna Perrone. Clarion, 1998. ISBN 0395829097. 32 pp. 4–8. Folklore.

Set in Tanzania, *Shadow Dance* tells of how ingratitude is given its just reward. Salome is happily singing when she hears the cries of a crocodile trapped in a gully. She saves him, only to be threatened by the crocodile that he will eat her unless she finds a better reason that he should not. With a pigeon's help and her own resourcefulness, Salome outwits the crocodile and he is trapped once again. Music for Salome's songs and translations from Kiswahili are included. (KYR)

8.57　Moore, Christopher, reteller. **Ishtar and Tammuz: A Babylonian Myth of the Seasons.** Illustrated by Christina Balit. Kingfisher, 1996. ISBN 0753450127. 24 pp. 6–10. Folklore.

Here is a creation myth from Mesopotamia that predates the similar Greek story of Persephone. In this story Tammuz, a male fertility figure, is killed and then rescued from the underworld by the mercurial and all-powerful goddess Ishtar. Based on early textual references, the author chose to make Tammuz Ishtar's son in this retelling, which makes her grief and resolve to rescue him ring rather hollow after she has killed him. The stunning art, in both bright action poses and edging, are reminiscent of Gustav Klimt and the *art nouveau* style. These illustrations are so bright and thick that they give the illusion that they are raised up off the page, as if made of gold leaf. (KL)

8.58　Morin, Paul. **Animal Dreaming: An Aboriginal Dreamtime Story.** Silver Whistle / Harcourt Brace, 1998. ISBN 0152000542. Unpaged. 5–9. Folklore.

A hauntingly beautiful book with aboriginal art tells the story of the "dreamtime" when animals of long ago created a world where all lived in peace and harmony. An elder tribesman tells a young boy the aboriginal story of Earth's formation and ancestral spirits. The soft land formations and the sacred dotted patterns of dreamtime art found in rock paintings are represented well in the rich illustrations of this book. (MP)

Notable Social Studies Trade Books for Young People, Notable Books for a Global Society

8.59   Normandin, Christine, editor. **Echoes of the Elders: The Stories and Paintings of Chief Lelooska.** Illustrated by Chief Lelooska. DK Ink, 1997. ISBN 078942455X. 38 pp. 9–12. Folklore.

The five stories told by Chief Lelooska of the Kwakiutl tribe of Vancouver are vibrantly illustrated by authentic stylized illustrations. This oversized book includes an audio CD with Chief Lelooska reading the stories aloud. In the introduction, the reader will learn about the Kwakiutl tribe of the Northwest coast and more about Chief Lelooska's drawings and carvings and how he planned to record these stories when he knew his life was at an end. Children aged ten and up will enjoy reading and hearing these tales. (MP)

A LA Notable Books for Children, Notable Social Studies Trade Books for Young People, Notable Books for a Global Society

8.60   Normandin, Christine, editor. **Spirit of the Cedar People: The Stories and Paintings of Chief Lelooska.** Illustrated by Chief Lelooska. DK Ink, 1998. 38 pp. 6–10. Folklore.

Chief Lelooska again brings us stories of spirits and animals from the Kwakiutl tribe, as fables for children to learn how to live in harmony with nature. Accompanied by the delightful Kwakiutl illustrations and words, this book is a fascinating collection of folktales. The latest edition also contains a CD featuring Chief Lelooska telling the legends and performing traditional chants and drumming. (KW)

Notable Social Studies Trade Books for Young People

8.61   Pearson, Maggie, reteller. **The Fox and the Rooster and Other Tales.** Illustrated by JoAnne Moss. Little Tiger, 1997. ISBN 18884444177. 80 pp. 4–8. Folklore.

Folktales from around the world and a brief introduction of the history behind storytelling are presented in this book. "Anansi,"

"The Snow Child," "Raven Boy," and "The King with Dusty Feet" are a few of the fourteen folktales featured. The illustrations realistically depict characters from each folktale and evoke definite visual images of the characters and the settings in which the stories evolve. (MS)

8.62   Porte, Barbara Ann, reteller. **Hearsay: Strange Tales from the Middle Kingdom.** Illustrated by Rosemary Feit Covey. Greenwillow / Morrow, 1998. ISBN 068815381X. 144 pp. 10 and up. Folklore.

The author has researched the folklore of China to compile the fifteen stories of this volume. Some of the stories are based on legends, while others of her own creation incorporate traditional Chinese motifs and lore. The sources for the stories are given at the end of the book. Porte weaves the stories together with her own words to create an intimate picture of Chinese life over countless generations. Rosemary Feit Covey has created wood engravings to augment the text. (MP)

8.63   Rattigan, Jama Kim, reteller. **The Woman in the Moon: A Story from Hawaii.** Illustrated by Carla Golembe. Little Brown, 1996. ISBN 0316734462 Unpaged. 4–8. Folklore.

This is the retelling of an old Hawaiian legend of Hina, the goddess who lives on the moon. Poorly treated and overworked, Hina, a *tapa* maker, spends her days searching for freedom and happiness. This is a story of a strong female character and her desire to find a tranquil place that she can call her own. A glossary of Hawaiian words is provided at the front of the book. The author has also added a note at the end explaining some aspects of the culture and heritage of Hawaii. (MS)

8.64   Rosen, Michael J., reteller. **The Dog Who Walked with God.** Illustrations by Stan Fellows. Candlewick, 1998. ISBN 0763604704. 40 pp. 4–8. Folklore.

Michael Rosen retells the creation story of the Kato Indians of northern California, in which the world begins covered by water. God, the "Great Traveler," accompanied by his dog companion, then sets out to fashion the earth. As they create and name creatures, plants, and landforms, they express the purposes of these creations and affirm their goodness. The author's note describes how the Kato Indians valued dogs so much that they believed the Great Traveler needed a dog to help with the difficult task of creating the world. Expressive, colorful watercolor illustrations complement this folktale. (KYR)

8.65 Ross, Gayle, reteller. **The Legend of the Windigo: A Tale from Native North America.** Illustrated by Murv Jacob. Dial, 1996. ISBN 0803718985. 32 pp. 4–8. Folklore.

The Windigo, a giant stone creature, is taller than the tallest tree, can change his shape at will, and feeds on humans. When people begin to disappear, the Windigo is near! A young boy encourages the people to outsmart the Windigo, but their victory is bittersweet. This riveting story holds the reader spellbound from the outset and carries the imagination to a dramatic and surprising conclusion. This book is very similar to *The Windigo's Return* by Douglas Wood (see **8.87**). Ross's colorful storytelling is coupled well with vibrant illustrations. (GG)

8.66 Roth, Susan L. **The Biggest Frog in Australia.** Illustrated by Susan L. Roth. Simon & Schuster, 1996. ISBN 0689804903. 32 pp. 5–7. Folklore.

When the biggest frog in Australia gets thirsty, he begins to drink everything in sight. Starting with the puddles, then the billabongs, rivers, lakes, and ocean, the biggest frog drinks up even the water from the rain clouds. When the rest of the land and animals become thirsty, they attempt to make the frog laugh to make the water spill out of his mouth. One by one they try, but it is two silly eels tying themselves into knots while trying to dance that make the frog laugh and return all the water back to where it came from. The brightly colored cut-paper collages help portray this very comical Australian folktale. (MR)

8.67 Rumford, James. **The Island-below-the-Star.** Houghton Mifflin, 1998. ISBN 0395851599. 32 pp. 4–8. Folklore.

Five brothers, all with different abilities to read nature's signals (stars, waves, clouds, winds, and birds), prepare to sail from their Polynesian home to the islands below the star Arcturus, today's Hawaiian Islands. Blending myth and history, Rumford's tale is an entertaining explanation of how ancient explorers navigated the vast oceans in search of new lands without the use of navigational instruments. Flowing watercolor illustrations capture the power and beauty of the sea and the personalities and courage of its characters. (KYR)

8.68 San Souci, Robert D. **Cendrillon: A Caribbean Cinderella.** Illustrated by Brian Pinkney. Simon & Schuster, 1998. ISBN 068980668X. Unpaged. 4–9. Folklore.

Although this Caribbean Cinderella story follows the basic plot of Perrault's version, it is told from the godmother's affectionate point of view. She is a washerwoman who has known Cendrillon since birth, and who possesses a magic mahogany wand that can change things only in order to help someone else. The godmother's language contains an assortment of French Creole expressions and a lively cadence. (A glossary is included.) The illustrations explode with tropical colors and details of the island setting. Some are framed by vines, fruits, trees, and water fountains that grow magically from an object within the picture. The characters' expressive faces and purposeful actions convincingly reflect their strong feelings throughout the story. (SJ)

ALA Notable Books for Children

8.69 San Souci, Robert D., reteller. **The Faithful Friend.** Illustrated by Brian Pinkney. Simon & Schuster, 1998. ISBN 0027861317. 38 pp. 8–12. Folklore.

San Souci portrays the love that the brothers Clement and Hippolyte have towards each other in his retelling of this folktale. Clement falls in love with a picture of Pauline, and Hippolyte agrees to accompany him on his journey to find her. When they arrive, Clement asks for Pauline's hand in marriage. Pauline's father is infuriated and has zombies cast spells on the couple to thwart the marriage. San Souci's writing flows as it describes how good ultimately triumphs over evil. Pinkney's use of scratchboard techniques creates depth and motion in his illustrations, although it is sometimes hard to distinguish between the brothers. (CMH)

Caldecott Honor Book, Coretta Scott King Illustrator Honor Book

8.70 San Souci, Robert D. **A Weave of Words.** Illustrated by Raul Colón. Orchard, 1998. ISBN 0531300536 (trade). ISBN 0531330532 (paperback). 32 pp. 5–10. Folklore.

This thrilling feminist tale from Armenia, with its folklore pedigree detailed, contains a compelling story line, lots of cultural and historic information, and a cliffhanger ending in which Prince Vashagan is saved by Anait, a weaver's daughter on horseback wielding a sword and chopping off the three heads of a monster. Best of all, the prince, who at first knows only how to hunt, learns to read, write, and weave to gain Anait's consent to marry him. His newfound skills even save his own life as he cleverly weaves a warning, while in captivity, into the border of a carpet, alerting Anait that he has been captured. Three cheers for reading, women on horseback, and weaving men! Rich, copper-tinted paintings further enhance the charm of this story. See also *The Golden Bracelet* (**8.33**). (KL)

8.71 Shepard, Aaron, reteller. **The Crystal Heart: A Vietnamese Legend.** Illustrated by Joseph Daniel Fiedler. Atheneum, 1998. ISBN 0689815514. 32 pp. 4–8. Folklore.

This beautifully illustrated Vietnamese legend tells of Mi Nuong, the daughter of a mandarin, who is sheltered in her father's palace. In her solitude, she hears the beautiful song of a man outside the palace. Thinking he might be her true love, Mi Nuong longs to meet this man but is shocked to learn that he is only a fisherman. She sends the man away, and he soon dies of a broken heart. Remaining in the fisherman's boat, however, is a crystal that the mandarin has fashioned into a cup. When Mi Nuong drinks from the cup, she sees the fisherman's face and hears his lonely song. (CP)

8.72 Sierra, Judy, reteller. **Nursery Tales around the World.** Illustrated by Stefano Vitale. Clarion, 1996. ISBN 0395678943. 114 pp. 4–8. Folklore.

Tales from a variety of cultures are grouped into categories of "Runaway Cookies," "Incredible Appetites," "The Victory of the Smallest," "Chain Tales," "Slowpokes and Speedsters," and "Fooling the Big Bad Wolf." Each category contains three tales and begins with an explanation of the story type. Familiar stories such as "The Gingerbread Man" and "The House That Jack Built" are retold along with lesser-known tales like "Odon the Giant" and "The Cat and the Parrot." Each page is bounded by colorful borders that complement the text. An introduction provides background information on nursery tales and tips on storytelling. Extensive notes on each retelling are included. (CC)

ALA Notable Books for Children

8.73   Sierra, Judy, reteller. **Wiley and the Hairy Man.** Illustrated by Brian Pinkney. Dutton, 1996. ISBN 0525674772. 32 pp. 5–8. Folklore.

Even though his father has been carried off by the Hairy Man, Wiley manages to outwit the ugly malefactor when they meet alone in the swamp. Wiley's mother tells him he must fool the Hairy Man three times before he will leave them alone. Wiley uses his wits and his mother uses her conjure magic to do just that. This favorite African American folktale is enriched by the vibrant colors of Pinkney's painted scratchboards. (SG)

8.74   Simms, Laura, reteller. **The Bone Man: A Native American Modoc Tale.** Illustrated by Michael McCurdy. Hyperion, 1997. ISBN 0786820748. 32 pp. 4–9. Folklore.

Be careful of the Bone Man! In this Native American Modoc story, Nulwee lives in fear of the day that he will have to face the Bone Man. On the day that he was born, it was prophesied that he would be the one to face the Bone Man and bring back all the people that the Bone Man has devoured. This wonderful story of heroism and bravery will inspire children to develop their own inner courage. Michael McCurdy's scratchboard illustrations add to the overall mystery and drama of the story. (KW)

ALA Notable Books for Children

8.75   Spooner, Michael, and Lolita Taylor, retellers. **Old Meshikee and the Little Crabs.** Illustrated by John Hart. Henry Holt, 1996. ISBN 0805034870. 32 pp. 6–12. Folklore.

Meshikee the turtle is revered in Ojibwe culture as the wise trickster. Like Coyote, Brer Rabbit, Till Eulenspiegel, Mullah Nasr-ed Din, and Anansi, Meshikee seems to be the victim of a plot by the mean and dull-witted crabs, but emerges smiling at the end. Wonderful wrap-around illustrations make each page an integrated design of text and art. This would be a good choice for a multicultural unit on tricksters. (KL)

8.76 Taylor, Harriet Peck, reteller. **When Bear Stole the Chinook: A Siksika Tale.** Illustrated by Harriet Peck Taylor. Farrar, Straus and Giroux, 1997. ISBN 0374109478. 32 pp. 5–8. Folklore.

An orphan boy lives among the Siksika people, but his only companions are the animals. The Siksika are suffering through an endless winter. Although the *chinooks* (warm spring breezes) are past due, they do not arrive. The boy sets out with his animal companions to find the *chinook*. This *pourquoi* tale also offers an explanation for bears' hibernation habits. (SF)

8.77 Tompert, Ann, reteller. **How Rabbit Lost His Tail.** Illustrated by Jacqueline Chwast. Houghton Mifflin, 1997. ISBN 0395822815. 31 pp. 4–8. Folklore.

Rabbit, with his long tail, thinks very highly of himself and celebrates by running feverishly around a willow tree. Believing that his running is making it snow, he continues until the snow is piled high and he is thoroughly exhausted. He steps up to one of the branches, falls asleep, and hibernates until spring. When he finally wakes up he has no idea how to get down because all the snow that melted has left a great distance. He fearfully asks several animals for help but only receives ridicule and sarcasm. Squirrel, the last animal, has a reasonable solution for Rabbit: Jump, he says. When Rabbit jumps his tail gets caught in the crotch of the tree, and he is left with the stubby tail known today. This legend seems to have an underlying moral, but the message is somewhat muddled in this telling. Chwast's illustrations are cartoon-like and lose the authenticity of the Seneca culture by dressing the animals in cute outfits. (CMH)

8.78 Van Laan, Nancy, reteller. **Shingebiss: An Ojibwe Legend.** Illustrated by Betsy Bowen. Houghton Mifflin, 1997. ISBN 0395827450. 30 pp. 8 and up. Folklore.

This cherished Ojibwe legend is beautifully retold and exquisitely illustrated. The storyteller relates the tale of a little merganser duck who, in his search for food, is forced to face the fierce Winter Maker. He triumphs, however, as he successfully meets each challenge throughout the bitter winter months. The retelling captures the mood of the oral storytelling tradition, incorporating Ojibwe words throughout the text. The highly detailed text is woven into the colorful and fanciful illustrations, producing a captivating interaction between the words and images. With rich text and intricate illustrations, this book offers an opportunity to share an enchanting literary experience. (SSG)

Notable Social Studies Trade Books for Young People

8.79 Van Laan, Nancy, reteller. **So Say the Little Monkeys.** Illustrated by Yumi Heo. Atheneum, 1998. ISBN 0689810385. 4–8. 32 pp. Folklore.

This Brazilian Indian *pourquoi* tale explains why small black-mouth monkeys sleep the way they do. The book's swinging rhymes make it one children will enjoy as a read-aloud. The pencil, oil, and torn-paper pictures give the book a simple folk-art quality. The author's retelling of this tale, originally told by the indigenous people of Brazil's Rio Negro, will delight children as they learn a new story. (MP)

8.80 Wahl, Jan, reteller. **The Singing Geese.** Illustrated by Sterling Brown. Dutton / Lodestar, 1998. ISBN 0525674993. 32 pp. 4–8. Folklore.

In this tall tale from West Virginia, Sam Bombel, the African American protagonist, departs from his home to shoot his dinner. He succeeds in shooting a goose, but the bird sings a mysterious song as it falls to the ground. Sam brings home the goose and asks his wife to cook it. Strange things happen as she plucks the goose and puts it into the oven. Dinner is served, but as Sam starts to carve the bird, a flock of geese comes back to rescue their fallen member. As a result, Sam Bombel's appetite for hunting is changed forever. Readers capable of suspending disbelief will enjoy this story, although the clarity and realism of the illustrations may make this difficult. Curiously, the goose is rarely resistant to its fate; it sits quietly with its head erect and its bill parted while the wife plucks its feathers, places it in the oven, and finally serves it at the dinner table. The author notes on the book jacket that he heard this tall tale from an elderly African American man in West Virginia. Children may enjoy singing the goose's song, music for which is located on the last page of the book. (JHC and CC)

8.81 Walker, Barbara K., reteller. **A Treasury of Turkish Folk Tales for Children.** Shoe String, 1998. ISBN 0208022066. 155 pp. 5–12. Folklore.

This author, a librarian and archivist, and her husband collected three thousand Turkish folktales on tape, many of which are retold in this impressive anthology. Walker has faithfully retained the "spicy proverbs, the excitement of suspense or joy the teller expresses, and the rich variety of endings." There is every bit as much variety as in any European fairy tale collection. These stories are suitable for reading aloud or silently, and could be used in comparative studies of fairy tales and folktales from around the world. (KL)

8.82 Wardlaw, Lee, reteller. **Punia and the King of Sharks: A Hawaiian Folktale.** Illustrated by Felipe Davalos. Dial, 1997. ISBN 0803716826 (trade). ISBN 0803716834 (library binding). 32 pp. 4–8. Folklore.

In this Hawaiian trickster tale, Punia is the clever, daring son of a father who was eaten by the King of Sharks, guardian of the lobster cave. Punia schemes to capture succulent lobsters for himself and his mother and to win back the use of the lobster cave for his village. Children will enjoy Punia's wily tricks, and the humorous and colorful illustrations add to the excitement. This story is a welcome addition to trickster tales that also introduces Hawaiian language and village life. (KYR)

Notable Social Studies Trade Books for Young People

8.83 Wells, Ruth, reteller. **The Farmer and the Poor God: A Folktale from Japan.** Illustrated by Yoshi. Simon & Schuster, 1996. ISBN 0689802145. Unpaged. 6–11. Folklore.

In this authentically illustrated Japanese tale, a poor, unhappy farmer and his family plan to move, leaving behind the "Poor God" who lives in their attic and is blamed for their misfortunes. Hearing of their plans, the Poor God uses straw from the farmer's rice fields to weave sandals for their journey. But the journey is postponed, the sandal business grows, and the farmer's family learns that what they needed for happiness was right there all along. Japanese words are printed in capital letters within clear contexts to help readers understand their meaning. The beautiful illustrations, painted on silk, accurately depict the landscape, clothing, houses, pottery, and straw sandals of rural Japan. (KB)

8.84 Whetung, James, reteller. **The Vision Seeker.** Illustrated by Paul Morin. Stoddart Kids, 1996. ISBN 0773729666. 32 pp. 9–12. Folklore.

This book tells one version of how the Anishinabe, a nation of people who trace their history back to the beginning of time, got the Sweat Lodge. *The Vision Seeker* begins with families fighting against families until they begin to die off from hunger. As they become weaker and weaker, Little Boy seeks to help his people. He is told to go to the high place and seek a vision. Little Boy leaves home with four grains of corn, which he has to ration over the next four days until he reaches the top of the mountain. Once there, Little Boy fasts until he has a dream. In his dream, he travels to a lodge in which there are seven grandfathers. Each of the grandfathers gives him a gift. Little Boy, the vision seeker, receives the gifts of knowledge, love, honesty, strength, bravery, respect, and humility. When Little Boy returns home his people build the Sweat Lodge, which symbolizes the connection of the Anishinabe people with their past. (CH)

8.85 Wolkstein, Diane, reteller. **Bouki Dances the Kokioko: A Comical Tale from Haiti.** Illustrated by Jesse Sweetwater. Gulliver / Harcourt, 1997. ISBN 0152000348. 28 pp. 4–8. Folklore.

The king of Haiti, who loves dancing, devises a plan to have dancers perform for him every night. He makes up a dance, the Kokioko, and offers a reward for anyone who can perform it for him. His subjects line up for a chance to win the reward. Malice, the king's gardener, sees the king dancing the Kokioko and secretly memorizes the dance. He convinces his friend, Bouki, to learn the steps and collect the reward. Bouki is not a good dancer, but he practices and subsequently wins. Malice and Bouki rejoice by dancing in the forest and Bouki is tricked out of his reward. This trickster tale is illustrated with vibrant color, and the excitement of the new dance is palpable. (ER)

8.86 Wolkstein, Diane. **White Wave: A Chinese Tale.** Illustrated by Ed Young. Gulliver / Harcourt, 1979/1996. ISBN 0152002936. 30 pp. 4–9. Folklore.

Kuo Ming, a lonely farmer, happens upon a beautiful snail shell as he walks home from working in the fields. He takes the snail home with him and places it in a pot with some leaves. The next day, when he returns from the fields, his dinner is waiting for him and the leaves are gone. He is sure that it is the snail's doing. His curiosity gets the best of him and he pretends to go off to work but instead watches from the window to see what happens. He finds the shell is inhabited not by a snail but by a lovely moon goddess, White Wave. One day, Kuo Ming can no longer contain himself and he rushes in to talk to her. In doing so, he must then lose what he holds so dear—White Wave—because he yearns for more than he is given. Ed Young's pencil illustrations make the tale come alive as they move like the spirals of the shell. (ER)

8.87 Wood, Douglas. **The Windigo's Return: A North Woods Story.** Illustrated by Greg Couch. Simon & Schuster, 1996. ISBN 0689800657. 32 pp. 4–8. Folklore.

The Windigo's Return is based on an Ojibwe legend that tells of the winter when the people of the North Woods began to disappear. As they vanish one by one, the people remain in fear of the terrible Windigo, until a young girl outsmarts him. The Windigo's dying curse—to come back and eat the tribe and all future generations—seems to come true the following summer, when mosquitoes plague the tribe with bites. The tale and its wonderful illustrations capture the ebb and flow of the seasons themselves. (GG)

8.88 Yep, Laurence, reteller. **The Khan's Daughter: A Mongolian Folktale.** Illustrated by Jean Tseng and Mou-Sien Tseng. Scholastic, 1997. ISBN 0590483897. Unpaged. 9–12. Folklore.

In this retelling of a Mongolian folktale, Mongke, a confident shepherd, must accomplish three difficult tasks in order to fulfill his father's prophecy that he will marry the Khan's beautiful daughter. Yep's artful retelling and the Tsengs' colorful, detailed illustrations transport the reader to the rugged plains and tent cities of Central Asia where the very human characters match wits. In this action-filled story, Mongke meets all the challenges, including the most difficult one presented by the Khan's daughter. (KB)

Appendix A:
Award-Winning Books

This appendix lists the winners of major awards in the field of children's literature, particularly those that honor multicultural books. Many multicultural books are listed as winners, but not all books cited are multicultural. Other awards are described in brief paragraphs, and winners of those awards that are reviewed in this volume are noted as such in their annotations. Awards are typically given the year following the book's publication, so only the awards for 1997, 1998, and 1999, the years that are covered in this third edition of *Kaleidoscope*, are listed here.

Jane Addams Award

The Jane Addams Award, established in 1953, is given annually to the book for young people that most effectively promotes peace, social justice, world community, or equality of the sexes and of all races. It is given by the Women's International League for Peace and Freedom and the Jane Addams Peace Association.

1997   **Longer Book**

Bartoletti, Susan Campbell. *Growing Up in Coal Country.* Houghton Mifflin.

Picture Book

Krull, Kathleen. *Wilma Unlimited.* Illustrated by David Diaz. Harcourt Brace.

1998   **Longer Book**

Nye, Naomi Shihab. *Habibi.* Simon & Schuster.

Picture Book

Hearne, Betsy. *Seven Brave Women.* Illustrated by Bethanne Andersen. Greenwillow.

1999   **Longer Book**

Wolff, Virginia Euwer. *Bat 6.* Scholastic.

Picture Book

Aliki. *Marianthe's Story: Painted Words / Marianthe's Story: Spoken Memories.* Greenwillow.

Américas Award for Children's and Young Adult Literature

The Américas Award is given in recognition of U.S. works of fiction, poetry, folklore, or selected nonfiction—from picture books to works for young adults—published in the previous year in English or Spanish, that authentically and engagingly portray Latin America, the Caribbean, or Latinos in the United States. By combining and linking the Americas, the award reaches beyond geographic and multicultural boundaries, focusing instead upon cultural heritages within the hemisphere. The award is sponsored by the national Consortium of Latin American Studies Programs (CLASP).

The award winners and commended titles are selected for their (1) distinctive literary quality; (2) cultural contextualization; (3) exceptional integration of text, illustration and design; and (4) potential for classroom use.

1997 **Award Winners**

Hanson, Regina. *The Face at the Window*. Illustrated by Linda Saport. Clarion.

Jiménez, Francisco. *The Circuit*. University of New Mexico.

Honorable Mentions

Ancona, George. *Mayeros: A Yucatec Maya Family*. Morrow.

Bloom, Valerie. *Fruits: A Caribbean Counting Poem*. Illustrated by David Axtell. Henry Holt.

Commended Books

Ada, Alma Flor. *Gathering the Sun: An Alphabet in Spanish and English*. Illustrated by Simón Silva. Lothrop, Lee & Shepard.

Ada, Alma Flor. *The Lizard and the Sun / La lagartija y el sol*. Illustrated by Felipe Dávalos. Doubleday.

Alarcón, Francisco X. *Laughing Tomatoes and Other Spring Poems / Jitomates risueños y otros poemas de primavera*. Illustrated by Maya Christina González. Children's Book Press.

Almada, Patricia. *From Father to Son / De padre a hijo*. Photographs by Marianno de López. Rigby.

Capellinni, Mary. *The Story of Doña Chila / El cuento de Doña Chila*. Illustrated by Gershom Griffith. Rigby.

Ehlert, Lois. *Cuckoo / Cucu*. Translated by Gloria de Aragón Andújar. Harcourt Brace.

Garay, Luis. *Pedrito's Day*. Orchard.

González, Lucía M. *Señor Cat's Romance and Other Favorite Stories from Latin America*. Illustrated by Lulu Delacre. Scholastic.

González-Jenson, Margarita. *Mexico's Marvelous Corn / El maravilloso maiz de Mexico*. Rigby.

Hernández, Jo Ann Yolanda. *White Bread Competition*. Piñata.

Horenstein, Genry. *Baseball in the Barrio*. Gulliver / Harcourt Brace.

Johnston, Tony, and Jeanette Winter. *Day of the Dead*. Harcourt Brace.

Keane, Sofía Meza. *Dear Abuelita / Querida Abuelita*. Illustrated by Enrique O. Sánchez. Rigby.

Kroll, Virginia. *Butterfly Boy*. Illustrated by Gerardo Suzán. Boyds Mills.

López, Loretta. *Birthday Swap / Que sorpresa de cumpleaños!* Lee & Low.

Martínez, Floyd. *Spirits of the High Mesa*. Arte Público.

Mora, Pat. *Tomas and the Library Lady*. Illustrated by Raul Colón. Knopf.

Moretón, Daniel. *La Cucaracha Martina: A Caribbean Folktale / La cucaracha Martina: Un cuento folklorico del Caribe*. Illustrated by Daniel Moretón. Turtle.

Orozco, Jose-Luis, selector. *Diez deditos / Ten Little Fingers and Other Play Rhymes and Action Songs from Latin America*. Illustrated by Elisa Kleven. Dutton.

Rahaman, Vashanti. *A Little Salmon for Witness: A Story from Trinidad*. Illustrated by Sandra Speidel. Lodestar.

Sisnett, Ana. *Grannie Jus' Come*. Illustrated by Karen Lusebrink. Children's Book Press.

Solá, Michéle. *Angela Weaves a Dream*. Photographs by Jeffrey Jay Foxx. Hyperion.

Soto, Gary. *Buried Onions*. Harcourt Brace.

Stevens, Jan Romero. *Carlos and the Skunk / Carlos y el zorrillo*. Illustrated by Jeanne Arnold. Rising Moon.

Viesti, Joe, and Diane Hall. *Celebrate in Central America*. Photographs by Joe Viesti. Lothrop, Lee & Shepard.

1998   **Award Winners**

Carling, Amelia Lau. *Mama and Papa Have a Store*. Dial.

Ancona, George. *Barrio: José's Neighborhood*. Harcourt Brace.

Honorable Mention

San Souci, Robert D. *Cendrillon: A Caribbean Cinderella*. Illustrated by Brian Pinkney. Simon & Schuster.

Commended Books

Ada, Alma Flor. *Under the Royal Palms: A Childhood in Cuba*. Atheneum.

Alarcón, Francisco X. *From the Bellybutton of the Moon and Other Summer Poems / Del ombligo de la luna y otros poemas de verano*. Illustrated by Maya Christina González. Children's Book Press.

Ancona, George. *Fiesta Fireworks*. Lothrop, Lee & Shepard.

Chambers, Veronica. *Marisol and Magdalena: The Sound of Our Sisterhood.* Hyperion.

Cowley, Joy. *Big Moon Tortilla.* Illustrated by Dyanne Strongbow. Boyds Mills.

Gershator, Phillis, and David Gershator. *Greetings, Sun.* Illustrated by Synthia Saint James. DK Ink.

Hausman, Gerald, and Ashley Wolff. *Doctor Bird: Three Lookin' Up Tales from Jamaica.* Philomel.

Heide, Florence Parry, and Roxanne Heide Pierce. *Tio Armando.* Illustrated by Ann Grifalconi. Lothrop, Lee & Shepard.

Isadora, Rachel. *Caribbean Dream.* Putnam.

Loya, Olga. *Momentos Magicos: Tales from Latin America Told in English and Spanish.* August House.

Luenn, Nancy. *A Gift for Abuelita: Celebrating the Day of the Dead / Un regalo para Abuelita: En celebracion del Dia de los Muertos.* Illustrated by Robert Chapman. Rising Moon.

Reeve, Kirk. *Lolo and Red-Legs.* Rising Moon.

Slate, Joseph. *The Secret Stars.* Illustrated by Felipe Dávalos. Cavendish.

Soto, Gary. *Big Bushy Mustache.* Illustrated by Joe Cepeda. Knopf.

Soto, Gary. *Petty Crimes.* Harcourt Brace.

Torres, Leyla. *Liliana's Grandmothers.* Farrar, Straus and Giroux.

Van Laan, Nancy. *The Magic Bean Tree: A Legend from Argentina.* Illustrated by Beatriz Vidal. Houghton Mifflin.

Van West, Patricia E. *The Crab Man / El hombre de los cangrejos* (dual editions). Illustrated by Cedric Lucas. Turtle.

1999 **Award Winner**

Herrera, Juan Felipe. *Crashboomlove.* University of New Mexico.

Honorable Mentions

Lomas Garza, Carmen. *Magic Windows / Ventanas mágicas.* Spanish translation by Francisco X. Alarcón. Children's Book Press,

Wolf, Bernard. *Cuba: After the Revolution.* Dutton.

Commended Books

Alarcón, Francisco X. *Angels Ride Bikes / Los angeles andan en bicicleta.* Illustrated by Maya Christina Gonzalez. Children's Book Press.

Ancona, George. *Carnaval.* Harcourt Brace.

Belafonte, Harry, and Lord Burgess. *Island in the Sun.* Illustrated by Alex Ayliffe. Dial.

Chin-Lee, Cynthia, and Terri de la Peña. *A Is for Americas.* Illustrated by Enrique O. Sánchez. Orchard.

Holtwijk, Ineke. *Asphalt Angels.* Translated from the Dutch by Wanda Boeke. Front Street.

Holzwarth, Werner. *I'm José and I'm Okay; Three Stories from Bolivia.* Translated from the German by Laura McKenna. Story idea and illustrations by Yatiyawi Studios. Kane / Miller.

Madrigal, Antonio Hernández. *Erandi's Braids.* Illustrated by Tomie dePaola. Putnam.

Rodríguez, Luis J. *It Doesn't Have to Be This Way: A Barrio Story / No tiene que ser así: Una historia del barrio.* Illustrated by Daniel Galvez. Children's Book Press.

Taylor, Harriet Peck. *Two Days in May.* Illustrated by Leyla Torres. Farrar, Straus and Giroux.

The Mildred L. Batchelder Award

Given annually (unless no book is deemed worthy) to a United States publisher, the Batchelder Award honors the most outstanding book originally published in a language other than English in a country other than the United States. Established in 1968, it is given by the Association of Library Service to Children of the American Library Association.

1997   Farrar, Straus and Giroux: *The Friends,* by Kazumi Yumoto. Translated from the Japanese by Cathy Hirano.

1998   Henry Holt: *The Robber and Me,* by Josef Holub. Translated from the German by Elizabeth D. Crawford.

Honor Books

Viking: *Nero Corleone: A Cat's Story,* by Elke Heidenrich. Translated from the German by Doris Orgel.

Scholastic: *Hostage to War: A True Story,* by Tatjana Wassiljewa. Translated from the German by Anna Trenter.

1999   Dial: *Thanks to My Mother,* by Schoschana Rabinovici. Translated from the German by James Skofield.

Honor Book

Viking: *Secret Letters from 0 to 10,* by Susie Morgenstern. Translated from the French by Gill Rosner.

2000   Walker: *The Baboon King,* by Anton Quintana. Translated from the Dutch by John Nieuwenhuizen.

Honor Books

Front Street: *Asphalt Angels,* by Ineke Holtwijk. Translated from the Dutch by Wanda Boeke.

R. & S.: *Vendela in Venice,* by Christina Bjork. Translated from the Swedish by Inga-Karin Eriksson.

Farrar, Straus and Giroux: *Collector of Moments,* by Quint Buchholz. Translated from the German by Peter F. Neumeyer.

The Pura Belpré Award

The Pura Belpré Award, established in 1996, is presented every two years to a Latino/Latina writer and a Latino/Latina illustrator whose work best portrays, affirms, and celebrates Latino culture. It is cosponsored by the Association for Library Service to Children (ALSC), a division of the American Library Association (ALA), and the National Association to Promote Library Services to the Spanish Speaking (REFORMA), an ALA affiliate.

The award is named after Pura Belpré, the first Latina librarian at the New York Public Library. As a children's librarian, storyteller, and author, she enriched the lives of Puerto Rican children in the United States through her pioneering work of preserving and disseminating Puerto Rican folklore.

1998 **Medal Winner for Narrative**

Martinez, Victor. *Parrot in the Oven: Mi Vida.* Joanna Cotler / HarperCollins.

Medal Winner for Illustration

Soto, Gary. *Snapshots from the Wedding.* Illustrated by Stephanie Garcia. Putnam.

Honor Books for Narrative

Alarcón, Francisco X. *Laughing Tomatoes and Other Spring Poems / Jitomates risueños y otros poemas de primavera.* Illustrated by Maya Christina Gonzalez. Children's Book Press.

Martinez, Floyd. *Spirits of the High Mesa.* Arte Público.

Honor Books for Illustration

Ada, Alma Flor. *Gathering the Sun: An Alphabet in Spanish and English.* English translation by Rosa Zubizarreta. Illustrated by Simón Silva. Lothrop, Lee & Shepard.

Jaffe, Nina. *The Golden Flower: A Taino Myth from Puerto Rico.* Illustrated by Enrique O. Sánchez. Simon & Schuster.

Lomas Garza, Carmen. *In My Family / En mi familia.* Children's Book Press.

2000 **Medal Winner for Narrative**

Ada, Alma Flor. *Under the Royal Palms: A Childhood in Cuba.* Atheneum.

Medal Winner for Illustration

Lomas Garza, Carmen. *Magic Windows.* Children's Book Press.

Honor Books for Narrative

Alarcón, Francisco X. *From the Bellybutton of the Moon and Other Summer Poems / Del ombligo de la luna y otros poemas de verano.* Illustrated by Maya Christina Gonzalez. Children's Book Press.

Herrera, Juan Felipe. *Laughing Out Loud, I Fly: Poems in English and Spanish.* Illustrated by Karen Barbour. HarperCollins.

Honor Books for Illustration

Ancona, George. *Barrio: José's Neighborhood.* Harcourt Brace.

Carling, Amelia Lau. *Mama and Papa Have a Store.* Dial.

Slate, Joseph. *The Secret Stars.* Illustrated by Felipe Dávalos. Cavendish.

Randolph Caldecott Medal

Given annually since 1938, the Caldecott Medal honors the illustrator of the most distinguished picture book published in the United States in the preceding year. Illustrators of winning books and of honor books must be citizens or residents of the United States. This award is conferred by the Association for Library Services to Children of the American Library Association.

1997 **Medal Winner**

Wisniewski, David. *Golem.* Clarion.

Honor Books

Ho, Minfong. *Hush! A Thai Lullaby.* Illustrated by Holly Meade. Melanie Kroupa / Orchard.

Pelletier, David. *The Graphic Alphabet.* Orchard.

Pilkey, Dav. *The Paperboy.* Richard Jackson / Orchard.

Sis, Peter. *Starry Messenger.* Foster / Farrar, Straus and Giroux.

1998 **Medal Winner**

Zelinsky, Paul O. *Rapunzel.* Dutton.

Honor Books

Myers, Walter Dean. *Harlem.* Illustrated by Christopher Myers. Scholastic.

Stewart, Sarah. *The Gardener.* Illustrated by David Small. Farrar, Straus and Giroux.

Taback, Simms. *There Was an Old Lady Who Swallowed a Fly.* Viking.

1999 **Medal Winner**

Martin, Jacqueline Briggs. *Snowflake Bentley.* Illustrated by Mary Azarian. Houghton Mifflin.

Honor Books

Pinkney, Andrea Davis. *Duke Ellington: The Piano Prince and His Orchestra.* Illustrated by Brian Pinkney. Hyperion.

Shannon, David. *No, David!* Scholastic.

Shulevitz, Uri. *Snow.* Farrar, Straus and Giroux.

Sis, Peter. *Tibet through the Red Box.* Foster / Farrar, Straus and Giroux.

The Coretta Scott King Award

These awards and honor designations have been given annually since 1969 to African American authors and illustrators for books that are outstanding inspirational and educational contributions to literature for children and young people. They are given by the Social Responsibilities Round Table of the American Library Association.

1997   **Author Award**

Myers, Walter Dean. *Slam.* Scholastic.

Author Honor Book

McKissack, Patricia C., and McKissack, Fredrick L. *Rebels against Slavery: American Slave Revolts.* Scholastic.

Illustrator Award

Schroeder, Alan. *Minty: A Story of Young Harriet Tubman.* Illustrated by Jerry Pinkney. Dial.

Illustrator Honor Books

Adedjouma, Davida, editor. *The Palm of My Heart: Poetry by African American Children.* Illustrated by Gregorie Christie. Lee & Low.

Lauture, Denize. *Running the Road to ABC.* Illustrated by Reynold Ruffin. Simon & Schuster Books for Young Readers.

English, Karen. *Neeny Coming, Neeny Going.* Illustrated by Synthia Saint James. BridgeWater.

1998   **Author Award**

Draper, Sharon M. *Forged by Fire.* Atheneum.

Author Honor Books

Hansen, Joyce. *I Thought My Soul Would Rise and Fly: The Diary of Patsy, a Freed Girl.* Scholastic.

Haskins, James. *Bayard Rustin: Behind the Scenes of the Civil Rights Movement.* Hyperion.

Illustrator Award

Steptoe, Javaka, editor. *In Daddy's Arms I Am Tall: African Americans Celebrating Fathers.* Illustrated by Javaka Steptoe. Lee & Low.

Illustrator Honor Books

Bryan, Ashley. *Ashley Bryan's ABC of African American Poetry.* Jean Karl / Atheneum.

Diakité, Baba Wagué. *The Hunterman and the Crocodile.* Scholastic.

1999   **Author Award**

Myers, Walter Dean. *Harlem.* Illustrated by Christopher Myers. Scholastic.

Johnson, Angela. *Heaven.* Simon & Schuster.

Author Honor Books

Grimes, Nikki. *Jazmin's Notebook.* Dial.

Hansen, Joyce, and Gary McGowan. *Breaking Ground, Breaking Silence: The Story of New York's African Burial Ground.* Henry Holt.

Johnson, Angela. *The Other Side: Shorter Poems.* Orchard.

Illustrator Award

Igus, Toyomi. *i see the rhythm.* Illustrated by Michele Wood. Children's Book Press.

Illustrator Honor Books

Thomas, Joyce Carol. *I Have Heard of a Land.* Illustrated by Floyd Cooper. Joanna Cotler / HarperCollins.

Curtis, Gavin. *The Bat Boy and His Violin.* Illustrated by E. B. Lewis. Simon & Schuster.

Pinkney, Andrea Davis. *Duke Ellington: The Piano Prince and His Orchestra.* Illustrated by Brian Pinkney. Hyperion.

NCTE Award for Excellence in Poetry for Children

Established in 1977, this award is presented every three years to a living American poet for an aggregate body of work for children aged three to thirteen.

1997   Eloise Greenfield

NCTE Orbis Pictus Award
for Outstanding Nonfiction for Children

This award commemorates John Comenius's book, *Orbis Pictus: The World in Pictures,* published in 1657, and historically considered to be the first book actually intended for children. The selection committee chooses one outstanding nonfiction book each year on the basis of accuracy, organization, design, writing style, and usefulness for classroom teaching.

1997   Stanley, Diane. *Leonardo da Vinci.* Morrow.

Honor Books

Freedman, Russell. *The Life and Death of Crazy Horse.* Holiday House.

Blumberg, Rhoda. *Full Steam Ahead: The Race to Build a Transcontinental Railroad.* National Geographic.

Osborne, Mary Pope. *One World, Many Religions: The Ways We Worship.* Knopf.

1998   Pringle, Laurence. *An Extraordinary Life: The Story of a Monarch Butterfly.* Orchard.

Honor Books

Wick, Walter. *A Drop of Water: A Book of Science and Wonder.* Scholastic.

Dorros, Arthur. *A Tree Is Growing.* Scholastic.

Giblin, James Cross. *Charles A. Lindbergh: A Human Hero.* Clarion.

Hampton, Wilborn. *Kennedy Assassinated! The World Mourns: A Reporter's Story.* Candlewick.

1999   Armstrong, Jennifer. *Shipwreck at the Bottom of the World: The Extraordinary True Story of Shackleton and the* Endurance. Crown.

Honor Books

Burleigh, Robert. *Black Whiteness: Admiral Byrd Alone in the Antarctic.* Simon & Schuster.

Holmes, Thom. *Fossil Feud: The Rivalry of the First American Dinosaur Hunters.* Julian Messner.

Jenkins, Steve. *Hottest, Coldest, Highest, Deepest.* Houghton Mifflin.

Lobel, Anita. *No Pretty Pictures: A Child of War.* Greenwillow.

John Newbery Medal

The Newbery Medal and honor book designations have been given annually since 1922 to the most distinguished contributions to children's literature published in the United States during the preceding year. The award is given by the Association for Library Service to Children of the American Library Association.

1997   Konigsburg, E. L. *The View from Saturday.* Atheneum.

Honor Books

Farmer, Nancy. *A Girl Named Disaster.* Orchard.

McGraw, Eloise. *Moorchild.* Simon & Schuster.

Turner, Megan Whalen. *The Thief.* Greenwillow.

White, Ruth. *Belle Prater's Boy.* Farrar, Straus and Giroux.

1998   Hesse, Karen. *Out of the Dust.* Scholastic.

Honor Books

Giff, Patricia Reilly. *Lily's Crossing.* Delacorte.

Levine, Gail Carson. *Ella Enchanted.* HarperCollins.

Spinelli, Jerry. *Wringer.* HarperCollins.

1999   Sachar, Louis. *Holes.* Farrar, Straus and Giroux.

        Honor Book

        Peck, Richard. *Long Way from Chicago.* Dial.

2000   Curtis, Christopher Paul. *Bud, Not Buddy.* Delacorte.

        Honor Books

        Couloumbus, Audrey. *Getting Near to Baby.* Putnam.

        dePaola, Tomie. *26 Fairmount Avenue.* Putnam.

        Holm, Jennifer L. *Our Only May Amelia.* HarperCollins.

Notable Books for a Global Society

The annual list of Notable Books for a Global Society comprises books selected by a committee of the Children's Literature and Reading Special Interest Group of the International Reading Association. The purpose of the list is to identify outstanding trade books for enhancing readers' understanding of people and cultures throughout the world. For a book to be eligible, it must have been published in the United States for the first time in the preceding year. The annotated list is published annually in *The Dragon Lode* and in *The Reading Teacher.*

1997   Balgassi, Haemi. *Peacebound Trains.* Illustrated by Chris K. Soentpiet. Clarion.

        Bash, Barbara. *In the Heart of a Village: The World of the Indian Banyan Tree.* Sierra Club Books for Children.

        Breckler, Rosemary. *Sweet Dried Apples: A Vietnamese Wartime Childhood.* Illustrated by Deborah Kogan Ray. Houghton Mifflin.

        Bruchac, Joseph. *Between Earth and Sky: Legends of Native American Sacred Places.* Illustrated by Thomas Locker. Harcourt Brace.

        Freedman, Russell. *The Life and Death of Crazy Horse.* Illustrated by Amos Bad Heart Bull. Holiday House.

        Ho, Minfong, translator and compiler. *Maples in the Mist: Children's Poems from the Tang Dynasty.* Illustrated by Jean Tseng and Mou-Sien Tseng. Lothrop, Lee & Shepard.

        Igus, Toyomi. *Going Back Home: An Artist Returns to the South.* Illustrated by Michele Wood. Children's Book Press.

        Lewin, Ted. *Markey.* Lothrop, Lee & Shepard.

        Lomas Garza, Carmen. *In My Family / En mi familia.* Children's Book Press.

        Martin, Rafe, reteller. *Mysterious Tales of Japan.* Illustrated by Tatsuro Kiuchi. Putnam.

Mora, Pat. *Confetti: Poems for Children.* Illustrated by Enrique Sanchez. Lee & Low.

Onyefulu, Ifeoma. *Ogbo: Sharing Life in an African Village.* Harcourt Brace.

Osofsky, Audrey. *Free to Dream: The Makings of a Poet: Langston Hughes.* Lothrop, Lee & Shepard.

Pausewang, Gudrun. *The Final Journey.* Translated by Patricia Crampton. Viking/Penguin.

Rinaldi, Ann. *Hang a Thousand Trees with Ribbons: The Story of Phillis Wheatley.* Harcourt Brace.

Schroeder, Alan. *Minty: A Story of Young Harriet Tubman.* Illustrated by Jerry Pinkney. Dial.

Schur, Maxine Rose. *When I Left My Village.* Illustrated by Brian Pinkney. Dial.

Sisulu, Elinor Batezat. *The Day Gogo Went to Vote: South Africa, April 1994.* Little Brown.

Smalls, Irene. *Irene Jennie and the Christmas Masquerade: The Johnkankus.* Illustrated by Melodye Rosales. Little Brown.

Staples, Suzanne Fisher. *Dangerous Skies.* Farrar, Straus and Giroux.

Tamar, Erika. *The Garden of Happiness.* Illustrated by Barbara Lambase. Harcourt Brace.

Tunnell, Michael O., and George W. Chilcoat. *The Children of Topaz: The Story of a Japanese American Internment Camp.* Holiday House.

White, Ruth. *Belle Prater's Boy.* Farrar, Straus and Giroux.

Wisniewski, David. *Golem.* Houghton Mifflin.

Yep, Laurence. *Ribbons.* Putnam.

1998   Bentley, Judith. *"Dear Friend": Thomas Garrett and William Still, Collaborators on the Underground Railroad.* Cobblehill / Dutton.

Bial, Raymond. *Mist Over the Mountains: Appalachia and Its People.* Houghton Mifflin.

Bruchac, Joseph. *Lasting Echoes: An Oral History of Native American People.* Illustrated by Paul Morin. Harcourt Brace.

Buettner, Dan. *Africatrek: A Journey by Bicycle through Africa.* Lerner.

Davol, Marguerite. *The Paper Dragon.* Illustrated by Robert Sabuda. Atheneum.

Demi. *One Grain of Rice: A Mathematical Folktale.* Scholastic.

Dolphin, Laurie. *Our Journey from Tibet: Based on a True Story.* Photos by Nancy Jo Johnson. Dutton.

Dorris, Michael. *The Window.* Hyperion.

Hamilton, Virginia. *A Ring of Tricksters: Animal Tales from America, the West Indies, and Africa.* Illustrated by Barry Moser. Scholastic.

Hest, Amy. *When Jessie Came across the Sea.* Illustrated by Patrick J. Lynch. Candlewick.

Hurmence, Belinda. *Slavery Time: When I Was Chillun.* Putnam.

King, Martin Luther, Jr. *I Have a Dream.* Illustrated by Coretta Scott King Award and Honor Book Artists. Scholastic.

Lee, Milly. *Nim and the War Effort.* Illustrated by Yangsook Choi. Farrar, Straus and Giroux.

Mastoon, Adam. *The Shared Heart: Portraits and Stories Celebrating Lesbian, Gay, and Bisexual Young People.* Illustrated with photographs. Morrow.

McKissack, Patricia C. *Ma Dear's Aprons.* Illustrated by Floyd Cooper. Atheneum.

Meyer, Carolyn. *Jubilee Journey.* Gulliver.

Mochizuki, Ken. *Passage to Freedom: The Sugihara Story.* Illustrated by Dom Lee. Lee & Low.

Myers, Walter Dean. *Harlem.* Illustrated by Christopher Myers. Scholastic.

Normandin, Christine, editor. *Echoes of the Elders: The Stories and Paintings of Chief Lelooska.* DK.

Nye, Naomi Shihab. *Habibi.* Simon & Schuster.

Rappaport, Doreen. *The Flight of the Red Bird: The Life of Zitkala-Sa.* Dial.

Schur, Maxine Rose. *Sacred Shadows.* Dial.

Spivak, Dawnine. *Grass Sandals: The Travels of Basho.* Illustrated by Demi. Atheneum.

Wood, Nancy, editor. *The Serpent's Tongue: Prose, Poetry, and Art of the New Mexico Pueblos.* Dutton.

Young, Ed. *Voices of the Heart.* Scholastic.

1999   Aliki. *Marianthe's Story: Painted Words / Marianthe's Story: Spoken Memories.* Greenwillow.

Ayers, Katherine. *North by Night: The Story of the Underground Railroad.* Delacorte.

Bennett, James W. *Blue Star Rapture.* Simon & Schuster.

Bierman, Carol, and Barbara Hehner. *Journey to Ellis Island: How My Father Came to America.* Hyperion / Toronto.

Bunting, Eve. *So Far from the Sea.* Illustrated by Chris K. Soentpiet. Clarion.

Flake, Sharon G. *The Skin I'm In.* Jump at the Sun / Hyperion.

Fletcher, Susan. *Shadow Spinner.* Atheneum.

Gollub, Matthew. *Cool Melons—Turn to Frogs! The Life and Poems of Issa.* Illustrated by Kazuko G. Stone. Lee & Low.

Hoyt-Goldsmith, Diane. *LaCrosse: The National Game of the Iroquois.* Photos by Lawrence Migdale. Holiday House.

Khan, Rukhsana. *The Roses in My Carpet.* Illustrated by Ronald Himler. Stoddart Kids.

Kurtz, Jane. *The Storyteller's Beads.* Harcourt Brace.

Lewin, Ted. *The Storytellers.* Lothrop, Lee & Shepard.

Lobel, Anita. *No Pretty Pictures: A Child of War.* Greenwillow.

Luenn, Nancy. *A Gift for Abuelita: Celebrating the Day of the Dead / Un regalo para Abuelita: En celebración del Dia de los Muertos.* Illustrated by Robert Chapman. Rising Moon / Northland.

Morin, Paul. *Animal Dreaming: An Aboriginal Dreamtime Story.* Silver Whistle / Harcourt Brace.

Myers, Walter Dean. *Amistad: A Long Road to Freedom.* Dutton.

Nye, Naomi Shihab. *The Space between Our Footsteps: Poems and Paintings from the Middle East.* Simon & Schuster.

Park, Frances, and Ginger Park. *My Freedom Trip: A Child's Escape from North Korea.* Illustrated by Debra Reid Jenkins. Boyds Mills.

Rinaldi, Ann. *Cast Two Shadows: The American Revolution in the South.* Gulliver / Harcourt Brace.

San Souci, Robert D. *Fa Mulan: The Story of a Woman Warrior.* Illustrated by Jean Tseng and Mou-Sien Tseng. Hyperion.

Swann, Brian. *Touching the Distance: Native American Riddle-Poems.* Illustrated by Maria Rendon. Harcourt Brace.

Waldman, Neil. *Masada.* Morrow.

Wyeth, Sharon Dennis. *Something Beautiful.* Doubleday.

Zemser, Amy Bronwen. *Beyond the Mango Tree.* Greenwillow.

Scott O'Dell Award for Historical Fiction

Established in 1981, the Scott O'Dell Award is given to a distinguished work of historical fiction for children or young adults. The author must be a citizen or resident of the United States, the work must be written in English and published in the United States, and the story must be set in the New World (North, South, or Central America). The award is given annually (if a worthy book has been published) by the Advisory Committee of the Bulletin of the Center for Children's Books.

1997   Paterson, Katherine. *Jip: His Story.* Lodestar.

1998   Hesse, Karen. *Out of the Dust.* Scholastic.

1999   Robinet, Harriette Gillem. *Forty Acres and Maybe a Mule.* Atheneum.

Booklists

In addition to recognition awarded to a handful of selected titles, several organizations issue annual lists of recommended books. While such lists are too lengthy to include in this volume, we include descriptions of the booklists that would be of interest to readers of *Kaleidoscope* and indicate how to obtain these booklists.

American Library Association Best Books for Young Adults

The Young Adult Library Services Association of the American Library Association each year chooses the fiction and nonfiction titles that best satisfy the criteria of good literary quality and popular appeal to young adult readers. The complete list is published each year in the April 1 issue of *Booklist*, or you may receive a copy by sending a self-addressed stamped business-sized envelope to YALSA, 50 E. Huron Street, Chicago, IL 60611.

American Library Association Notable Children's Books

The Notable Children's Books Committee of the Association for Library Service to Children, a division of the American Library Association, selects notable books each year on the basis of literary quality, originality of text and illustration, design, format, subject matter of interest and value to children, and likelihood of acceptance by children. The complete list of Notable Children's Books appears yearly in the March 15 issue of *Booklist*, a journal published by the American Library Association.

American Library Association Quick Picks for Young Adults

The ALA's Young Adult Library Services Association also publishes a list each year of books with high appeal to young adult readers who, for whatever reason, do not like to read. The complete list is published each year in the April 1 issue of *Booklist*, or you may receive a copy of sending a self-addressed stamped business-sized envelope to YALSA, 50 E. Huron Street, Chicago, IL 60611.

International Reading Association Children's Choices, Teachers' Choices, Young Adults' Choices

The International Reading Association each year asks children, young adults, and teachers to vote on a list of books recommended by recognized sources such as *Booklist*, *Horn Book*, and *Journal of Reading*. The top vote-getters in each group are listed in IRA journals each year and may also be obtained from the IRA directly. The complete list of Children's Choices appears yearly in the November issue of *The Reading Teacher*, the Young Adults' Choices appear in the November issue of *Journal of Reading*, and the Teachers' Choices appear in the November issue of *The Reading Teacher*. Single copies of any of the lists may be obtained at no charge by sending your request along with a stamped (4 oz.), self-addressed 9" × 15" envelope to The International Reading Association, Order Department, 800 Barksdale Road, P.O. Box 8139, Newark, DE 19714-8139.

Notable Children's Trade Books in the Field of Social Studies

A Book Review Committee appointed by the National Council for the Social Studies, in cooperation with the Children's Book Council, selects books published in the United States each year that (1) are written primarily for students in grades K–8, (2) emphasize human relations, (3) represent a diversity of groups and are sensitive to a broad range of cultural experiences, (4) present an original theme or a fresh slant on a traditional topic, (5) are easily readable and of high literary quality, and (6) have a pleasing format and, when appropriate, illustrations that enrich the text. The complete list of these notable books appears yearly in the April/May issue of *Social Education*, the journal of the National Council for the Social Studies. Single copies may be obtained at no charge by sending a stamped (3 oz.), self-addressed 6" × 9" envelope to the Children's Book Council, 568 Broadway, Suite 404, New York, NY 10012.

Appendix B: Publisher Addresses

To help teachers and librarians order books featured in *Kaleidoscope*, following is a list of publishers' addresses and phone numbers. Current information can also be found in *Books in Print* and in *Literary Market Place*, both published annually by R. R. Bowker; through reference libraries; and on the World Wide Web.

Atheneum / Simon & Schuster
1230 Avenue of the Americas,
4th Floor
New York, NY 10020
(212) 698-7200

August House Littlefolk
201 East Markham Street
Little Rock, AR 72201
(501) 372-5450

Bantam Doubleday Dell
1540 Broadway
New York, NY 10036
(212) 354-6500

Barefoot Books
37 West 17th Street, 4th Floor East
New York, NY 10011
(212) 604-0505

**The Blue Sky Press /
Scholastic Inc.**
555 Broadway
New York, NY 10012
(212) 343-4498

Boyds Mills
815 Church Street
Honesdale, PA 18431
(800) 490-5111

Browndeer Press / Harcourt Brace
525 B Street, Suite 1900
San Diego, CA 92101
(619) 231-6616

Candlewick Press
2067 Massachusetts Avenue
Cambridge, MA 02140
(617) 661-3330

Carolrhoda Books, Inc.
The Lerner Group
241 First Avenue North
Minneapolis, MN 55401
(800) 328-4929

Marshall Cavendish
99 White Plains Road
Tarrytown, NY 10591
(914) 332-8888

Children's Book Press
6400 Hollis Street
Emeryville, CA 94608
(510) 655-3395 FAX (510) 655-1978

(Distributed by Bookpeople)
7900 Edgewater Drive
Oakland, CA 94621
(800) 999-4650

Chronicle Books
Attn.: Customer Service
85 2nd Street, 5th Floor
San Francisco, CA 94105
(800) 722-6657

Clarion Books
215 Park Avenue South
New York, NY 10003
(212) 420-5800

Cobblehill Books / Penguin USA
375 Hudson Street
New York, NY 10014
(212) 366-2800

Crown Publishers, Inc.
1540 Broadway
New York, NY 10036
(212) 782-9000

**Delacorte / Bantam Doubleday
Dell Publishing Group, Inc.**
1540 Broadway
New York, NY 10036
(212) 782-9000

Dial / Penguin Putnam, Inc.
375 Hudson Street
New York, NY 10014
(212) 366-2800

DK Ink / DK Publishing, Inc.
95 Madison Avenue
New York, NY 10016
(212) 213-4800

**Doubleday / Bantam Doubleday
Dell Group, Inc.**
1540 Broadway
New York, NY 10036
(212) 782-9000

**Dutton / Cobblehill / Penguin
Putnam, Inc.**
375 Hudson Street
New York, NY 10014
(212) 366-2000

Farrar, Straus and Giroux, Inc.
19 Union Square West
New York, NY 10003
(212) 741-6900

Frances Foster Books / FSG
19 Union Square West
New York, NY 10003
(212) 741-6900

Fulcrum Publishing
350 Indiana Street, Suite 350
Golden, CO 80401-5093
(800) 992-2908 or (303) 277-1623

**Greenwillow Books /
HarperCollins Children's Books**
1350 Avenue of the Americas
New York, NY 10019
(212) 261-6500

**Groundwood / Douglas &
McIntyre Children's Books**
1700 Fourth Street
Berkeley, CA 94710
(800) 788-3123

Gulliver Books / Harcourt Trade Publishers
15 E. 26th Street, 15th Floor
New York, NY 10010
(212) 952-1190

Harcourt Brace Children's Books
525 B Street, Suite 1900
San Diego, CA 92101
(619) 231-6616

HarperCollins Children's Books
1350 Avenue of the Americas
New York, NY 10019
(212) 261-6500

Holiday House, Inc.
425 Madison Avenue
New York, NY 10017
(212) 688-0085

Henry Holt and Company, Inc.
115 W. 18th Street
New York, NY 10011
(212) 886-9200

Houghton Mifflin
222 Berkeley Street
Boston, MA 02116
(617) 351-5000

Hyperion Books for Children
114 Fifth Avenue
New York, NY 10011
(212) 633-4400

Kids Can Press
4500 Whitmer Estates
Niagara Falls, NY 14305-1386

Send Correspondence To:
29 Birch Avenue
Toronto, Ontario M4V 1E2 Canada

Kingfisher / Larousse Kingfisher Chambers
95 Madison Avenue
New York, NY 10016
(212) 686-1060

Alfred A. Knopf, Inc.
1540 Broadway
New York, NY 10036
(212) 782-8668

Lee & Low Books
95 Madison Avenue
New York, NY 10016
(212) 779-4400

Lerner Publishing Group
241 First Avenue North
Minneapolis, MN 55401
(800) 328-4929

Linnet Book / The Shoe String Press, Inc.
2 Linsley Street
P.O. Box 657
North Haven, CT 06473-2517
(203) 239-2702

Little, Brown & Company
3 Center Plaza
Boston, MA 02108
(617) 227-0730

Little Tiger Press
N16 W23390 Stoneridge Drive
Waukesha, WI 53188

Lodestar Books / Penguin USA
375 Hudson Street
New York, NY 10014
(212) 366-2000

Lothrop Lee / Greenwillow / William Morrow
1350 Avenue of the Americas
New York, NY 10019
(212) 261-6500

Margaret K. McElderry Books / Simon & Schuster Children's Publishing
1230 Avenue of the Americas
New York, NY 10020
(212) 698-7200

The Millbrook Press, Inc.
2 Old Milford Road
Brookfield, CT 06804
(203) 740-2220

Morrow Junior Books / William Morrow and Company, Inc.
1350 Avenue of the Americas
New York, NY 10019

Orca Book Publishers
P.O. Box 468
Custer, WA 98240-0468

Orchard Books
95 Madison Avenue
New York, NY 10016
(212) 951-2641

Pelican Publishing Company, Inc.
P.O. Box 3110
Gretna, LA 70054
(504) 368-1175

Philomel Books / Penguin Putnam, Inc.
375 Hudson Street
New York, NY 10016
(212) 951-8700

Puffin Books / Penguin Putnam, Inc.
375 Hudson Street
New York, NY 10014
(212) 366-2000

G. P. Putnam's Sons / Penguin Putnam, Inc.
375 Hudson Street
New York, NY 10014
(212) 951-8700

Rabbit Ears / Rabbit Ears Productions, Inc.
Published by Simon & Schuster, Inc.
1230 Avenue of the Americas
New York, NY 10020
(212) 698-2851

Rising Moon / Northland Publishing Company
P.O. Box 1389
Flagstaff, AZ 86002-1389

Runestone Press / Lerner Publishing Group
241 First Avenue North
Minneapolis, MN 55401
(800) 328-4929

Scholastic Inc.
555 Broadway
New York, NY 10012
(212) 343-6100

Sierra Club
85 Second Street
San Francisco, CA 94105-3441
(415) 977-5500

Silver Whistle / Harcourt Trade Publishers
15 East 26th Street
New York, NY 10011
(212) 592-1135

Simon & Schuster
1230 Avenue of the Americas
New York, NY 10020
(212) 698-2851

Stoddart Kids Publishing
PMB 128
4500 Whitmer Industrial Estates
Niagara Falls, NY 14305-1386
(800) 805-1083

Troll
Subsidiary of Education Reading
Services
100 Corporate Drive
Mahwah, NJ 07430
(800) 526-5289

Viking Children's Books / Penguin Putnam, Inc.
375 Hudson Street
New York, NY 10014
(212) 366-2000

Zino Press Children's Books
P.O. Box 52
Madison, WI 53701
(800) 356-2303

Author Index

Illustrator Index

Subject Index

Title Index

Editor

Junko Yokota is associate professor in the Reading and Language Department of the National College of Education at National-Louis University, where she teaches children's literature, multicultural literature, and preservice courses in reading and language arts. During the first ten years of her career, she was a public school classroom teacher and school librarian.

Her work in children's literature focuses primarily on multicultural literature, and she is a recipient of the Virginia Hamilton Award for Contribution to Multicultural Literature. Born and raised in Japan, Yokota maintains an interest in international children's literature. She is currently the president of the U.S. national section of the International Board on Books for Young People (USBBY), the major international organization focused on literature for children and adolescents. Her work in children's literature has resulted in speaking engagements in countries such as China, Japan, Malaysia, Singapore, and Bahrain.

Yokota has served on numerous book award committees, including the Caldecott Award Committee, the Batchelder Committee, the International Reading Association's Children's Book Award Committee, and the Notable Books for a Global Society Committee. She is also a co-author of the college textbook *Children's Books in Children's Hands*.

This book was typeset in Palatino and Helvetica by Precision Graphics.
Typefaces used on the cover were University Roman and Palatino.
The book was printed on 50 lb. White Williamsburg by Versa Press.